MODELLING NONLINEAR
ECONOMIC RELATIONSHIPS

D0139541

Modelling Nonlinear Economic Relationships

CLIVE W. J. GRANGER

and

TIMO TERÄSVIRTA

OXFORD UNIVERSITY PRESS

Oxford University Press, Great Clarendon Street, Oxford OX2 6DP

Oxford New York
Athens Auckland Bangkok Bogota Bombay
Buenos Aires Calcutta Cape Town Dar es Salaam
Delhi Florence Hong Kong Istanbul Karachi
Kuala Lumpur Madras Madrid Melbourne
Mexico City Nairobi Paris Singapore
Taipei Tokyo Toronto Warsaw
and associated companies in
Berlin Ibadan

Oxford is a trade mark of Oxford University Press

Published in the United States by
Oxford University Press Inc., New York

First published 1993
Reprinted 1994, 1996, 1997

British Library Cataloguing in Publication Data
Data available

Library of Congress Cataloging in Publication Data
Data available
ISBN 0 19 877319 6 (hbk)
ISBN 0 19 877320 X (pbk)

Printed in Great Britain
on acid-free paper by
Biddles Ltd., Guildford and King's Lynn

Preface

Time series econometrics is largely concerned about modelling relationships between economic variables and it seems to be generally agreed, particularly by theorists, that relationships are often nonlinear. We started this book when we realized that, at that time, there was no discussion of how to model nonlinear relationships between series. There were plenty of accounts of multivariate linear modelling and some of univariate nonlinear series modelling, so our objective was to see if we could mould these together into a more complete discussion. The result should be considered a first attempt, and doubtless, as experience is gained with the success or otherwise of the models and techniques proposed, these methods will evolve and improve. An obvious difficulty is that there are vast numbers of possible models for nonlinear relationships and economists are just learning which are useful. Although statistical theory is emphasized here, our ultimate object is to provide usable techniques and it will be the experience obtained from their use which will determine how this area of research will evolve.

Most of the book was written whilst the authors were at the Economics Department of the University of California, San Diego, which provided a nurturing environment, with plenty of helpful discussion from our colleagues and the many excellent visitors. Timo Teräsvirta also had a chance to work on the book at University of Göteborg, the Research Institute of the Finnish Economy, Helsinki, and the Bank of Norway, Oslo. We received very good computing help from Jin-Lung Lin, Zhuanxin Ding, and Chor-Yiu Sin. Timo Teräsvirta is grateful to the Yrjö Jahnsson Foundation for financial support. We would particularly like to thank Paula Lindsay for being responsible for typing the text and making changes with a continual cheerful disposition. Clive Granger would like to thank National Science Foundation grants SES 90-23037 and SES 89-02950 for summer support.

We have received a great deal of help from many people but retain responsibility for any errors or difficulties that remain.

Contents

1

Basic Concepts

1.1 General Introduction

It seems to be generally accepted that the economy is nonlinear, in that major economic variables have nonlinear relationships. Economic theorists suggest models with floors and ceilings, buffer stocks, and switching regimes. Investment functions, production functions, and Phillips' curves are usually specified in nonlinear forms. Given any particular nonlinear model, with known specification but unknown parameters, econometricians can suggest ways of estimating these parameters and produce some asymptotic properties of these estimators (see, for instance, Judge *et al*. 1985 and White 1984). However, most economic theories only suggest plausible nonlinear specifications, usually are incomplete, and often do not agree with actual data, particularly in the dynamic structure. There thus seems to be a need for exploratory statistical techniques to produce sound models, perhaps used in conjuction with appropriate theories. In the time-series analysis area, linear techniques are well developed for single series and for fairly small vector, multivariate series, as described for example in Granger and Newbold (1986). There has been worthwhile development in nonlinear univariate time-series models (see Tong 1990 for a survey), and more recently attention has been turned to multivariate systems. This book will attempt to summarize the more practical components of these new developments and thus hopefully to encourage econometricians to use nonlinear models.

The stages of progress in the linear techniques were basically from univariate structures, the ARIMA models of Box–Jenkins, to the multiple input, single output cases, where one variable is explained by several, such as ARMAX models, and finally to systems such as VAR or VARMA models. These three stages of development will doubtlessly occur with nonlinear models. It is difficult to jump from fairly general univariate models to practical multivariate systems. Although some system results will be discussed here, particular attention is paid to the case of a single dependent variable modelled by a few explanatory variables and the lagged dependent variable in nonlinear form.

Only discrete time-series will be considered for the purely pragmatic reason that all economic measurements are made at discrete time-intervals, hours, days, weeks, quarters, and so forth, which can be taken to be constant in length. Whether or not economic variables are generated in continuous time will not be specifically considered.

The question of whether an observed series is deterministic, rather than stochastic, only occurs with nonlinear models. This text will concentrate on stochastic situations, although some attention is given to chaotic series, which are deterministic but have some properties in common with stochastic processes (see Chapter 3). The existence of unexpected shocks or innovations to the economy, or to society at large, seems to be clear and this, plus measurement errors, strongly suggests that economic variables are stochastic. Some of the measurement error enters into the decisions of economic agents and is thus embedded into the system. Observed series are thus *not* simply signal plus noise, where noise is just measurement error which can perhaps be filtered out. Actual series may contain deterministic components, such as cycles and trends, and this possibility will have to be considered in any analysis.

One further division of models that occurs in nonlinear situations but not linear ones is into parametric and nonparametric. Parametric models involve specific mathematical functions, such as polynomial or trigono-metric series for example, but with unknown parameters. Questions that naturally arise are which classes of functions to consider, which lags to use, how to estimate the parameters, and then how to evaluate the resulting model. Nonparametric models allow a wider class of possible shapes, and in a sense they involve many more parameters although only some of these may be estimated. Nonparametric models are usually considered to be computer-intensive and, as they sometimes search over a wide range of possible models, the possibility of overfitting or data mining has to be checked. These models are discussed in Chapter 7.

The stages of analysis for linear models suggested by Box and Jenkins (1970) are:

  (i) model specification. Using various summary statistics, decide on a class of models to be used for a particular data set and also approximately the number of lags required.
 (ii) model estimation. Estimate the parameters of the selected model(s), and
(iii) model evaluation. Use a variety of inference statistics and specification tests to judge the quality of the model and, perhaps, compare it with other models. For example, the post-sample forecasting abilities of the models can be compared. If the model is unsatisfactory, consider a new specification.

Some components of this modelling strategy can be followed with nonlinear models and will be discussed in detail in later sections. Discussions of the question of what exactly is meant by nonlinearity will be postponed until Section 1.4.

The number of possible nonlinear models that can be applied to a data-set is already enormous and will certainly continue to grow. Although many of these models will be surveyed we have decided to emphasize fairly simple models that are applicable, and thus likely to be used by applied econometricians. Thus, a proposed model is likely to be judged on its practical usefulness as much as its reality in economics. So far there is little experience using nonlinear models with economic data and so little learning has occurred as to which nonlinear models or techniques are better than others. Because of the number and inherent flexibility of nonlinear models, the possibility of getting a spuriously good fit to any given set of data is high. We therefore strongly recommend the use of a test of linearity, as described in Chapter 6, before fitting models and also the use of post-sample evaluation of the nonlinear models with alternatives including a linear model, to determine the actual quality of the fitted model. There is a difficulty with this procedure in some situations if the post-sample periods happen to be particularly 'linear' in some way, but we still recommend use of post-sample evaluation. Forecasts from nonlinear models are discussed in Chapter 8.

1.2 Linear Models

The main building block of theoretical linear models is the series that is independent and identically distributed (i.i.d.). A series ε_t $t = 1, \ldots, T$ is i.i.d. if all terms are independent of the others and all have the same distribution. Thus, if $p_t(x)$ is the probability density function of ε_t, then $p_t(x) = p(x)$ for all t and the joint distribution of any set of n components of ε_t is just the product of the marginal distributions. If one observes the sequence up to time T, the value taken at time $T + 1$ will in no way be affected by the earlier values and will be drawn from the same distribution.

Rather strong restrictions are required for a process to be i.i.d. and for many purposes, particularly with linear models, it is sufficient to consider a simpler process, called 'white noise'. A sequence e_t, $t = 1, \ldots, T$ is called white noise if its mean, $m = E[e_t]$ is constant, its variance $\sigma^2 = \text{var}(e_t)$ is also a constant and all covariances $\text{cov}[e_t, e_s]$ are zero for $t \neq s$. Thus, just first and second moment properties are considered. These will be called 'the white noise properties' and clearly a series can possess them but not be i.i.d.

A closely related class of processes are 'martingale differences'. A series x_t is called a martingale if $E[x_t | x_{t-j}, j \geq 1] = x_{t-1}$ and a martingale difference is then $\Delta x_t = x_t - x_{t-1}$, so that $E[\Delta x_t | x_{t-j}, j \geq 1] = 0$. A martingale difference has the mean and covariance properties of a white noise series, but does not necessarily have a constant variance. Both white noise and martingale difference series have distinct linear properties but their nonlinear properties are unclear. Their definitions do not specify $E[x_t^p | x_{t-j}, j \geq 1]$ for an integer p for instance although information about such quantities are often required to study nonlinear processes.

Two important classes of linear models are the moving average and the autoregressive processes. If ε_t is an i.i.d. zero mean series, an example of a moving average is

$$y_t = \varepsilon_t + c_1 \varepsilon_{t-1} + c_2 \varepsilon_{t-2},$$

denoted as $y_t \sim \text{MA}(2)$ as just two lags of the input i.i.d. series are involved. An example of an autoregressive process is

$$y_t = a_1 y_{t-1} + a_2 y_{t-2} + \varepsilon_t$$

where again ε_t is i.i.d. and has zero mean. This model is denoted as AR(2) as again there are only two lags. Clearly, MA(q) and AR(p) processes are easily defined, for positive integer p and q. A wider class are the autoregressive moving average models, an example being

$$y_t = a_1 y_{t-1} + a_2 y_{t-2} + \varepsilon_t + c_1 \varepsilon_{t-1},$$

which is denoted as $y_t \sim \text{ARMA}(2, 1)$, having two lags of y_t and one of ε_t. The more general ARMA(p, q) model arises frequently, at least in the theory of linear processes. The main features of such a linear model are the length of its memory, which is summarized here by the values of p and q, and the particular input series involved, usually assumed to be i.i.d. or at least a martingale difference. In practice only the white noise properties are tested for ε_t.

Some linear models have a 'long-memory' property, so that $E[y_{t+h} | y_{t-j}, j \geq 0]$ does not necessarily tend to zero as h becomes large. If this quantity does tend to zero, it is called short-memory, a necessary condition being that $\text{cov}(y_{t+h}, y_t) \to 0$ as h becomes large. If y_t has constant mean, variance and covariance with $|\text{cov}(y_{t+h}, y_t)| < A\rho^h$ for h large and $|\rho| < 1$, it will be called stationary. (A more precise definition is given in Section 1.5.) An example of a long-memory series is one whose differences are stationary, denoted as ARIMA(p, 1, q) or more briefly $y_t \sim \text{I}(1)$. If d differences are required to obtain stationarity the series is called integrated of order d and denoted as I(d).

The ARIMA models defined here are univariate. The natural generalization is to a series y_t that is explained by a linear combination of p values of its own past, q values of lagged ε_t, and r lags of a vector $\mathbf{x}_t$ of other variables, so that

$$y_t = \sum_{j=1}^{p} a_j y_{t-j} + \sum_{j=1}^{r} \boldsymbol{\beta}_j \mathbf{x}_{t-j} + \sum_{j=1}^{q} c_j \varepsilon_{t-j} + \varepsilon_t.$$

This is called a transfer of ARMAX model, X here standing for 'exogenous'.

The next generalization is to a system such as a vector autoregressive (VAR) process, in which a vector $\mathbf{y}_t$ is modelled jointly, for example

$$\mathbf{y}_t = \sum_{j=1}^{p} \mathbf{a}_j \mathbf{y}_{t-j} + \boldsymbol{\varepsilon}_t$$

where $\mathbf{y}$ has n components, each $\mathbf{a}_j$ is an $n \times n$ matrix and $\boldsymbol{\varepsilon}_t$ is a vector i.i.d. input with

$$\begin{aligned} \text{cov}(\varepsilon_{jt}, \varepsilon_{ks}) &= 0 \qquad t \neq s \\ &= \sigma_{jk} \qquad t = s \end{aligned}$$

so that contemporaneous effects can occur within the inputs. These models are discussed in Granger and Newbold (1986), Harvey (1981), and elsewhere.

Clearly other linear models are possible, some being quite exotic, but they will not be discussed here.

1.3 Some Univariate Nonlinear Models

In this section a few simple univariate nonlinear models are introduced. Their properties are discussed more fully in later chapters where multivariate generalizations are considered.

An important, simple model is the nonlinear autoregressive of order one, where y_t is generated by

$$y_t = f(y_{t-1}) + \varepsilon_t \tag{1.3.1}$$

where ε_t is zero mean i.i.d. and y_t is then denoted as NLAR(1). A Markov process has the property that the conditional distribution of y_{t+1} given all y_{t-j}, $j \geq 0$ is the same as the conditional distribution of y_{t+1} given just y_t. Thus, all the information about the future of the series is contained in its most recent value. Clearly a NLAR(1) process is Markov. An alternative form is

$$y_t = g(y_{t-1}) \cdot y_{t-1} + \varepsilon_t \tag{1.3.2}$$

which is often more useful. The deterministic part of this model is

$$\bar{y}_t = g(\bar{y}_{t-1})\bar{y}_{t-1}$$

and this has $y = 0$ as an equilibrium point, and if $\bar{y}_s = 0$, then $\bar{y}_t = 0$ for all $t > s$. An obvious generalization to p lags is the NLAR(p) model

$$y_t = f(y_{t-j}, j = 1, \ldots, p) + \varepsilon_t, \tag{1.3.3}$$

which is not Markov if $p > 1$.

Various particular forms of the NLAR model have received attention in the univariate case, see Tong (1990). One example is the threshold autoregressive model (TAR) which has a form such as

$$\left.\begin{aligned} y_t &= a_1 y_{t-1} + \varepsilon_t \quad \text{if } y_{t-2} > 0 \\ &= a_2 y_{t-1} + \varepsilon_t \quad \text{if } y_{t-2} \leqslant 0 \end{aligned}\right\} \qquad (1.3.4)$$

with $a_1 \neq a_2$. Thus, the parameters of a linear model change through time due to a switching rule, which in this case depends on an earlier value of the series. There are clearly many possible generalizations, with several switching regimes, more lags, and the switching rule can also depend on other variables. In this form the parameter values switch rather abruptly, which may be thought to be unrealistic in some cases. A smoother switching form of the simple model is

$$y_t = a \cdot g(y_{t-2}) \cdot y_{t-1} + \varepsilon_t \qquad (1.3.5)$$

where $g(y)$ is a smooth nondecreasing function with $g(\underline{y}) = \alpha_1$, $g(\bar{y}) = \alpha_2$ and $\alpha_1 < g(y) < \alpha_2$ all other y. $g(y)$ is thus like a cumulative density function, or a logistic function. Such models are called smooth TAR, or perhaps better, smooth transition autoregressive models and thus denoted STAR. Other generalizations are obviously possible.

A further specific NLAR model that has received some attention is the exponential AR model, such as

$$y_t = a_1 y_{t-1} + a_2 y_{t-2} + \varepsilon_t$$

where

$$a_j = \phi_j + \pi_j \exp(-\alpha y_{t-1}^2) \quad j = 1, 2,$$

see Ozaki (1985). It is suggested that if the quantity

$$\frac{1 - \phi_1 - \phi_2}{\pi_1 + \pi_2}$$

is either negative or bigger than one, then the process will include limit cycles, so that the series includes an important periodic component for t large.

Nonlinear moving average models can take many forms such as

$$y_t = \varepsilon_t + h_1(\varepsilon_{t-1}) + h_2(\varepsilon_{t-2}), \qquad (1.3.6)$$

a simple version being

$$y_t = \varepsilon_t + b\varepsilon_{t-1}^2,$$

which could be denoted as NLMA(1).

A class of models intermediate between NLAR and NLMA are the bilinear models, such as

$$y_t = \varepsilon_t + b\varepsilon_{t-1} y_{t-2} \qquad (1.3.7)$$

or

$$y_t = ay_{t-1} + \varepsilon_t + b\varepsilon_{t-2}y_{t-2}.$$

Some of these models, such as (1.3.7) generate series which have the white noise properties, as shown in Granger and Andersen (1978). They thus provide an example of a series that is not forecastable linearly but may be forecastable nonlinearly.

The models considered so far all have had constant parameters, but as tastes, technology, and policy rules change it is easy to believe in time-varying parameters. If the causes of this change are unobserved, a class of models of the form

$$y_t = \beta_t x_{t-1} + \varepsilon_t$$

$$\beta_t = m + \alpha\beta_{t-1} + \eta_t$$

has been suggested, called time-varying parameter autoregressive models, VPAR(1) in this case. β_t is unobserved but can be estimated iteratively using the Kalman filter, as explained in Granger and Newbold (1986), Harvey (1981), and elsewhere. However, as β_t is estimated from the data, the actual model can equally well be thought of as being nonlinear rather than time-varying parameter. It is clear that it is difficult to distinguish these two types of models. The case $\alpha = 0$ gives a 'random coefficient' model, which is discussed in detail in Nicholls and Quinn (1982).

If the cause of the changing parameter is some observed variable, z_t, one gets a class of models known as 'doubly stochastic', discussed by Tjøstheim (1986). An example is

$$y_t = \beta x_{t-1}z_t + \varepsilon_t$$

where both x_t and z_t are observed series. This is an important class of models, which are not strictly univariate and are discussed more generally in Section 2.1.

1.4 Nonlinearity and Heteroskedasticity

A compact way of writing a generating mechanism for a series y_t, with explanatory variables $\mathbf{x}_t$ is

$$y_t = g(\mathbf{x}_{t-j}, j \geqslant 1, \varepsilon_{t-j}, j \geqslant 0) \tag{1.4.1}$$

where $\mathbf{x}_t$ will typically include y_{t-k}, $k \geqslant 0$ as well as other variables. However, a more useful form, bringing out an explicit innovation is

$$y_t = g(I_{t-1}) + h(I_{t-1})\varepsilon_t \tag{1.4.2}$$

where I_t is the information set $\mathbf{x}_{t-j}$, ε_{t-j}, $j \geqslant 0$. If $\mathbf{y}_t$ is a vector, then the kth component will have the representation

$$y_{kt} = g_k(I_{t-1}) + h_k(I_{t-1})\varepsilon_{kt} \qquad (1.4.3)$$

where I_t is $\mathbf{x}_{t-j}$, ε_{t-j} $j \geqslant 0$ and $\mathbf{x}_t$ includes $\mathbf{y}_t$.

If $h_k(I_{t-1}) \neq$ a constant, the series y_k is heteroskedastic, otherwise it is homoskedastic. If $g(I_{t-1})$ is linear in the components of I_{t-1}, then y_t may be said to be 'linear in mean'. If $h(I_{t-1})$ is also a constant, then y_t has a complete linear representation in terms of I_{t-1}, otherwise it is nonlinear. In the case when $h = 1$ and y coincides with x, so that $I_t : y_{t-j}$, $j \geqslant 0$, it may be possible to write

$$y_t = \varepsilon_t + f(\varepsilon_{t-j}, j \geqslant 0).$$

If $f(\ )$ is a linear function, then y_t can also be called a linear process in terms of the innovations. This definition is useful in theory but it has little practical value as ε_t is typically unobserved.

An example of heteroskedasticity is when

$$h(I_{t-1}) = \alpha + \beta_1 \varepsilon_{t-1}^2 + \beta_2 \varepsilon_{t-2}^2,$$

which provides a simple case of an 'autoregressive conditional heteroskedastic (or ARCH) model', as discussed by Engle (1982). It is clear that ARCH models can be linear in mean but are not completely linear. This can complicate tests for linearity, as discussed in Chapter 6.

It may be noted that if y_t is completely linear with respect to $\mathbf{x}_{t-1}$, then some instantaneous transform of y_t, such as y_t^3, is not linear in mean with respect to $\mathbf{x}_{t-1}$. It is thus seen that linearity is not a very robust concept. It is common practice to analyse instantaneously transformed dependent variables, particulary $\log y_t$ instead of y_t, wherever it is thought to be appropriate. This type of nonlinearity is not discussed in any detail in this text. The researcher is taken to have a variable of interest, for which forecasts perhaps have to be made, and that this variable is used directly in the analysis. Transformations of the explanatory variables will be discussed in later chapters.

Models (1.4.1) and (1.4.2) are essentially reduced forms. It can be argued that economic variables arise from decisions made by economic agents, that it takes time to gather necessary information and then to make and to implement the decision, so that there is a natural time-gap between the generation of the input variables $\mathbf{x}_{t-1}$ and the formation of y_t. Of course, this data generation period may well be (much) shorter than the observation period over which actual data are gathered. It follows that there may well be a temporal aggregation problem, in going from one period to the other, and that this can lead to apparent simultaneity in the system, so that current $\mathbf{x}_t$ effects y_t instantaneously. Thus $\mathbf{x}_t$ may seem to belong to the information set I_{t-1} in some of the above constructs. There are many well-known interpretational problems in linear models with the use of such information sets including contemporaneous variables, and these problems remain with nonlinear models. Forms such as (1.4.1) and (1.4.2) will be used in this text and possibly also contemporaneous information sets. The effects of temporal aggregation on nonlinear models will be briefly discussed in Section 8.1.

1.5 Stationarity and Invertibility

Denote by $\mathbf{x}_{t,m}$ the section of a series $\mathbf{x}_{t-j}$, $j = 0, \ldots, m - 1$, so that the section contains m consecutive terms. Let $p_{t,m}(x)$ denote the distribution function of $\mathbf{x}_{t,m}$. A series x_t is said to be (completely) stationary if $p_{t,m}(x)$ is not a function of t for every finite m. Thus, a series is stationary if its generating mechanism is time invariate and if the series is short-memory, so that the conditional distribution of $\mathbf{x}_{t+h,m}$ given $\mathbf{x}_{t-j}$, $j \geq 0$ is equal to the unconditional distribution, for h large. Stationarity is an extremely useful property for developing the statistical theory of a process but is very difficult, if not impossible, to test for in practice. Some particular aspects of stationarity can be tested, such as means or variances being constant over time or being short-memory, but testing the constancy of the full distribution is not easy. For a given model, stationarity can sometimes be established. For example, the linear autoregressive model

$$y_t = a_1 y_{t-1} + a_2 y_{t-2} + \varepsilon_t$$

is stationary if the roots of the polynomial

$$1 - a_1 z - a_2 z^2 = 0$$

all lie outside the unit circle $|z| = 1$ and if ε_t is i.i.d. This statement generalizes to the AR(p) model in the obvious way.

A process x_t is said to have second-order stationarity if its mean and variance are constant and its autocovariances $\text{cov}(x_{t+k}, x_t)$ depend only on k. These conditions are enough for analysis of linear processes but are only necessary conditions for complete stationarity, which is required for nonlinear processes.

A rather more difficult concept is that of ergodicity. Essentially a series is ergodic if estimates of essential parameters continuously improve in quality as extra terms of the series are added. Examples of nonergodic series are a constant or a pure sine wave. Hannan (1970) or White (1984) provide a full description of this idea. Again, testing if a particular finite series is ergodic is impossible but statements can be made for particular models. For example, the NLAR(1) process generated by

$$y_t = g(y_{t-1}) + \varepsilon_t$$

is ergodic if the function $g(y)$ is continuous, and is bounded by

$$|g(y)| \leqslant |y| - A \quad \text{for } |y| > H$$
$$|g(y)| \leqslant C \qquad\qquad |y| < H$$

for some constants C, H, and $A > E[|\varepsilon|]$. This is proved by Doukhan and Ghindés (1980). Thus, ergodicity is obtained essentially if

$$\left[\frac{|g(y)|}{|y|}\right] < 1 \text{ for } |y| \text{ large.}$$

A property that a process may have, and which is especially important for forecasting, is that of invertibility. If one starts with a model of the form

$$y_t = g(I_{t-1}) + \varepsilon_t \tag{1.5.1}$$

where $I_t : \mathbf{x}_{t-j}, \varepsilon_{t-j}, j \geqslant 0$ and $\mathbf{x}_t$ is a vector of explanatory variables, the question can be asked: can one estimate the ε_t sequence? This sequence is, of course, not usually directly observed. Simply reversing the equation gives

$$\varepsilon_t = y_t - g(I_{t-1}) \tag{1.5.2}$$

but one has to know earlier values of the ε series to obtain an estimate of the current value. Suppose that one guesses at enough 'starting-up' values of the ε sequence, say $\tilde{\varepsilon}_{-k}$, $k = 1, \ldots, q$ so that estimates can be obtained, $\hat{\varepsilon}_t$, $t = 0, 1, \ldots, T$. If $\hat{\varepsilon}_t \to \varepsilon_t$ in some fashion, so that for example $E([\hat{\varepsilon}_t - \varepsilon_t]^2) \underset{t}{\to} 0$, the process may be called invertible. In this case any sensible set of starting values will produce estimates $\hat{\varepsilon}_t$ that eventually tend to the true value, ε_t. However, for some processes this convergence does not occur. Examples of invertible models are

$$y_t = \varepsilon_t + 0.6\varepsilon_{t-1}$$

and

$$y_t = \varepsilon_t + \alpha y_{t-1}\varepsilon_{t-1},$$

with

$$|\alpha \sigma_\varepsilon| < 0.606,$$

Examples of noninvertible models are

$$y_t = \varepsilon_t + 1.3\varepsilon_{t-1}$$

and

$$y_t = \varepsilon_t + \alpha \varepsilon_{t-1}^2$$

and

$$y_t = \varepsilon_t + \alpha \varepsilon_{t-1} \varepsilon_{t-2}.$$

For complicated models, conditions for invertibility are sometimes available—see for instance Liu (1985) for some bilinear models—but these conditions are often too difficult to be used in practice. A pragmatic way to discover if a particular model is invertible, such as (1.5.1) with a specific function $f()$, is to generate data from the model with a known sequence ε_t, and then to use (1.5.2) to get estimates $\hat{\varepsilon}_t$ for some input $\tilde{\varepsilon}_{-k}$. Obvious starting values are $\tilde{\varepsilon}_{-k} = 0$, all k, but others can be used—provided that they are not the true starting values. By plotting $\hat{\varepsilon}_t$ against ε_t, which are known in a simulation, it should be clear if convergence is occurring. The exercise should be repeated several times to gain confidence in the result. It should be noted that stationarity and ergodicity are properties of a series whereas invertibility is a property of a model.

1.6 Stability, Memory, and Equilibrium

Questions of stability relate to the properties of a process with a specific generating mechanism after it has been running for a long period. For purposes of illustration, consider a simple NLAR(1) model of the form

$$y_t = f(y_{t-1}) + \varepsilon_t \tag{1.6.1}$$

with starting value y_0, where ε_t is a zero mean i.i.d. sequence. Assume that there is a solution to this equation of the form

$$y_t = y(\varepsilon_t, \varepsilon_{t-1}, \dots \varepsilon_1; y_0) \tag{1.6.2}$$

and that the conditional probability distribution function of y_t given y_0 is

$$\text{Prob}(y_t \leq x | y_0) = \Phi_t(x; y_0).$$

The process y_t can be called 'short-memory' if $\Phi_t(x:y_0) \to \Phi_h(x)$ as $t \to h$ for h large, so that after the process has been running for a long time, the starting value no longer affects the marginal distribution. The process is called 'stable' if

$$\lim_t \Phi_t(x; y_0) = \Phi(x; y_0)$$

so that y_t, y_s will both have the same marginal distribution for t, s large but this distributor may still depend on y_0. To illustrate these definitions consider the linear AR(1) process

$$y_t = \rho y_{t-1} + \varepsilon_t,$$

which has solution

$$y_t = \rho^t y_0 + \sum_{k=0}^{t-1} \rho^k \varepsilon_{t-k}. \tag{1.6.3}$$

If $|\rho| < 1$, the first term eventually becomes negligible and y_t is normally distributed $N(0, V)$ from the central limit however, where $\mathrm{var}(\varepsilon) = \sigma_\varepsilon^2$ and $V = \sigma_\varepsilon^2/(1 - \rho^2)$. Thus, if $|\rho| < 1$, y_t is both short-memory and stable. However, if $\rho > 1$, say, then the first term in (1.6.3) becomes large and the second term has variance $= O(\rho^{2k}\sigma_\varepsilon^2)$, so that the process is both long-memory and not stable. For the model

$$y_t = f(y_{t-1}, \varepsilon_t),$$

which includes (1.6.1) as a special case, Lasota and Mackey (1989) prove that, if

(i) $f(y, \varepsilon)$ is continuous in y

(ii) ε_t is i.i.d.

(iii) $E\|f(x, \varepsilon_t) - f(z, \varepsilon_t)\| < \|x - z\|$

and

$$E\|f(x, \varepsilon_t)^2\| \leq \sigma\|x\|^2 + \beta$$

and

$$0 < x < 1, \sigma > 0,$$

where $\|\ \|$ is any norm, not necessarily the Euclidean one, then y_t is short-memory and stable. Here y_t can be a vector but ε_t is taken to be a univariate random perturbation to the system. The first condition in (iii) is essentially that of continuity of f with respect to y and the second condition is a widely used sufficient condition for stability. Clearly these definitions can be used for any process and are easily generalized to systems, where $\mathbf{y}_t$ is a vector. Conditions for a generating mechanism to be stable are not always available, but can be found for some particular mechanisms, such as the bilinear. For example the bilinear model

$$y_t = b\varepsilon_{t-j}y_{t-k} + \varepsilon_t, \, j, \, k \geqslant 1$$

is stable if and only if $\log|b| + E[\log|\varepsilon_t|] \leqslant 0$, as shown by Quinn (1982).

    There are various ways in which a process can be unstable. For example the distribution $F_t(x)$ can be explosive in mean or variance, or in higher moments, or it can be periodic, so that

$$F_{t+p}(x) = F_t(x) \neq F_{t+j}(x) \qquad j = 1, \ldots, p - 1$$

for example. In this case the mean and/or some of the moments will be periodic, and the process is said to contain a limit cycle.

For the model (1.6.1), a necessary condition for stability in mean is that the deterministic process

$$\bar{y}_t = f(\bar{y}_{t-1}) \tag{1.6.4}$$

be stable. This sequence is said to have an equilibrium y^* if

$$y^* = f(y^*) \tag{1.6.5}$$

so that if ever $\bar{y}_t$ takes the value y^* it will remain at this value thereafter. y^* is said to be a stable equilibrium if $\bar{y}_t \to y^*$ so that every $|\bar{y}_t - y^*|$ is small for large t. Various other definitions of stable equilibrium exist for deterministic processes such as those generated by (1.6.5) but these are often of little relevance for series found in economics or their generating mechanisms. For example, if y_t is generated by

$$y_t = (a + e_t)y_{t-1} \tag{1.6.6}$$

with e_t as i.i.d. or some other random process then y_t will be stochastic but $y^* = 0$ is an equilibrium. Writing (1.6.6) as

$$\log|y_t| - \log|y_{t-1}| = \log|a + e_t|$$

it is seen that $\log|y_t|$ must be a long-memory, upward-trending process and so is not necessarily a good representation for an economic series.

The solutions to (1.6.4) can also be exploding or have limit cycles. Adding the random inputs, ε_t as in (1.6.1) will still produce explosive models and possibly limit cycles. For a given model it is often worth while to generate the deterministic solution $\bar{y}$ so that its properties can be investigated.

The relationship between the stochastic process y_t and its deterministic equivalent, $\bar{y}_t$, is not simple. In the case shown, Lord (1979) has derived some specific results. If $\bar{y}_t$ is the solution to (1.6.4), with starting value $\bar{y}_0$, denoted by $\bar{y}_t(\bar{y}_0)$ and similarly $y_t(y_0)$ is the solution to (1.6.1), with starting value y_0, Lord shows that there exists a series v_t such that

$$y_t(y_0) = \bar{y}_t(v_t)$$

and that

$$y_t(y_0) = \bar{y}_t(\bar{y}_0) + \psi_t(v_t, \bar{y}_0) \cdot (v_t - \bar{y}_0).$$

The series v_t is generated by

$$v_t = x_0 + \sum_{s=1}^{t} \psi_s^{-1}(v_s, v_{s-1}) \cdot \varepsilon_s$$

where

$$\psi_t(y_0, \bar{y}_0) = \int_0^1 \phi_t(\lambda \bar{y}_0 + (1 - \lambda)y_0) \, d\lambda$$

and

$$\phi_t(\bar{y}_0) = \frac{\partial \bar{y}_t(\bar{y}_0)}{\partial \bar{y}_0}.$$

Here $\psi^{-1} \equiv 1/\psi$. These results show that if $\bar{y}_t$ is explosive or contains a limit cycle, so will y_t.

For a nonlinear stochastic process, the equilibrium concept is usually less relevant, but if the process is stable with mean μ and finite variance, the mean can be considered as an attractor, as the optimum forecast of y_{t+h}, for h large, is equal to μ. Attractors are discussed further in Chapter 5.

The stability definition can be extended to the vector $\tilde{\mathbf{y}}_{t,k} = (y_t, y_{t-1}, \ldots, y_{t-k+1})$ and is then seen to be related to stationarity, as discussed in the previous section. If a process has been running for a long time, and if $\tilde{\mathbf{y}}_{t,k}$ is stable for all k, then it will also be stationary.

The question of how to determine stability for a multivariate model is considered in Chapter 4.

2

General Models and Tools
for Analysis

Preamble

This chapter considers two important topics—the form of some general models that have been proposed for nonlinear relationships and a discussion of some of the statistical tools that may be helpful in determining what model to use. The general models include a generalization of a linear moving average—called the Volterra representation—and a form of autoregressive model with time-varying coefficients, known as the 'state-space model'. In a sense all of the other, specific models considered later are special cases of these general models. However, the general models are often too general for practical use. The chapter also discusses frequency domain analysis, which generalizes the spectrum of linear processes. The resulting functions are interesting theoretically but of limited practical use.

The tools of analysis used for helping specify linear models are not always helpful with nonlinear models; this is particularly true of autocorrelations, cross-correlations, and partial correlations. Some alternatives are discussed at the end of the chapter, which have promise but which require further evaluation.

2.1 Some General Nonlinear Models

A number of general models have been proposed which are useful in theory but not always in practice. They are discussed here to provide a framework for discussing more useful models.

Suppose one has a situation where there is an output to a system, y_t, and a distinct vector input, $\mathbf{u}_t$, which is observed. For example, y_t could be the expenditures of a government department and u_t the series of allocations to it. A general model may then be

$$y_t = f(\mathbf{u}_t, \mathbf{u}_{t-1}, \ldots, \mathbf{u}_{t-q}) + \varepsilon_t \qquad (2.1.1)$$

if just q lags of the input series are used. If the function f is well behaved, the Taylor series around zero will give an expansion:

$$y_t = \mu + \text{(linear component)} + \text{(quadratic component)}$$

$$+ \text{(cubic component)} + \ldots + (m \text{ component)}$$

$$+ e_t \qquad\qquad (2.1.2)$$

where the cubic component, for example, contains all triple terms $u_{i,t}u_{j,s}u_{k,p}$, i, j, k, ranging over 1 to v, and t, s, p each ranging over 0 to q. Each term is premultiplied by a parameter. It is clear that the notation quickly becomes unwieldy and the number of parameters becomes very large. If the lag q is severely restricted to 1 or 2 say, and v is small, also 1 or 2, one still needs to restrict m, the number of the (power) components, to get a feasible model. One feature that is clear is that if the input consists of a single frequency, say $u_t = a \sin \theta_t + b \cos \theta_t$, the output will contain frequency θ plus all its harmonics. If u_t contains two frequencies θ_0 and θ_1 then y_t contains frequencies θ_0, θ_1, $\theta_0 + \theta_1$ and all $k_0\theta_0 + k_1\theta_1$ for integer k_0, k_1. Thus, frequency interpretations are much more difficult than in the linear situation.

A special case of these models is when $\mathbf{u}_t$ is unobserved and is, say, an i.i.d. vector $\boldsymbol{\varepsilon}_t$ and $e_t = 0$. The corresponding expansion will be

$$y_t = \mu + \sum_{i,j} b_{ij}\varepsilon_{i,t-j}$$

$$+ \sum b_{ij,kl}\varepsilon_{i,t-j}\varepsilon_{k,t-l}$$

$$+ \text{cubic component etc.} \qquad\qquad (2.1.3)$$

This is just a formal representation and to study the properties of y_t generated in this fashion, statements about the properties of the sums of the coefficients b_{ij}, etc., and their powers need to be given. These expansions were called Volterra series by Wiener (1958) and have been studied by Rugh (1981) and others; Priestley (1981) called (2.1.2) the 'dual' of the Volterra series. (2.1.3) is a nonlinear generalization of the Wold representation which says that any second-order stationary series x_t can always be represented by

$$\tilde{x}_t = \mu + \sum_{j=0}^{\infty} b_j\varepsilon_{t-j}$$

for some i.i.d. process ε_t and sequence b_j.

Thus, $\tilde{x}_t$ and x_t will have the same mean, variance, and autocovariances, but higher-order moment properties may be different.

As before, the Volterra series expansion is usually too complicated to use, unless it is severely truncated. In that case it is an example of a nonlinear moving average (NLMA) process. A simple case,

$$y_t = \varepsilon_t + \alpha\varepsilon_{t-1} + \beta\varepsilon_t\varepsilon_{t-1}$$

has been studied by Robinson (1977) who considered the parameter estimates and their asymptotic properties. These models have found little use in practice, partly because they are often noninvertible and so are difficult to use directly for forecasting. They can be used to model particular features of a series. For example Rocke (1982) considered y_t generated by

$$y_t = \varepsilon_t + b_1\psi(\varepsilon_{t-1}) + b_2\psi(\varepsilon_{t-2}) + \ldots$$

where $\psi(x) \leq x$ for all $x > 0$, $\psi(-x) = -\psi(x)$ and $\psi'(0) = 1$. This is called a 'limited-response model' and they are said to behave like linear ARMA models under small shocks but to react less strongly to large shocks than linear extrapolation would lead one to expect. A model that would be more useful in economies is one in which there is a reduced lagged effect for large shocks compared to ordinary-sized ones. A regular increase in an input price may be expected to be assimilated less quickly than an exceptionally large price increase, for example.

The obvious problem with input–output systems and Volterra series is that they are using the available information inefficiently, in that no direct use is made of lagged dependent variables. An alternative input–output model which does not have this objection is the 'state affine model', used by Sontag (1977), Guégan (1987), and others. Let $\mathbf{U}_{t,r} \equiv (U_t, U_{t-1}, \ldots, U_{t-r})$ be an input series and its lags and consider a generating mechanism

$$\sum_{k=0}^{q} P_k(\mathbf{U}_{t,r})y_{t-k} = Q(\mathbf{U}_{t,r}).$$

If $P_k(\ )$ and $Q(\ )$ are polynomials in the components of $U_{t,r}$, this system can be written as a state-space form:

$$\mathbf{Z}_{t+1} = F(U_t)\mathbf{Z}_t + H(U_t)$$

$$y_t = G(U_t)\mathbf{Z}_t + I(U_t)$$

where $\mathbf{Z}_t$ is the state vector which characterizes the 'state of the system' at time t, and F, H, G, and I are all polynomials. In the case where $U_t \equiv \varepsilon_t$, an i.i.d. input, Guégan shows that the resulting representation includes bilinear models, and conditions for stationarity and invertibility can be obtained, although these are not easy to use in practice.

A related, very general class of models, called 'state-dependent models', was introduced by Priestley (1980) and is discussed in more detail by him in Priestley (1988). Starting with a causal relationship of the form

$$\mathbf{y}_t = h(I_{t-1}) + \mathbf{e}_t,$$

where $I_t:\mathbf{y}_{t-j}$, $\mathbf{e}_{t-j}$ $0 \le j \le m$ is an information set, using first-order terms from a Taylor expansion, suggests a model

$$\mathbf{y}_t = \boldsymbol{\mu}(\mathbf{z}_{t-1}) - \sum_{j+1}^{p} \boldsymbol{\phi}_j(\mathbf{z}_{t-1})\mathbf{y}_{t-j}$$

$$+ \boldsymbol{\varepsilon}_t + \sum_{j+1}^{q} \boldsymbol{\theta}_j(\mathbf{z}_{t-1})\boldsymbol{\varepsilon}_{t-j}$$

where $\mathbf{z}_t$ is a vector of 'state-variables', which are themselves functions of the contents of I_t. Thus, $\mathbf{y}_t$ is generated by a vector ARMA model, whose coefficients change through time as the state variables evolve. The model is completed by specifying how the state variables are generated. For ease of notation, consider the univariate case, so y_t has just a single component. Priestley suggests making the parameters evolve as

$$\phi_j(\mathbf{z}_t) = \phi_j(\mathbf{z}_{t-1}) + \Delta \mathbf{w}_t' \boldsymbol{\beta}_j^{(t)} \quad j = 1, \ldots, p$$

where

$$\mathbf{w}_t \equiv (\varepsilon_{t-q}, \varepsilon_{t-q+1}, \ldots, y_{t-p}, \ldots, y_t)$$

so $\mathbf{w}$ has $p + q$ elements. Similarly

$$\mu(\mathbf{z}_t) = \mu(\mathbf{z}_{t-1}) + \Delta \mathbf{w}_t' \boldsymbol{\alpha}^{(t)}$$

and

$$\theta_j(\mathbf{z}_t) = \theta_j(\mathbf{z}_{t-1}) + \Delta \mathbf{w}_t' \boldsymbol{\gamma}_j^{(t)} \quad j = 1, \ldots, q.$$

Define

$$\mathbf{B}_t = (\boldsymbol{\alpha}^{(t)}; \beta_p^{(t)}, \beta_{p-1}^{(t)}, \ldots, \beta_1^{(t)}; \gamma_q^{(t)}, \ldots, \gamma_1^{(t)}),$$

which is the vector of all the α, β, γ components of the equations, then the final specification stage has

$$\mathbf{B}_{t+1} = \mathbf{B}_t + \mathbf{V}_{t+1}$$

where $\mathbf{V}_t$ is a sequence of independent matrix-valued random variables. The result is called a state-dependent model (SDM) and can be estimated using a Kalman algorithm.

A related class is the 'doubly stochastic models' introduced by Tjøstheim (1986). An example is the autoregressive form

$$y_t = \sum \theta_{jt} y_{t-j} + \varepsilon_t \tag{2.1.5}$$

where θ_{jt} is a stochastic process for each j, usually taken to be independent of ε_t. Various alternatives arise from specifying different generating mechanisms for the θ_{jt}. They are usually taken to be stationary, such as a simple moving average or autoregressive process. Particular special cases are the random coefficient models, in which $\theta_{jt} = m_j + e_{jt}$, where the m are constant and e_{jt} are i.i.d. series, as studied by Nichols and Quinn (1982). This class has insufficient dynamics for general use but produces rich models for heteroskedasticity. Another, rather different special case is the one where $\theta_t = (\theta_{1t}, \ldots, \theta_{kt})' = (\theta_1^{(1)}, \ldots, \theta_k^{(1)})'$ with probability p, $\theta_t = (\theta_1^{(2)}, \ldots, \theta_k^{(2)})'$ with probability $1 - p$, and $\{\theta_t\}$ is a vector Markov chain with two states. The number of states can be extended to exceed two. Tyssedal and Tjøstheim (1988) called (2.1.5) with these properties the suddenly changing autoregressive (SCAR) model. Its properties, the estimation of the parameters in particular, have also been discussed in Karlsen and Tjøstheim (1990).

The three general classes of model just considered, the state affine, state-dependent, and doubly stochastic, are all essentially linear AR or ARMA models with different forms of time-varying parameters, through which nonlinearities are introduced. Some theoretical results on stationarity and invertibility are available but are of little practical use. The simple, specific models, such as nonlinear autoregressive (including threshold models), nonlinear autoregressive, and bilinear models are all special cases of these general models or extended versions of them. In the following chapters multivariate extensions of the simple models are specifically considered and the general models are discussed further in Chapter 7.

2.2 Frequency Domain Analysis

If x_t is a zero mean, stationary process with autocovariances $R_k = \text{cov}(x_t, x_{t-k})$ the quantity

$$s(\omega) = \frac{1}{2\pi} \sum_{k=-\infty}^{\infty} R_k e^{-ik\omega} \quad \pi \leqslant \omega \leqslant \pi \qquad (2.2.1)$$

will exist and is called the power spectrum of the series. The quantity $\bar{s}(\omega) = s(\omega)/\text{var}(x)$ is the normalized spectrum. Both $s(\omega)$ and $\bar{s}(\omega)$ are positive and even functions in the frequency ω. There is a one-to-one relationship between the sequence of autocovariances and the power spectrum; each can be derived from the other, from (2.2.1), and from

$$R_k = \int_{-\pi}^{\pi} e^{ik\omega} s(\omega) \, d\omega. \qquad (2.2.2)$$

The spectrum has useful interpretations when searching for cycles or near cycles in a series. Replacing R_k by $Q_k = \text{cov}(x_t, y_{t-k})$ in (2.2.1) gives the cross-spectrum $c(\omega)$, which is generally a complex function and measures the lag between series at each frequency and also the strength of any relationship at the different frequencies. Interpretations are discussed in Granger and Hatanaka (1964) and questions of testing and estimation in Koopmans (1974).

These quantities can be generalized into concepts that are potentially useful for the analysis of the nonlinear properties of a series. Define the third-order central automoment of a stationary series x_t with mean m as

$$C(k, s) = E[(x_t - m)(x_{t+k} - m)(x_{t+s} - m)]. \qquad (2.2.3)$$

Several symmetry relationships will hold:

$$C(k, s) = C(s, k) = C(-k, s - k) = C(k - s, -s).$$

The bispectrum is defined as

$$f(\omega_1, \omega_2) = (2\pi)^{-2} \sum_k \sum_s C(k, s) \exp(-ik\omega_1 - is\omega_2) \quad -\pi \le \omega_1, \omega_2 \le \pi.$$

$$(2.2.4)$$

The inverse relationship is

$$C(k, s) = \int_{-\pi}^{\pi} \int_{-\pi}^{\pi} \exp(ik\omega_1 + is\omega_2) \cdot f(\omega_1, \omega_2) \, d\omega_1 \, d\omega_2.$$

Because of various symmetries it is only necessary to know the bispectrum over the region $0 \le \omega_1, \omega_2 \le \pi$, $\omega_1 + \omega_2 \le \pi$.

If x_t is a stationary, linear process generated by

$$x_t = \sum_{k=0}^{\infty} h_k \varepsilon_{t-k}$$

$$\equiv h(B)\varepsilon_t$$

where ε_t is i.i.d. with zero mean, then x_t has spectrum

$$s(\omega) = |h(z)|^2 \sigma_\varepsilon^2, \, z = e^{-i\omega}$$

and bispectrum

$$f(\omega_1, \omega_2) = s(\omega_1)s(\omega_2)s(\omega_1 + \omega_2)\lambda_3 \qquad (2.2.5)$$

where $\lambda_3 = E[\varepsilon_t^3]$. It follows that if $\lambda_3 = 0$, then $f(\omega_1, \omega_2) = 0$ at all frequencies, an example being a Gaussian process. The function

$$\bar{f}(\omega_1, \omega_2) = \frac{f(\omega_1, \omega_2)}{s(\omega_1)s(\omega_2)s(\omega_1 + \omega_2)} \qquad (2.2.6)$$

is called the 'normalized bispectrum' and it has the property that it is a constant over all frequencies if the series is linear. Thus, this function is potentially relevant for a study of possible nonlinearity. A test for linearity has been proposed using this function by Ashley, Patterson, and Hinich (1986). Estimation questions are discussed by Subba Rao and Gabr (1984) who also give various examples. Some difficulties with the approach are that interpretation of the diagram is not easy; it is often very jagged and has an unclear shape. Even simple nonlinear models, such as the NLAR(1) and bilinear, do not have distinctive bispectral shapes and some nonlinear models have $f(\omega_1, \omega_2) = 0$ for all frequencies and so this property is not a characterizing one for linearity. The first bispectral estimate using economic data was by Godfrey (1965), using ideas proposed by John Tukey (1959). The initial theory of the bispectrum, and also higher-order functions called polyspectra, was provided by Brillinger and Rosenblatt (1967a, b).

To investigate relationships between series, the cross-bispectrum can be defined. Let y_t, x_t be a pair of stationary series with means μ_y, μ_x respectively. Define the third-order cross-moment $(x \to y)$ by

$$\mu_{xx,y}(k, s) = E[(y_t - \mu_y)(x_{t+y} - \mu_x)(x_{t+s} - \mu_x)]$$

and the cross-bispectrum by

$$f_{xxy}(\omega_1, \omega_2) = (2\pi)^{-2} \sum_{k=\infty}^{\infty} \sum_{s=-\infty}^{\infty} \mu_{xx,y}(k, s) \exp(-i\omega_1 k - i\omega_2 s)$$

$$-\pi \leqslant \omega_1, \omega_2 \leqslant \pi.$$

If there is a one-way quadratic relationship this function may be interpretable. For example, if x_t is a Gaussian input series, and if

$$y_t = \sum_{j=0}^{q} \alpha_j x_{t-j} + \sum_{j,k=1}^{p} \beta_{jk}\{x_{t-j}x_{t-k} - R(j - k)\} + \varepsilon_t \quad (2.2.7)$$

where

$$R(j - k) = E[x_{t-j}x_{t-k}]$$

and defining

$$A(\omega) = \sum \alpha_j e^{-ij\omega}$$

and

$$B(\omega_1, \omega_2) = \sum \beta_{jk} e^{-ij\omega_1} \cdot e^{-ij\omega_2},$$

then Subba Rao and Nunes (1985) show that

$$A(\omega) = C_{xy}(\omega)/s_x(\omega)$$

and

$$B(\omega_1, \omega_2) = \frac{f_{xxy}(\omega_1, \omega_2)}{2s_x(\omega_1)s_x(\omega_2)}. \qquad (2.2.8)$$

It should be noted that the linear terms, x_{q-j} are orthogonal to the quadratic term involving $x_{t-j}x_{t-k}$ in (2.2.7) if x_t is Gaussian. In the simplest of all nonlinear cases, where

$$y_t = \sum \alpha_i x_{t-i} + \beta_{jk}(x_{t-j}x_{t-k} - R(j-k)) + \varepsilon_t$$

so that there is just a single quadratic term, (2.2.8), gives

$$f_{xxy}(\omega_1, \omega_2) \, \beta_{jk}[e^{-ij\omega_1}s_x(\omega_1)] \cdot x[e^{-ij\omega_2}s_x(\omega_2)],$$

so that, in principle, the lags j, k of the single quadratic term can be determined. This is too simple a case to be of much practical value and, anyway, it only has this interpretation when there is no feedback in the system, from y to x. If one has plenty of data, the bispectrum may be interesting to estimate and to use as a test for nonlinearity but in most realistic situations their poor estimation properties and difficulties with interpretation make them not a recommended technique for analysis.

2.3 Tools of Analysis

For linear, stationary processes a number of exploratory tools for use in specification searches have been developed and their interpretation is understood. The best known of these are the auto- and cross-correlations

$$\rho_k = \text{corr}(y_t, y_{t-k})$$

and

$$c_k = \text{corr}(y_t, x_{t-k}),$$

and their estimates. The partial correlations, such as

$$\bar{\rho}_k = \text{corr}(y_t, y_{t-k}|y_{t-j}, j = 1, \ldots, k-1)$$

are also useful. However, once one gets away from linear, stationary processes these tools become of dubious use. For example, if x_t, u_t are both Gaussian white noise and y_t is generated by

$$y_t = \beta y_{t-1} x_{t-1} + u_t,$$

then it is easily shown that ρ_k is zero for all $k \neq 0$ and c_k is zero for all k. Thus, y_t is not linearly forecastable from either its own past or the past of x_t and y_t. However, y_t is forecastable one step ahead non-linearly, with optimum forecast

$$f_{t,1} = \beta y_t x_t.$$

In another example, Blatt (1987) generated a series which was an explosive, deterministic oscillation constrained by a floor and ceiling. He found estimated autocorrelations that were indistinguishable from those of a stationary process. Similarly, data generated by an explosive AR(1) process will have autocorrelations that look like those from a stationary AR(1) series. Clearly, if tools are designed specifically for one situation but are used elsewhere, they can become misleading and difficult to interpret.

There are few simple explanatory tools for use to investigate possible nonlinear models. The bispectrum is one but is also usually difficult to interpret. There are a number of descriptive statistics designed for use with chaotic processes, such as the correlation dimension, Lyapunov exponents, and Kolmogorov entropy. These are all described in Lorenz (1989). Although they may be useful in distinguishing a deterministic chaotic process from a stochastic one, as discussed in Section 3.3, they are unhelpful when trying to distinguish one stochastic process from another.

A potentially useful statistical tool would measure the relatedness between y_t and y_{t-k} or x_{t-k}. Various measures of relatedness exist and could be used. For a pair of random variables y, x these include:

(a) the maximum correlation coefficient, defined as

$$m\rho = \text{corr}\,(g(y), f(x))$$

where the functions f, g are chosen to maximize $m\rho$.

(b) maximum mean correlation

$$mm = \text{corr}\,(y, f(x))$$

with f chosen to maximize mm, and

(c) maximum regression coefficient

$$mr = R^2 \text{ in the regression}$$

$$y = f(x) + \text{residual}$$

where f is chosen to maximize mr.

Used with time-series, y would be y_{t+k}, x would be either y_t, giving $m\rho_{yy}(k)$, etc., or x would be x_t, giving $m\rho_{yx}(k)$, etc. In $m\rho$ the functions can be estimated using the ACE algorithm proposed by Breiman and Friedman (1988); mm can be estimated using just the first step of ACE. The functions are usually taken to be cubic splines, or some nonparametric functions; mr can be estimated directly from an algorithm suggested by Tibshirani (1988). Approximations to mr can be found by just regressing y_{t+k} on a selection of parametric functions of y_t or x_t, such as $\log|x|$, x, x^2 and $\exp x$. The size of R_e^2 will indicate the potential relevance of a nonlinear relationship.

A further statistic which may be useful is the 'shadow autocorrelation' R, which is derived from the mutual information measure discussed in Pinsker (1964) and McEliece (1977). Let X, Y be a pair of random variables with joint probability distribution function $p(x, y)$ and marginals $p_1(x)$, $p_2(y)$ then the mutual information measure $I(X, Y)$ is defined by

$$I(X, Y) = \iint p(x, y)\log\left[\frac{p(x, y)}{p_1(x)p_2(y)}\right] dx\, dy.$$

From this, define

$$R^2(X, Y) = 1 - \exp(-2I(X, Y)).$$

It is shown in Granger and Lin (1991) that $R(X, Y)$ has the following useful properties:

(i) $R = 0$ if and only if X, Y are independent;
(ii) $R = 1$ if and only if $X = f(Y)$ where $f(\ )$ is some invertible, deterministic function, otherwise $0 \leqslant R \leqslant 1$;
(iii) R is unaltered if X, Y are replaced by instantaneous transformations, $g(X)$, $h(Y)$;
(iv) If X, Y are such that (possibly after some individual instantaneous transformations) the resulting variables have a joint Gaussian distribution with correlation ρ, then $R = |\rho|$. Of course, such a transformation need not exist.

If X, Y are replaced by x_t, x_{t-k} then $R_k \equiv R(x_t, x_{t-k})$ is a generalized (modulus of an) autocorrelation and can potentially be used to suggest appropriate lags to be used in a model, with the distribution functions involved in the definition being estimated nonparametrically.

Granger and Lin (1991) investigated the properties of $\hat{R}_k$ using simulations. When the expected value of R_k is zero, with an i.i.d. process, for example, the expected value of $\hat{R}_k$ is still positive as the estimate is constrained to be positive using a kernel density estimator with band width proportional to $n^{-1/5}$, with sample size n; the bias (i.e. mean) of $\hat{R}_1$ was as shown in Table 2.1.

The sizes for $\hat{R}_k$ at other lags are similar. For a sample size of 300, the 95% and 99% critical values for the null hypothesis $R_k = 0$ are 0.2045 and 0.2212 respectively. Thus, with this sample size, an estimate of $\hat{R}_k$ larger than these values suggests that x_t, x_{t-k} are not independent. As examples of the successful use of the shadow correlation,

TABLE 2.1

Sample size	Mean $\hat{R}_1$
100	0.203
200	0.179
300	0.164
500	0.149
1000	0.132
3000	0.101

samples of size 300 were generated 200 times from each of the models:

(1) $\qquad y_t = e_t + 0.8e_{t-3}^2 \quad$ (NLMA(3))

(2) $\qquad y_t = 0.6e_{t-1}y_{t-2} + e_t$ (bilinear)

(3) $\qquad y_t = 4y_{t-1}(1 - y_{t-1})$ (deterministic chaos)

where $e_t \sim N(0, 1)$, i.i.d. series in each.

Average, estimated $\hat{R}_k$ values were as shown in Table 2.2. The significant values correspond to relevant lags in the various models. The chaos series produced very low values compared to stochastic cases. The results, when used with linear and nonlinear autoregressive models, are also interesting. See, for example, the following three models.

(4) $\qquad y_t = |y_{t-1}|^{0.8} + e_t \quad$ (NLAR(1))

(5) $\qquad y_t = \text{sign}(y_{t-1}) + e_t$ (NLAR(1))

(6) $\qquad y_t = y_{t-1} + e_t.$ $\qquad$ (random walk)

Average $\hat{R}_k$ values are shown in Table 2.3. For the nonlinear AR(1)

TABLE 2.2

lag k	Model		
	1	2	3
1	0.171	0.217*	0.408*
2	0.173	0.234*	0.150
3	0.330*	0.188	0.059
4	0.172	0.189	0.060
5	0.171	0.177	0.062

* indicates significance at least at the 95% level.

TABLE 2.3

lag	Model		
k			
	4	5	6
1	0.460	0.498	0.655
2	0.298	0.304	0.612
3	0.232	0.221	0.580
4	0.201	0.194	0.558
5	0.185	0.188	0.542

models the shadow autocorrelations decline exponentially, similar to the autocorrelogram using the (linear) autocorrelations with a linear AR(1) model. Similarly, for a random walk $\hat{R}_k$ declines slowly as k increases, as for the linear autocorrelation case, but is downward biased at low lags.

A generalized partial autocorrelation can also be defined but is difficult to estimate, as k becomes large. A usable statistic is the Kendall partial tau (τ) which is defined in Quade (1976) as follows:

Consider the random variables X_t, Y_t, $\mathbf{Z}_t$ and only the cases where $\|\mathbf{Z}_t - \mathbf{Z}_s\| \leq L$, where $\| \|$ is some norm and L is a predetermined 'tolerance'. With this condition holding, define $\mu(t, s) = \text{sign}\left[(X_t - X_s)(Y_t - Y_s)\right]$ and $C_p =$ number of (t, s) pairs with $\mu(t, s)$ positive $D_p =$ number of (t, s) pairs with $\mu(t, s)$ negative with $0 \leq t \leq T$, and let N_p be the number of (t, s) pairs where the constant holds. Finally, define

$$\tau_p = (C_p - D_p)/N_p.$$

In the time-series context, take $X = x_t$, $Y = x_{t-k}$ and $\mathbf{Z}_t = x_{t-1}, \ldots, x_{t-k+1}$. A test based on this statistic, and its asymptotic normal $N(0, 1)$ distribution, was found to be helpful in choosing the correct lags for the simple nonlinear autoregressive models but did not work well with nonlinear moving average models. The pair of statistics, the shadow autocorrelation, and the partial Kendall tau appear to be useful as analogous of the auto- and partial auto-correlations used with linear models.

A final pair of tools that are sometimes useful are designed to help decide how many components to use in a model. To illustrate the idea, suppose that y_t is being modelled in terms of just two observed inputs x_t, w_t with a model of the form

$$y_t = \sum_{j=1}^{p} \alpha_j g_j(x_t) + \sum_{j=1}^{q} \beta_j h_j(w_t) = e_t.$$

Two statistics have been found to be helpful in choosing values for p and q:

$$\text{AIC}(p, q) = \log \sigma_{p,q}^2 + 2(p + q)/n$$

$$\text{BIC}(p, q) = \log \sigma_{p,q}^2 + (p + q) \frac{\log n}{n}$$

where $\sigma_{p,q}^2$ is the estimated variance of the residual e_t for a particular choice of p and q, and n is the sample size utilized in the maximum-likelihood estimation of the parameters α, β. These statistics are estimated for many possible values of p and q and the p_0, q_0 that minimize the statistic is chosen. If it is believed that the true value of p or q is infinite and the question is what finite values of p_0, q_0 produce the best approximation to the true infinite model, given sample size n, then the AIC statistic is recommended. If it is believed that the true generating mechanism has finite p, q values, then the BIC statistic is recommended. There is no test of significance associated with these statistics, to see if a model based on p_0, q_0 is significantly better than $p_0 - 1$, $q_0 - 1$, say. In practice there will usually be more than two inputs and so there will be several model size parameters $p_1, \ldots, p_m$ to chose from rather than just the pair p, q. The statistics provide alternative penalties for choosing large models, that is involving many parameters. Their uses are discussed in Judge *et al*. (1985). Here the inputs are assumed to be known, but for many modelling procedures the functions are actually linear combinations of several inputs, such as the neural network or nonparametric models discussed in Chapter 7 where a function might be $\phi(\sum c_j x_{t-j})$. In these cases there are now many more parameters involved—those inside the functions and those multiplying the functions. If there are p such functions, each involving different linear combinations of r inputs, the total number of parameters is now pr. Rissanen (1989) has suggested using the BIC criterion, with p replaced now by pr, and calls this a complexity criterion. As before, p is chosen to minimize the criterion but no tests of significance are yet available.

3

Nonlinear Models in Economic Theory

Preamble

There are many nonlinear models that have been suggested by economic theory and they are briefly reviewed here to see if they suggest models that econometricians should consider. One class that does seem to be potentially relevant involves switching regimes.

One difficulty is that theorists often discuss deterministic models—involving bifurcation, catastrophes, and chaotic processes—whereas econometricians probably believe strongly that the economy is inherently stochastic due to measurement errors, unexpected shocks to the system, and unmeasured variables. The chapter briefly looks at these deterministic models.

3.1 Some Suggested Nonlinear Models

Economic theorists have by no means studied just linear models and they have suggested various forms of nonlinearity to try to explain real aspects of the economy. It should be emphasized that the specifications are often merely suggestions of appropriate forms and are not derived from some deep theory. The examples discussed here are largely taken from macroeconomics, although plenty occur elsewhere in economics.

Sometimes the nonlinear specification is rather vague, such as a savings function:

$$\text{Savings} = S(Y, K)$$

where Y = income and K is capital stock, but with S being a sigmoid function in Y with K fixed, non-decreasing as Y with $S_K > 0$ and $0 < S_y < 1$, where S_x = partial derivative. An example might be a logistic function.

Other models are more specific with one variable being related to a particular function of another. An example is the 'prey–predator' model used by Desai (1986) based on a well-known theory of Richard Goodwin. If w = real wages, v = employment rate, u = share of wages in national income, $Z_1 = \log u$, $Z_2 = \log v$, the system used is;

$$\Delta Z_1 = -a + b \exp(Z_2)$$
$$\Delta Z_2 = c - b \exp(Z_1)$$

Some models are very nonlinear in form but can be made linear by instantaneous transformation. An example is the Cobb–Douglas production function;

$$Y = \sigma L^\gamma K^\beta$$

where L = labour input, K = capital stock, and Y is production. Clearly the model is linear in the logs of the variable. Similarly the CES production function given by

$$Y^\gamma = aL^\gamma + bK^\gamma$$

is linear in the variables raised to the power γ.

Models can also involve products of variables, such as a translog cost function where cost of output = linear terms in $\log p_1$, $\log p_2 +$ $\gamma \log p_1 \cdot \log p_2$ where p_1, p_2 are prices of inputs. An example of a dynamic specification that is nonlinear in various ways is an extension of a classical growth model discussed by Glombowski and Krüger (1986). If K is capital stock, β the degree of employment, π profits, and λ the share of wages in GNP, a four-equation version of the system is:

$$\Delta \log K_t = c_1 + c_2(1 - \lambda_t)$$
$$\Delta \log \beta_t = c_3 + c_4 \Delta \log K_t$$
$$\Delta \log \lambda_t = c_5 + c_6(\epsilon \beta_t + (1 - \epsilon)\beta_{t-1})$$

and

$$\Delta \log \pi_t = \Delta \log(1-\lambda_t) + \Delta \log K_t + \Delta \log(1-\lambda_t) \cdot \Delta \log K_t$$

where c_1, c_2 etc. are constants. As given here, everything is simultaneous and so data would be difficult to generate from this model.

A different type of model involves ceilings and floors. For example, Thio (1986) builds a model of the business cycle which is mostly linear or log linear, but includes an investment function of the form $I_t = I(y_{t-1})$ where

$$y_t = Y_t - Y_t^c$$

and

$$Y_t = \text{value of output,}$$
$$Y_t^c = \text{capacity of production}$$

where

$$I(y_{t-1}) = \min\,[gy_{t-1},\, \phi Y^c_{t-1}] \quad \text{if } Y_{t-1} \geqslant Y^c_{t-1}$$
$$\phantom{I(y_{t-1})} = \max\,[gy_{t-1},\, \psi Y^c_{t-1}] \quad \text{if } Y_{t-1} \leqslant Y^c_{t-1}$$

with $\phi > 0$, $\psi < 0$ (see Fig. 3.1).

In a related analysis Blatt (1983) discusses a series which would have explosive oscillations but is constrained by a ceiling and a floor. An extension of this idea is that of Miller and Orr (1966) concerning holdings of cash. Because of transfer costs, companies or individuals do not continually adjust their money holdings but allow them to wander between upper and lower thresholds. If a threshold is crossed, a transfer between money and a near-money asset is triggered, giving a new portfolio balance and bringing money held back to some point within the thresholds. This behaviour can also be considered as an example of regime switching, where a rule of behaviour switches according to whether a variable lies in a particular region or not. Ferri and Greenberg (1989) discuss such models of labour supply which switch in form as one gets near to full employment.

A different type of regime switching occurs in disequilibrium analysis where

$$\text{sales} = \min\,(X^d,\, X^s)$$

where X^d is the quantity demanded and X^s the quantity supplied to some market, and

$$X^d = a_1 Z_d + \varepsilon_d$$
$$X^s = a_2 Z_s + \varepsilon_s.$$

Z_d is the set of variables affecting demand with corresponding parameters a_1, ε_d is a demand disturbance term, and similarly for the supply side. Quandt (1982) has discussed the econometrics of this situation.

A further example of switching regimes are models with kinked budget constraints, as discussed by Moffitt (1990). Other examples,

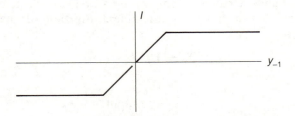

FIG. 3.1. Plot of investment function

taken from stock-market literature discussing efficient market theory are given in Granger (1992).

This very superficial survey illustrates the variety of models that have been suggested and, if true, have to be discoverable by the statistical techniques discussed in later chapters. Some of the models are specifically covered by smooth transition switching and general regression specifications, others can be expected to be adequately approximated by flexible techniques such as nonparametric estimates. A brief history of nonlinear dynamics in economics has been provided by Rostow (1992).

In his discussion of the choice of functional forms in economic analysis, Lau (1986) lists five criteria for consideration:

(i) theoretical consistency—so that the form chosen is capable of possessing the theoretical properties required of the economic relationship;

(ii) domain of attraction—so that the variables involved can take a wide and appropriate set of possible values (some values, such as zero and infinity, may produce unacceptable forms of the relationship);

(iii) flexibility—the form chosen should be able to approximate other likely forms for some choice of parameter values;

(iv) computational facility; and

(v) factual conformity.

Once a model has been constructed, it is certainly worth considering these criteria. They can also be useful when comparing alternative models. Lau shows that some apparently sensible function forms can be rejected by use of such criteria.

One property of most of the nonlinear models discussed above that is disturbing to econometricians is that they are all actually, or essentially, deterministic. Economic theorists often propose theories as though the economy were deterministic, and this often makes the theory of limited use to the econometrician or applied economist when specifying a model. Further aspects of this tendency by theorists are discussed in the next two Sections.

3.2 Bifurcation and Catastrophe

The outputs from a simple nonlinear deterministic model can have a variety of properties, such as leading towards an equilibrium, or towards a limit cycle, or appearing to have some properties in common with stochastic processes—so-called chaos, which will be discussed in the next section. To illustrate these ideas, consider a univariate deterministic generator:

$$x_t = f(x_{t-1}, \mu) \qquad (3.2.1)$$

where μ is some parameter. The process generated from this 'iterative map', given a starting value x_0, is said to have an equilibrium or fixed point x^* if

$$x^* = f(x^*, \mu)$$

and to have a 2-cycle if there exists a value $\bar{x}$ such that:

$$\bar{x} \neq f(\bar{x}, \mu),$$

but

$$\bar{x} = f[f(\bar{x}, \mu), \mu].$$

Thus, for a fixed point, if x_t ever becomes x^* it will remain at this value forever. Similarly if x_t takes the value $\bar{x}$ it will take this value at times $t + 2$, $t + 4$, $t + 6$, ... and so will contain a cycle of period 2. If x_t is generated by

$$x_t = bx_{t-1}(1 - x_{t-1}) \tag{3.2.2}$$

and

$$0 < x_0 < 1, \, b > 0,$$

then x_t will have a fixed point for b small, for large b values it will produce cycles, and for $b = 4$ will produce chaos.

An example of a simple model that produces cycles is given by Ferri and Greenberg (1989: 69). If

$$\Delta \log w_t = F(e_t)$$

where e_t is employment rate, w_t is nominal wage, and $F(e)$ is a function that is nondecreasing for $\alpha \leq e \leq \beta$, with

$$\lim_{e \to \alpha} F(e) = -\infty$$

$$\lim_{e \to \beta} F(e) = +\infty$$

Then consider the system of equations:

$$\Delta x_t = x_t E(x_t)[H(x_t) - F(e_t)], \quad E' > 0$$

$$\Delta v_t = v_t[n - g(x_t)]$$

$$e_t = X_t/v_t$$

where $x = N/K$ is the employment/capital ratio, $v = N^s/K$ is the labour supply/capital ratio, $E(x)$ is the firm's derived demand for labour, and $H(x)$ measures the inflation of expected demand prices. In the x–v plane, this model can produce limit cycles.

Some nonlinear generators, such as (3.2.1) have the property that a small change in parameter values can lead to large changes in the long-run properties, from one fixed point to another quite different one, or from a fixed point to a cycle. This effect is called a bifurcation and reflects the idea that as one searches over parameter values one is actually considering models with quite different long-run properties.

Lorenz (1989) gives a full and interesting discussion of bifurcation and provides the following example. Suppose that the growth rate of some variable, N_t, depends linearly on the size of the variable, so that

$$\frac{N_{t+1} - N_t}{N_t} = \mu\left(1 - \frac{N_t}{m}\right) - 1,$$

say. N_t could be the size of a population and, with $N_0 > 0$, $\mu > 0$, m could be the saturation level, so that $N_t \leq m$ for all t. Rewriting the equation gives

$$N_{t+1} = \mu N_t\left(1 - \frac{N_t}{m}\right).$$

Except for $N_t = 0$, which is extinction, the only fixed point is

$$N^* = m(1 - \mu^{-1}).$$

Lorenz's analysis suggests that if $\mu < 3$, the process will tend towards this fixed point, but if $\mu = 3$, population level will be characterized by a permanent 2-cycle.

There are several types of bifurcation and these are discussed by Lorenz. For univariate and bivariate models limited to be less than fourth-order powers in the variable it can be shown that only a few types of bifurcation can occur. This is the basis of catastrophe theory, also discussed by Lorenz (1989). In just a few of these cases very substantial changes in the motion of the process can occur with small changes in parameter values, hence the use of the word 'catastrophe'. An example would be a group of runners who regularly go around a cross-country track but who look just at the track. They are unaware that at one point the track goes along the top of a substantial cliff. A small change in the location of the track could lead them to fall over the cliff. In economics the analogy would be if a small policy change affects values of parameters in a small way but leads to a large change in some important economic variable such as unemployment or the inflation rate. These problems occur in deterministic models and may be less relevant for stochastic models, where the inherent shocks to the system effectively greatly extend the experience of the economy.

3.3 Chaos

The extensive use of deterministic models in much of economic theory leads to a difficulty as most economic data appear to contain important random elements. A possible escape from this impasse is to consider chaotic processes, which have received wide attention in physics and other fields. For the moment a 'white chaotic process' will be defined as a process generated by a deterministic difference equation:

$$x_{t+1} = f(x_{t-j}, j = 0, \ldots, p)$$

such that x_t does not tend to a constant or a cycle (of finite power) and has estimated autocovariances that are very small or zero, so that $\hat{cov}(x_t, x_{t-k}) \simeq 0$, for $k = 1, 2, \ldots, m$, m large. An example of such a process is generated by the 'logistic map':

$$x_{t+1} = 4x_t(1 - x_t)$$

with $0 < x_0 < 1$. Liu (1990) generated six thousand terms from this model and found the autocorrelations for x_t and for x_t^2 as shown in Table 3.1.

The series has the same autocorrelation properties as a white noise but it is clearly not i.i.d. as the square of the series has a significant first-order correlation. (The approximate 95% confidence interval is given by $\pm 2/\sqrt{n}$. Here $n = 6,000$, so the interval is ± 0.026.) There are many generating mechanisms that produce chaos series and others can produce series having autocorrelation identical to other stationary linear processes. The existence of these processes suggests that economic data, taken to be stochastic by econometricians, could be deterministic but chaotic. It has been shown by economic theorists that deterministic theories could lead to chaotic outcomes, see, for example, the special edition of the *Journal of Economic Theory*, 40/1 (1986), and the books

TABLE 3.1.   Autocorrelations for terms from logistic map and for squared terms

Lag k	corr(x_t, x_{t-k})		corr(x_t^2, x_{t-k}^2)	
1	.016		−.222	
2	.007		.001	
3	.005		.002	
4	.006		.005	
5	−.000		.004	
6	−.025		−.027	
7	.004		.011	
8	−.003		−.003	
9	−.002		−.004	
10	.012		.014	
	mean	0.498	mean	0.374
	variance	0.126	variance	0.132

by Puu (1989), Lorenz (1989), and Chen and Day (1992). However, what is important is not whether economic can be chaos in theory, but whether it occurs in practice.

Visually, a white chaos series will appear to be a stochastic white noise, and chaotic series can be constructed that appear visually to be very similar to other stochastic linear processes such as those generated by ARMA models. There are in fact many types of chaotic processes and a variety of statistics has been designed to differentiate between them and to characterize the basic properties of the processes. Only two such statistics will be mentioned here, the Lyapunov exponent and the correlation dimension. If the process is generated by

$$x_t = f(x_{t-1}),$$

suppose that two sequences $x_t^{(j)}$ $j = 1$, 2 are generated with slightly different starting values $x_0^{(j)}$ $j = 1$, 2 and denote $d_t = x_t^{(1)} - x_t^{(2)}$, the distance between the processes, then for d_0 sufficiently small and for t not too big,

$$d_t = d_0 \cdot 2^{\lambda t}$$

is found to hold for chaotic processes, where λ is the Lyapunov exponent, which is necessarily positive.

For a single chaotic series x_t, define $x_{t,m}$ to be the set of m adjacent values x_{t+j}, $j = 0 \ldots m - 1$ and let the m-correlation integral $C_m(\varepsilon)$ be defined by

$$C_m(\varepsilon) = \lim_{N \to \infty} N^{-2}\{\text{number of pairs } (i, j)$$

$$|x_i - x_j| < \varepsilon, \ |x_{i+1} - x_{j+1}| < \varepsilon \ldots |x_{i+m-1} - x_{j+m-1}| < \varepsilon\} \quad (3.3.1)$$

so that a pair x_{i+m}, x_{j+m} are ε-close if every pair of corresponding components are within ε of each other. The idea is that if x_i, x_j are close in value, then so will be subsequent pairs for a chaotic series, but this will not occur for a stochastic sequence. It has been shown that for a chaotic process

$$C_m(\varepsilon) \simeq \varepsilon^{v_m}$$

for small ε, and

$$v_m = \bar{v}$$

for $m > \bar{v}$, where $\bar{v}$ is a measure called the dimension of the process, $\bar{v}$ need not be an integer. If $\bar{v}$ is large, say 10 or so, it is difficult to estimate and the pseudo-random numbers generated on computers are chaotic processes with large dimension. It follows that high-dimensional chaotic processes are indistinguishable from stochastic processes even when using samples of much greater sizes than are available in economics. There still remains the possibility of distinguishing a low-dimensional white chaotic process from a stochastic i.i.d. series. This may be achieved using estimators of $v_m = d \log C_m(\varepsilon)/d\varepsilon$, which should be approximately constant as m increases for a chaotic process but should be equal to m for a stochastic process. In Liu (1990) and Liu, Granger, and Heller (1992) a series of simulations were conducted, with conclusions:

(i) If a series is generated by a white chaotic process, such as the tent map discussed above, the technique using the estimated correlation dimension works successfully. Similarly, an i.i.d. process produces estimates of v_m which are virtually identical to m. These results hold both for large ($n = 1,000$) and small ($n = 200$) samples.

(ii) If a process is the sum of a white chaos, with variance v_1, and an i.i.d. series with variance v_2, then $\hat{v}_m$ will be inclined to steadily increase with m, even when v_1 is twenty times v_2. Thus, if an economic variable is white chaos but is observed with a small stochastic measurement error, then the estimated correlation dimension procedure will not be able to distinguish the large chaotic component;

(iii) and the actual economic variables considered will appear to be stochastic rather than chaotic.

Brock, Deckert, and Scheinkman (1987) have devised a test concerning chaos, and this is discussed and applied, for example in Brock and Sayers (1988) and very frequently in the analysis of financial time-series. The test is described in Chapter 6, where it is called the BDS Test and uses the correlation dimension. It has as its null hypothesis, in the univariate case, $H_0: y_t$ is i.i.d. and is designed to have power against white noise chaos processes. However, the test also has power against a variety of nonlinear stochastic processes. At present, there is evidence for nonlinearity in economic data but little evidence for this also being chaos. This is probably in agreement with the prior beliefs of most econometricians and applied economists.

4

Particular Nonlinear Multivariate Models

Preamble

This chapter reviews several specific nonlinear models that are useful in practical analysis. The models are fairly obvious generalizations of well-known univariate models, such as autoregressive, moving average, and bilinear models. Some specific nonlinear autoregressive models are likely to be the most practical: these are all concerned with modelling the mean or conditional expectation or a series. The final section discusses simple models for conditional variance.

4.1 Nonlinear Autoregressive and Regression Models

If $\mathbf{y}_t$ is a vector, with m components, a nonlinear vector autoregressive system (NLVAR(p)) has the form

$$\mathbf{y}_t = \mathbf{f}(\mathbf{y}_{t-j}, j = 1, \ldots, p) + \mathbf{e}_t \tag{4.1.1}$$

where $\mathbf{e}_t$ is zero mean i.i.d. The two obvious questions are: what is the vector of functions $\mathbf{f}' = (f_1, f_2, \ldots, f_m)$, and what is the lag p? For a particular component of $\mathbf{y}_t$, one has the multiple input, single output model:

$$y_{kt} = f_k(\mathbf{y}_{t-j}, j = 1, \ldots, p) + e_{kt},$$

or

$$y_{kt} = g_k(y_{k,t-j}, \mathbf{x}^{(k)}_{t-k}, j = 1, \ldots, p) + e_{kt} \tag{4.1.2}$$

where $\mathbf{x}^{(k)}$ is the vector of 'other' explanatory variables $\mathbf{x}' = (y_1, y_2, \ldots, y_{k-1}, y_{k+1} \ldots, y_m)$. Necessary and sufficient conditions of stability for the system (4.1.1) with $p = 1$ are, according to Tweedie (1975), and Lasota and Mackey (1989), that

$$\|\mathbf{f}(\mathbf{y})\| \leq \alpha \|\mathbf{y}\| \quad \text{for } \|\mathbf{y}\| \geq c \tag{4.1.3a}$$

where

$$|\alpha| < 1,$$

and

$$\|f(\mathbf{y})\| \text{ finite for all finite } \mathbf{y} \qquad (4.1.3b)$$

where $\|\mathbf{f}\|$ is any norm of $\mathbf{f}$, such as the Euclidean norm $(\sum_{j-1}^{m} f_j^2)^{1/2}$. Thus, for large enough values of $\mathbf{y}$, the functions $\mathbf{f}$ have essentially to be dominated by a linear function with slope less than one. This is analogous to the univariate AR(1) model

$$y_t = \alpha y_{t-1} + e_t,$$

which is stable if $|\alpha| < 1$ with the condition as given. The process can be locally unstable, and could trend upward, for example, until the stable, constraining region is reached, rather like an exploding AR(1) with an upper barrier. A stricter stability condition (4.1.3a) has holding for all $\mathbf{y}$ values, which is the same as taking $c = 0$ in (4.1.3a). If $\mathbf{y}$ is stable then so are all components, but conditions for stability of a single component y_{kt} cannot be achieved easily.

In particular, the x can be unstable but functions of them, such as sums, may be stable, in analogy with cointegration.

It may be noted that by repeated substitution in (4.1.1), $\mathbf{y}_t$ can be given as a function of e_{t-j}, $j \geqslant 0$ and then by expansion of this function, a Volterra series representation is found, as discussed in Chapter 2. Similarly, by repeated substitution in (4.1.2), y_{kt} can be given as a function of $\mathbf{x}_{t-j}^{(k)}$, $e_{k,t-j}$ $j \geqslant 0$. However, in practice the original equations are usually more usable than derived ones for purposes of estimation and forecasting.

If the function $\mathbf{f}$ in (4.1.1) or g_k in (4.1.2) are known exactly, apart from a set of parameters β, say, then these can be estimated by least-squares (as discussed in Judge *et al.* 1985 or Gallant 1987) and maximum-likelihood (see Gallant and White 1988) techniques. Under suitable conditions, these estimates will be consistent and normally distributed and constraints on these parameters can be tested. The reality and necessity of the conditions are not clear in practice and they are generally very difficult to test. It follows that the asymptotic results, such as confidence intervals for a parameter should be used with caution and considered to be approximations at best to true intervals for finite samples.

An example of a simple NLAR(1) model is;

$$\mathbf{y}_t = \mathbf{a}_1'\mathbf{y}_{t-1} + \exp\left(-\gamma(\mathbf{a}_3'\mathbf{y}_{t-1}^2)\right)\mathbf{a}_2'\mathbf{y}_{t-1} + \mathbf{e}_t$$

where $a_3 = (a_{31}, \ldots, a_{3p})'$, $\sum a_{3j} = 1$, $\gamma > 0$ which is an obvious generalization of the exponential AR model. Here $\mathbf{y}_t^2$ is the vector of squared components of $\mathbf{y}_t$. A further generalization would replace $\mathbf{a}_3'\mathbf{y}_{t-1}^2$ by a positive definite form in the components of $\mathbf{y}$.

4.2 Smooth Transition Regression Models

Many parts of economic theory include the idea that the economy behaves differently if some variable lies in one region rather than in another. One might have savings having a different structural model if interest rates are decreasing rather than increasing, or industry may change its decisions if capacity is nearly full or the employment rate is high.

These models can be grouped under the heading of 'regime-switching' theories. They can take many forms and thus give rise to a variety of non-linear time-series models. A very simple single-equation form might be:

$$y_t = \alpha_0 + \alpha_1 x_{t-1} + (\beta_0 + \beta_1 x_{t-1})F(x_{t-1} - \mu) + e_t \qquad (4.2.1)$$

where e_t is i.i.d. Furthermore, $F(x)$ is a continuous function which may be either even or odd, x_t is an explanatory variable, α the time-delay, and x_{t-1} is the transition variable. For example, $F(x)$ may be an odd, monotonically increasing function with $F(-\infty) = 0$, $F(+\infty) = 1$. Bacon and Watts (1971) and Maddala (1977: 396) were early proponents of such models which are here called smooth transition regression (STR) models. The cumulative distribution of a $N(\mu, \sigma^2)$ variable is a possibility; see for example Goldfeld and Quandt (1973), who, however, made that assumption just to estimate the parameters of a switching-regression model by maximum likelihood. Likewise, $F(x)$ may be an even function with $F(\pm\infty) = 0$, $F(0) = 1$, and in that case F may equal the density function of a $N(\mu, \sigma^2)$ variable. If F is odd and monotonically increasing, $|x_{t-1} - \mu|$ is large and $x_{t-1} < \mu$, y_t is effectively generated by the linear model

$$y_t = \alpha_0 + \alpha_1 x_{t-1} + e_t. \qquad (4.2.2)$$

If $|x_{t-1} - \mu|$ is large and $x_{t-1} > \mu$, y_t is virtually generated by

$$y_t = (\alpha_0 + \beta_0) + (\alpha_1 + \beta_1)x_{t-1} + e_t. \qquad (4.2.3)$$

Intermediate values of x_{t-1} give mixtures of these values. Note that if $\sigma^2 \to 0$ F becomes the Heaviside function: $F = 0$, $x_{t-1} < \mu$; $F = 1$, $x_{t-1} \geq \mu$; and (4.2.1) is the switching-regression model of Quandt (1983) and Goldfeld and Quandt (1973) with switching variable x_{t-1}. If x_{t-1} is replaced by y_{t-1}, (4.2.1) is a special case of the Smooth-Transition Autoregressive (STAR) model (see Chan and Tong 1986, Luukkonen *et al*. 1988, and Teräsvirta 1990*b*, 1993). When $\sigma^2 \to 0$, the above STAR model becomes the two-regime (single threshold) Threshold Autoregressive (TAR) model; for extensive discussions of TAR models see Tong (1990). Economic theory usually considers just switching or threshold models, with a sharp switch, but if the economy consists of many individuals or firms, each of whom switches sharply but at different times, a smooth model seems more appropriate for the aggregate. If σ^2 is very large, it is very difficult to distinguish (4.2.1) from a linear model unless the number of observations is extremely large.

If F is even, y_t is practically generated by (4.2.3) whenever $|x_{t-1} - \mu|$ is large and by (4.2.2) if $x_{t-1} \approx \mu$. If x_{t-1} is replaced by y_{t-1}, then (4.2.1) becomes univariate and is another special case of the STAR model.

If F is assumed to be even, many other functions than the normal density could be used. For instance, one may assume

$$F(z) = 1 - e^{-z^2}. \tag{4.2.4}$$

That makes (4.2.1) a multivariate generalization of the univariate exponential autoregressive (EAR) model of Haggan and Ozaki (1981); for further discussion of the EAR model see Priestley (1988). Throughout the present exposition, a rather more general situation is achieved if $F(x_{t-1})$ is replaced by $F(x_{t-d})$, some $d > 0$ in 4.2.1.

A much more general model with a vector $\mathbf{x}_t$ of m explanatory variables can be written using the vector

$$\mathbf{w}_t' = (y_{t-1}, \ldots, y_{t-p}, x_{1t}, x_{2t}, \ldots, x_{kt}),$$

and a model

$$y_t = \alpha_0 + \alpha' \mathbf{w}_t + (\beta_0 + \beta' \mathbf{w}_t) F(z_t) + e_t \tag{4.2.5}$$

where

$$z_t = \gamma(\delta' \mathbf{w}_t - c), \ \delta = (\delta_1, \ldots, \delta_m)', \ m = p + k \tag{4.2.6}$$

and where e_t is a zero mean sequence of independent variables whose variance may also be a function of the indicator function z_t. As little is known about the function F, except for its general distribution function shape, it is often convenient to assume that it is logistical if it is odd, i.e.

$$F(z) = \frac{1}{1 + \exp(-z)}. \tag{4.2.7}$$

Model (4.2.1) is then called a logistic STR (LSTR) model. The coefficient γ is the smoothness parameter if the δ_j are normalized so that the sum of all the elements of δ equals unity. Bacon and Watts (1971) among other things proposed the hyperbolic tangent function in place of (4.2.7) (see also Seber and Wild 1989, sect. 9.4). Other choices and further generalizations are possible, including the use of variables in z_t that do not appear elsewhere in the model.

If $\mathbf{x}_t$ has m components, model (4.2.5) contains $3(m + 1)$ coefficients to be estimated, ignoring any possible heteroskedasticity. If p is known, the coefficients can be estimated using maximum likelihood or least squares and some optimization procedure (see Chapter 7). However, in practice p is not known and the number of parameters to be estimated may be too large, given the limited size of most actual samples. This suggests that there may be some practical advantages in using a constrained model rather than a fully general one. An obvious simplification is to consider indicator functions with only one transition variable

$$z_t = \gamma(x_{t-d} - c),$$

or

$$z_t = \gamma(y_{t-d} - c).$$

This is what is often assumed in univariate LSTAR and ESTAR models. Alternatively, one could assume δ is known. This reduces the number of parameters to be estimated to $2(m + 1) + 2$ and greatly simplifies the optimization procedure.

Another particular logistic STR model can be defined by letting $z_t = \gamma(y_{t-d} - \alpha_0 - \alpha' \mathbf{w}_{t-d})$ in (4.2.5) instead of (4.2.6). Then the non-linearity is a function of the deviation from the linear path if either

$$F(z_t) = (1 + \exp\{z_t\})^{-1} - 1/2,$$

or as in (4.2.4). This may be generalized to $z_t = \gamma(\sum_{j=1}^{q} (y_{t-j} - \alpha_0 - \alpha' \mathbf{w}_{t-j}))$, $\gamma > 0$. The model is called the STR-Deviation (STR-D) model and the univariate version is the STAR-D model. The motivation for this model family is discussed in Chapter 6.

If we want to apply STR models to practical economic modelling problems, the first question is testing linearity against STR. If linearity is rejected, the next issues will be the specification of the model (selecting the appropriate STR family), estimating its parameters, and evaluating the estimated model. Those will be discussed in Chapter 7.

In the above STR models the transition variable was assumed observable, and the same was true for the special case, the switching-regression models. However, it is also possible to assume that the switching variable is independent of other variables and unobservable. The switching-regression model with two regimes then has the form

$$y_t = \alpha_0 + \alpha' \mathbf{w}_t + (\beta_0 + \beta' \mathbf{w}_t)s_t + e_t \tag{4.2.8}$$

where $s_t = 0$ or 1, $Ee_t = 0$, $\mathrm{var}(e_t|s_t) = \sigma_0^2 + s_t\sigma_1^2 > 0$, and s_t is generated by a two-state Markov chain with constant transition probabilities over time. Goldfeld and Quandt (1973) considered this model among other switching-regression models. If $\mathbf{w}_t = (y_{t-1}, \ldots, y_{t-p})'$ the model is uni-variate; Tyssedal and Tjøstheim (1988) called (4.2.8) the Suddenly Changing Autoregressive model and Karlsen and Tjøstheim (1990) discussed its properties and presented estimation algorithms and applications. The model is used for locating switch-points from one regime to the other in situations where at least two regimes are known to occur a priori.

4.3 Bilinear Models

A general form for the generating mechanism of a univariate bilinear series is:

$$y_t = \sum_{i=1}^{p} a^i y_{t-i} + e_t + \sum_{i=1}^{q} b^i e_{t-i} + \sum_{i=1}^{r} \sum_{j=1}^{s} c^{ij} y_{t-i} e_{t-j} \qquad (4.3.1)$$

where a^i is a simplified notation for $a^{(i)}$ and is not a power. Thus, the bilinear generating mechanism is that of an ARMA(p, q) plus the bilinear terms multiplying lagged e_t and y_t, where the input e_t is zero mean i.i.d., with finite variance. It is seen that the model (4.3.1) involves $p + q + rs$ coefficients, plus the variance of e to be estimated, and may be called a BL(p, q, r, s) model. It is often more convenient to write these models in Markovian or 'state-space' form. For example, the simple BL $(p, 0, p, 1)$ model is:

$$y_t = \sum_{i=1}^{p} a^i y_{t-i} + e_t + \sum_{i=1}^{p} c^{il} y_{t-1} e_{t-1}, \qquad (4.3.2)$$

and can be written in the form

$$\mathbf{x}_t = \mathbf{A}\mathbf{x}_{t-1} + \mathbf{C}\mathbf{x}_{t-1} e_{t-1} + \mathbf{D} e_t$$
$$y_t = \mathbf{H}'\mathbf{x}_t \qquad (4.3.3)$$

where

$$\mathbf{A} = \begin{bmatrix} a_1 & a_2 & \cdots & a_p \\ 1 & 0 & \cdots & 0 \\ \vdots & \vdots & & \vdots \\ 0 & 0 & & 0 \end{bmatrix}, \quad \mathbf{C} = \begin{bmatrix} c^{11} & c^{21} & c^{31} & \cdots & c^{p1} \\ 0 & 0 & & \cdots & \vdots \\ \vdots & \vdots & \vdots & & \vdots \\ 0 & 0 & 0 & & 0 \end{bmatrix}.$$

$D' = (1, 0, 0, \ldots, 0, 0)$ and $H' = (1, 0, \ldots, 0)$. An alternative form, provided by D. T. Pham (1985) has

$$\left. \begin{aligned} \mathbf{z}_t &= (\mathbf{A} + \mathbf{C}e_t)\mathbf{z}_{t-1} + (\mathbf{A} + \mathbf{C}e_t)\mathbf{D}e_t \\ \mathbf{x}_t &= \mathbf{z}_{t-1} + \mathbf{D}e_t \\ y_t &= \mathbf{H}'\mathbf{x}_t. \end{aligned} \right\} \qquad (4.3.4)$$

For various special cases of the general univariate model (4.3.1) theoretical papers have discussed conditions for stationarity, invertibility, and Markovian representations, Volterra representations, and expressions for the bispectrum. References include Granger and Andersen (1978), Lin (1985), Subba Rao (1985), Terdik (1985), Subba Rao and Gabr (1986), Guégan (1987), Guégan and Pham (1989), and various papers in the *Journal of Time Series Analysis*. Most of these results are of considerable theoretical interest but are of little relevance in practice. The conditions for stationarity and invertibility, for instance, are too complicated to be used as constraints on parameters in actual models.

There have been relatively few studies of multivariate bilinear systems, although considerable progress in the theory has been made by Stensholt and Tjøstheim (1987) and later by Stensholt and Subba Rao (1987). Let $\mathbf{y}_t' = [y_{1t}, y_{2t}, \ldots, y_{mt}]$ be an m-component vector of observed variables. The system or vector bilinear model has for the kth component

$$y_{kt} = e_{kt} + \sum_{i=1}^{p} \sum_{u=1}^{m} a_{ku}^{i} y_{u,t-i}$$

$$+ \sum_{i=1}^{q} \sum_{u=1}^{m} b_{ku}^{i} e_{u,t-i}$$

$$+ \sum_{i=1}^{r} \sum_{j=1}^{s} \sum_{u=1}^{m} \sum_{v=1}^{m} c_{kuv}^{ij} y_{u,t-i} e_{v,t-j} \qquad (4.3.5)$$

where $\mathbf{e}_t' = (e_{1t}, \ldots, e_{mt})$ is an i.i.d. vector with $E[\mathbf{e}_t] = 0$, $E[\mathbf{e}_t \mathbf{e}_t'] = G$. Each equation of the system involves $rsm^2 + pm + qm$ parameters. If we simplify by taking $p = q = r = s$, this gives a total of $p^2 m^3 + 2pm^2$ parameters to be estimated for the system, plus the $(n + 1)n/2$ components of G. Thus, a rather modest system with $m = 5$ components and $p = 3$, gives a total of 1290 parameters. The system is clearly too general to be of practical use and so only special cases will be considered. A further difficulty with the system in its general form is that one cannot estimate a single equation from it, as residuals from the other equations are usually required for estimation of any one equation.

For the 'subdiagonal' case when $c^{ij} = 0$ all $i < j$, so that only bilinear terms of the form $e_{t-u-s} x_{t-u}$, $s > 0$, such as $e_{t-2} x_{t-10}$, appear in the model, Stensholt and Tjøstheim (1987) find conditions for stationarity and an expression for the Volterra expansion and give a Markov representation. They also obtain expressions for the mean, and higher-order autocovariance matrices. From this they deduced a potentially important theorem:

If, in the model (4.3.5) and in the subdiagonal case, $p = r$ and $q = s$, then the autocovariance matrices of the process are the same as for a vector ARMA(p, q) process.

Thus, if a linear vector ARMA(p, q) process is fitted by standard techniques (see Granger and Newbold 1986, ch. 3), so that p and q are chosen by some model selection procedure such as AIC or BIC (as described in Judge *et al*. 1985) then these same values of p and q can be used to suggest upper bounds on the lags r and s for the bilinear terms in (4.3.5). Although one cannot necessarily rely entirely on this theorem for the specification of bilinear models, particularly for small samples, it can be helpful with this specification.

It is clearly going to be necessary to concentrate on a special class of system bilinear models which are very parsimonious compared to the general class. Estimation and specification questions are considered in Chapter 7.

4.4 Nonlinear Moving-Average Models

With an i.i.d. vector $\mathbf{e}_t$, a system nonlinear MA model takes the form;

$$\mathbf{y}_t = f(\mathbf{e}_{t-j}, j \geq 1) + \mathbf{e}_t, \tag{4.4.1}$$

and the problems of analysis are similar to those for the NLAR models, but now $\mathbf{e}_t$ is not observed. Experience suggests that the process will often be noninvertible, so that if one just observes $\mathbf{y}_t$, it will be impossible to obtain good estimates for $\mathbf{e}_t$, even if the function f is known. Rather than consider the general case, just the linear quadratic case is considered, so that each component of $\mathbf{y}_t$ is generated by a linear sum of lagged $\mathbf{e}_t$ components plus quadratic terms of the form

$$\beta_{pq}^{(ij)} e_{p,t-i} e_{q,t-j}.$$

The level of complexity is similar to that encountered with bilinear models and possible methods of specification and estimation are similar. A crude estimate of $\mathbf{e}_t$ can be found by building a vector AR model and using its residuals in place of the actual e in exploratory analysis and specification searches. The quadratic form is essentially the same as taking the first two terms of the Volterra expansion, discussed in Section 2.1. Because of difficulties with invertibility and with practical analysis, these models seem to have been little used with real data.

Some models of this form include terms such as $\gamma e_t e_{t-2}$, but we view these as a conditional heteroskedasticity in the series.

A specific (univariate) nonlinear moving-average model is the asymmetric moving-average model Wecker (1981) proposed. It is defined as

$$y_t = e_t + \sum \beta_j^+ e_{t-j}^+ + \sum \sigma_j^- e_{t-j}^- \tag{4.4.2}$$

where $e_{t-j}^+ = \max(e_{t-j}, 0)$, and $e_{t-j}^- = \min(e_{t-j}, 0)$, $j = 1, \ldots, q$. Model (4.4.2) allows a shock to have fundamentally different dynamic effects depending on whether it is positive or negative. The model can of course be generalized to contain autoregressive structure or exogenous regressors to make it multivariate.

4.5 Heteroskedasticity and Random Coefficient Models

If the conditional mean of a process is found to involve certain variables, there is every reason to expect these, and possibly other variables, to affect higher moments. Usually, the variance is the next most important moment, after the mean. For an information set I_t, the conditional mean and variance are;

$$m_t = E[y_t|I_t],$$

and

$$h_t^2 = E[(y_t - m_t)^2|I_t]$$

where m_t and h_t^2 are functions of the components of I_t. If h_t^2 is not a constant y_t is said to be heteroskedastic. If this is not realized in the estimation of the parameters in m_t it is well known that inefficient estimations will occur. An obvious problem is that if m_t is misspecified, such as when important variables are missing from I_t, then this will affect the estimate of h_t^2 and it is likely that the extent of heteroskedasticity will be overestimated. A particular case of this occurs when m_t is assumed to be a linear function of components of I_t but when its correct specification is a nonlinear one.

An obvious way of modelling h_t^2 is to form $(y_t - \hat{m}_t)^2$ and to regress this on positive functions of components of I_t. The same types of models can be used as described in Chapter 7, with either parametric or nonparametric forms.

Two classes of models for heteroskedasticity have received a lot of attention in the literature. The first class is the group of random coefficient models, the second one has become popular particularly in the analysis of financial data and is called the ARCH (autoregressive conditional heteroskedasticity) class. It was originally introduced by Engle (1982) and surveyed by Engle and Bollerslev (1986) and by Bollerslev, Chou, and Kroner (1992), and Bera and Higgins (1993).

Consider the model

$$y_t = \boldsymbol{\beta}(t)'\mathbf{x}_t + u_t \tag{4.5.1}$$

where $u_t \sim$ i.i.d., $Eu_t = 0$, $\text{var}(u_t) = \sigma^2$, $Eu_t\mathbf{x}_t = 0$, $Eu_t\boldsymbol{\beta}(s) = 0$, $\forall t, s$, $\boldsymbol{\beta}(t) = (\beta_1(t), \ldots, \beta_k(t))'$, $E\boldsymbol{\beta}(t) = \boldsymbol{\beta}$, $\text{var}(\boldsymbol{\beta}(t)) = \Phi$, $\text{cov}(\boldsymbol{\beta}(s), \boldsymbol{\beta}(t)) = \mathbf{0}$, $s \neq t$. In (4.5.1),

$$E(y_t|I_t) = \boldsymbol{\beta}'\mathbf{x}_t$$

and

$$h_t^2 = \text{var}\,(\mathbf{y}_t|I_t) = \sigma^2 + \mathbf{x}_t'\Phi\mathbf{x}_t.$$

If $\mathbf{x}_t = (y_{t-1}, \ldots, y_{t-p})'$, then (4.5.1) is the Random Coefficient Autoregressive (RCA) model surveyed in Nicholls and Quinn (1982).

The ARCH class may also be viewed as a class of random coefficient models. However, there are extensions of ARCH models that do not fit into this framework. Consider (4.5.1) with $\boldsymbol{\beta}(t) \equiv \boldsymbol{\beta}$, $\forall t$, but

$$u_t = \sum_{j=1}^{\infty} \alpha_j(t)u_{t-j} + e_t \tag{4.5.2}$$

where $e_t \sim \text{i.i.d.}(0, \alpha_0)$, $E\alpha_j(t) = 0$, $\text{var}\,(\alpha_j(t)) = \alpha_j$, $j = 1, \ldots, \infty$, $\sum_{j=1}^{\infty}|\alpha_j| < \infty$, $\text{cov}\,(\alpha_j(t), \alpha_j(s)) = 0$, $i \neq j$, $\forall s, t$. $Ev_t\alpha_j(s) = 0$ for all t, s. The error term thus has an infinite RCA representation. If (4.5.2) holds,

$$h_t^2 = \alpha_0 + \sum_{j=1}^{\infty} \alpha_j u_{t-j}^2.$$

If $\alpha_j = 0$, $j > q$, (4.5.1) with (4.5.2) is a regression model with ARCH(q) errors. If it is assumed that $\sum_{j=1}^{\infty}\alpha_j z^j$ is a rational polynomial,

$$\sum_{j=1}^{\infty} \alpha_j z^j = \left(\sum_{j=1}^{q} \theta_j z^j\right)\Bigg/\left(\varphi_0 - \sum_{j=1}^{p} \varphi_j z^j\right), \quad \varphi_0 = 1, \tag{4.5.3}$$

it is seen that the GARCH(p, q) models where

$$h_t^2 = \alpha_0' + \sum_{j=1}^{p} \varphi_j h_{t-j}^2 + \sum_{j=1}^{q} \theta_j u_{t-j}^2 \tag{4.5.4}$$

satisfy (4.5.2). As an example, for GARCH(1, 1) we obtain

$$\alpha_1 = \theta_1, \ \alpha_2 = \varphi_1\theta_1, \ \ldots, \ \alpha_k = \varphi_1^{k-1}\theta_1, \ \ldots.$$

This requires φ_1, $\theta_1 > 0$, because α_j's are variances. Assume now that $\alpha_j = 0$, $j > q$, but $\text{cov}\,(\alpha_i(t), \alpha_j(t)) = \alpha_{ij}$; $i, j \leq q$. Then

$$\text{var}\,(y_t|I_t) = \alpha_0 + \mathbf{w}_t'A\mathbf{w}_t$$

where $\mathbf{w}_t = (u_{t-1}, \ldots, u_{t-q})'$ and $A = [\alpha_{ij}]$. Tsay (1987) suggested this generalization. Asymmetric ARCH fits in as well if correlation between the error e_t and random coefficients is allowed. As a simple example, let $\alpha_j = 0$, $j > 1$, in (4.5.2) and set $e_t = \alpha_0(t)$, $\boldsymbol{\alpha}(t) = (\alpha_0(t), \alpha_1(t))'$ and assume

$$\text{cov}\,(\boldsymbol{\alpha}(t)) = A = \begin{bmatrix} \alpha_{00} & \alpha_{01} \\ \alpha_{10} & \alpha_{11} \end{bmatrix}.$$

Set $\widetilde{w}_t = (1, u_{t-1})'$ and $\zeta_{01} = \alpha_{01}/(\alpha_{00}\alpha_{11})^{1/2}$. Then

$$E(u_t|I_{t-1}) = 0$$

$$\begin{aligned}
\operatorname{var}(u_t|I_{t-1}) = \widetilde{w}_t' A \widetilde{w}_t &= \alpha_{00} + \alpha_{11}u_{t-1}^2 + 2\alpha_{01}u_{t-1} \\
&= \alpha_{00} - \alpha_{01}^2/\alpha_{11} + \alpha_{11}(u_{t-1}^2 + 2\alpha_{01}u_{t-1}/\alpha_{11} + \alpha_{01}^2/\alpha_{11}^2) \\
&= \alpha_{00}(1 - \zeta_{01}^2) + \alpha_{11}(u_{t-1} + \alpha_{01}/\alpha_{11})^2
\end{aligned}$$

as in the asymmetric ARCH(1) model.

A number of alternative specifications have been suggested without the above random coefficient interpretation. For instance, h_t^2 may be replaced by $\log h_t^2$ in (4.5.3) and possibly u_{t-j}^2 by $|u_{t-j}|$. This is called the exponential GARCH model, see Nelson (1990). A multivariate GARCH model has also been proposed in which h_{it}^2 is the variance of the residual of the ith equation of a system and is a function of lagged h_j^2 and e_j^2 terms for $j = i$ and also from other equations. This type of specification involves rather too many parameters, so that a factor form involving many fewer parameters has been proposed by Engle (1987).

A model of particular interest arises from the strong belief that for speculative prices, of stocks and commodities for example, there is a direct relationship between the return of an asset, like m_t, and the level of risk, perhaps measured by h_t^2. Thus, if m_t is a linear function of I_t, the ARCH in mean or ARCH $-$ m model would be:

$$y_t = m_t + \alpha h_t^2 + u_t$$

where u_t obeys (4.5.2) with (4.5.4) holding. This model and its estimation are discussed by Engle, Lillian, and Robins (1987). Once more, multivariate extensions are obviously available.

Neither the random coefficient model nor ARCH, or its generalization, arise naturally from economic theory. The latter can be considered as a pragmatic and successful method of modelling the heteroskedasticity that is found to occur in economic, and particulary, financial series. Random coefficient models are a very special subclass of time-varying parameter (TVP) models, where the parameters usually change smoothly, as discussed in Chow (1984). The state-space models proposed by Priestley (1980) and discussed in Section 2.1 provide a further generalization. The smooth transition regression models introduced above in Section 4.2 can also be considered to be a special case of a TVP model, where parameters can change rapidly.

5

Long-Memory Models

Preamble

Most of the models considered so far have been assumed to be stationary, or at least stable. In most cases these models are short-memory, in that a shock to the variable today will not have an effect on the value of the variable in the distant future. However, it seems that some economic variables are long-memory, containing 'permanent' components, and different models then need to be considered. If x_t, y_t are both long-memory there may be some simple function of them in short-memory which produces a generalization of the concept of cointegration, which has proved to be a useful one in linear models.

5.1 Integrated Series

An important pair of classes of series can be illustrated as follows: let x_t be an AR(1) series generated by:

$$x_t = \alpha x_{t-1} + e_t \tag{5.1.1}$$

where $-1 < \alpha < 1$, so that x_t is stationary. Suppose that a second series y_t is generated by:

$$y_t - y_{t-1} = x_t \tag{5.1.2}$$

then one can also write:

$$y_t = \sum_{j=0}^{t-1} x_{t-j} + y_0. \tag{5.1.3}$$

As y_t involves an accumulation or summation it is called an 'integrated' series, a notation introduced by Box and Jenkins (1970). As a stationary series is produced after one differencing of y_t, it is called 'integrated of order one', and denoted $y_t \sim I(1)$. If y_t produces a stationary series only after being differenced d times, it would be denoted as $y_t \sim I(d)$. From this notation, x_t (given by 5.1.1) is an example of an $I(0)$ series, as it is stationary without being differenced. As (5.1.1) can be written as:

$$(1 - \alpha B)x_t = e_t,$$

it follows that the generating model for y_t is:

$$(1 - \alpha B)(1 - B)y_t = e_t. \tag{5.1.4}$$

The autoregressive component of the model is zero if $B = 1$, and so y_t is also called a unit root process. It should be emphasized that in this case, x_t is an example of an $I(0)$ process and y_t is an example of an $I(1)$ process. The two series are seen to have quite different properties (as shown in Granger and Newbold 1986, ch. 1). If α is not near one, x_t will fluctuate around a mean (of zero if $E[e] = 0$), will frequently cross the value $x = 0$ and has a spectrum that is bounded at all frequencies and is positive at zero frequency. In contrast, y_t will fluctuate less, has no natural mean, will cross any particular value infrequently and is dominated by a long-swing component which is indicated by the fact that the spectrum of y_t is infinite at zero frequency. If x_t has a constant variance, then the variance y_t will approximately increase as a linear function in time.

It is convenient to define a series x_t to have (linear) short-memory in mean if, with

$$f_{t,h}^L = E[x_{t+h}|x_{t-j}, j \geq 0]$$

the optimum linear forecast of x_{t+h} given values of x_t available at time t, then

$$\lim_h f_{t,h}^L \to m \tag{5.1.5}$$

when m is the unconditional mean of x_t. Thus, distant past values of x_t have no linear information about current values. If $f_{t,h}^L$ continues to depend on x_{t-j}, $j \geq 0$ as h becomes large, the process can be said to be (linear) long-memory in mean. x_t generated by (5.1.1) is an example of a short-memory process and y_t (given by 5.1.2) is an example of a long-memory process as, from (5.1.2):

$$y_{t+h} = y_t + \sum_{j=0}^{h-1} x_{t+h-j}$$

and so $f_{t,h}^L(y)$ will always include y_t, the current value of the series.

A useful definition of an $I(0)$ process is one that is linear short-memory in mean. This class will include stationary series but also various non-stationary ones, including those with time-varying, but bounded variance, and AR(1) process (given by 5.1.1) but with parameter α that varies deterministically through time within the region $-1 < \alpha_t < 1$. If an $I(0)$ series possesses a spectrum $f(\omega)$, it will be bounded above and will be positive at zero frequency. If it does not have a spectrum, a similar property can be required of the average time-varying spectrum (see Priestley 1981) or pseudo-spectrum (see Hatanaka and Suzuki 1967).

y_t is said to be $I(1)$ if its difference is $I(0)$. If it has a spectrum, $f_y(\omega)$ will be approximately proportional to ω^{-2} for small ω values. As before, an $I(0)$ x_t and an $I(1)$ y_t will have quite different long-run properties, similar to those discussed above.

It is clear from a casual glance at many macroeconomic series that they appear to have long-run properties that do not correspond to those of $I(0)$ series, such as apparent deterministic trends, often linear or broken linear in the logarithms of the variables, plus long swings corresponding to important low-frequency components. There is evidence (such as in Nelson and Plosser 1982), that many series contain unit roots in their generating mechanisms, although this is still being debated in the literature. However, there is no doubt of the importance of low-frequency components. The grouping of series into $I(0)$ or $I(1)$ is often convenient, but it should be emphasized that many series probably do not strictly belong to either group, even after trend removal. A non-stationary series may switch from one classification to the other through time or may be $I(d)$ with $d > 1$, for example.

The definitions given here are both linear and univariate and so need to be generalized for this text. It is clear that a series y_t cannot be linear short-memory in mean with the information set y_{t-j}, $j \geqslant 0$ but long-memory in mean with the larger set y_{t-j}, w_{t-j}, $j \geqslant 0$ where w_t is some other series. Otherwise y_{t-h} could be forecast from w_{t-s}, as could y_t, with h, s both large. But it would follow that y_{t+h} can be forecast by y_t, by a simple regression argument. Nonlinear memory definitions are discussed in the next section.

An important extension of these ideas occurs when a pair of $I(1)$ series, y_{1t}, y_{2t} have a linear combination:

$$z_t = y_{1t} - ay_{2t}$$

which is $I(0)$. The pair are then said to be cointegrated. For this to occur, there must be representation of the form:

$$y_{1t} = aW_t + \tilde{y}_{1t}$$

$$y_{2t} = W_t + \tilde{y}_{2t}$$

where $\tilde{y}_{jt}$ $j = 1$, 2 are each $I(0)$ and W_t is $I(1)$. The W_t series is an $I(1)$ common factor which makes both the original series $I(1)$, but also allows cointegration to occur. Certain simple types of equilibria can be equated with cointegration. The idea is discussed in Granger (1986) and the book of readings edited by Engle and Granger (1991). Questions of testing for $I(1)$ and for cointegration are discussed in these sources and also in Johansen (1991).

5.2 Long-Memory and Nonlinearity

When considering nonlinear relationships, the definitions given in the previous section are no longer appropriate, as they are based just on linearity. Some natural generalizations are as follows:

(i) consider the conditional distribution of x_{t+h}, given the information set $I_t:x_{t-j}, j \geq 0$, i.e. $F_h(x) = \text{prob}(x_{t+h} \leq x|I_t)$. The series is said to be short-memory in distribution (SMD) if:

$$\lim_h F_h(x) = \bar{F}(x) \tag{5.2.1}$$

does not depend on I_t. Thus, $|\text{prob}(x_{t+h} \in C_1|x_{t-j} \in C_2) - \text{prob}(x_{t+h} \in C_1)| \to 0$ as $h \uparrow$ for all sets C_1, C_2 such that $\text{prob}(x_{t-j} \in C_2 \neq 0)$, plus the obvious generalizations of this statement using various subsets of $x_{t-j}, j \geq 0$. If $\bar{F}(x)$ always depends on I_t, the series may be called long-memory in distribution (LMD). These definitions are too general for practical use and so more constrained definitions need to be considered;

(ii) define $f_{t,h} = E[x_{t+h}|I_t]$ to be the optimum (least-squares) forecast of x_{t+h} using the information in I_t, not necessarily linearly. If:

$$\lim_h f_{t,h} = D \tag{5.2.2}$$

where D is some random variable, then x_t is said to be short-memory in mean (SMM) if the distribution of D does not depend on I_t. The case of most interest is where D has a singular distribution, so that D is just a constant. However, limit cycles and chaotic strange attractors can be included in the definition, but are not considered here. If $f_{t,h}$ continues to depend on I_t as h increases, the series will be called long-memory in mean (LMM). It is clear that SMD implies SMM but not vice versa, and that LMM implies LMD, but not necessarily vice versa, as a series can be short-memory in mean but long-memory in variance, for example. If one runs the regression:

(a) $$x_{t+h} = \alpha_{1h} + \beta_{1h}x_t + e_{1t} \tag{5.2.3}$$

(b) $$x_{t+h} = \alpha_{2h} + \beta_{2h}g(x_t) + e_{2t} \tag{5.2.4}$$

where the function $g()$ is chosen to maximize R^2, then necessary conditions for SMM are that β_{1h}, β_{2h} tend to zero as h increases, but neither are sufficient conditions. If either β_{1h} or β_{2h} does not tend to zero, this is a sufficient condition for LMM. $I(0)$ series are an example of SMM and $I(1)$ of LMM. If x_t is LMD then some functions, $f(x_t)$ will be LMM;

(iii) suppose that a single series x_t has a Volterra series expansion in terms of a single i.i.d. zero mean series ε_t, as discussed in Chapter 2. x_t will then be the sum of components such as

$$\varepsilon_{t-1}^{\alpha}\varepsilon_{t-2}^{\beta}\varepsilon_{t-3}^{\gamma} \quad \text{etc.}$$

multiplied by a coefficient. Conditioning out all parts except those involving ε_{t-h}, for a fixed h, gives

$$E[x_t|\varepsilon_{t-h}] = \sum_j a_j \varepsilon_{t-h}^j$$

$$= A_h(\varepsilon_{t-h}).$$

If $A_h(x)$ does not tend to zero as h becomes large, the variable x_t can be considered to be long-memory.

Results of the effects on memory of taking instantaneous transformations of variables are needed for the following sections. Thus, if x_t is LMM, say, the question is: what memory properties will $y_t = f(x_t)$ have? No general results are available but when x_t is a Gaussian random walk, so that:

$$x_t = x_{t-1} + e_t \tag{5.2.5}$$

where e_t is i.i.d. and normally distributed $N(0, \sigma_e^2)$ some results are available in Granger and Hallman (1989, 1991a, b) and in Ermini and Granger (1991). It is shown, using both theory and simulations, that for several monotonic and power functions, such as $|x|$, x^2, x^3, $\log(x + c)$, then, with x_t a Gaussian random walk, the transformed series y_t is long-memory in mean. This is also true for the transform

$$y_t = \text{sgn}(x_t) = \begin{array}{ll} 1 & \text{if } x_t \geq 0 \\ = -1 & \text{if } x_t < 0. \end{array}$$

However, if $y_t = \sin(x_t)$, then y_t is short-memory in mean. If $y_t = \exp(x_t)$, then:

$$E[y_{t+h}|y_t] = c^h y_t$$

where $c = \exp(1/2\sigma_e^2) > 1$. Clearly y_t is LMM but it is found that the autocorrelations of y_t, $\rho_k = \text{corr}(y_t, y_{t-k})$ tend to zero as k increases. Thus regression (5.2.3) gives the correct indication, but the correlogram does not.

As the variance of the transformed series is not always increasing, as expected for an $I(1)$ process, it is found in Granger and Hallman (1991a) that a standard unit root test, due to Dickey and Fuller, can give misleading results. Essentially the difference between an $I(1)$ series and a LMM series is being indicated. An alternative test, based on the ranks of series, is found to have better power.

In their 1989 paper, Granger and Hallman consider pairs of series. The results can be illustrated with a simple case. If e_t, η_t are i.i.d. normally distributed with zero means, unit variances, and contemporaneous correlation ρ, let:

$$x_{1t} = ax_{1,t-1} + e_t$$

$$x_{2t} = bx_{2,t-1} + \eta_t.$$

If a and b are less than one in magnitude, the series are $I(0)$, if $a = 1$, then x_{1t} is $I(1)$. It is found that if both series are $I(0)$ then their product is SMM. If one series is $I(0)$ and the other $I(1)$, the product is SMM, but long-memory in variance. If both series are $I(1)$, the product is LMM and the variance increases at the rate $o(t^2)$ if $\rho \neq 0$. Thus, the product does not have the standard $I(1)$ properties.

Turning to cointegration properties, it is shown that:

(i) if x_t is $I(1)$ then x_t and $g(x_t)$ cannot be cointegrated unless $g(\ )$ is linear; and

(ii) if x_{1t}, x_{2t} are cointegrated then $g(x_{1t})$, $g(x_{2t})$ are cointegrated only if $g(x)$ is a homothetic function, so that $g(\lambda x) = \lambda^k g(x)$.

5.3 Attractors

A deterministic vector sequence $\mathbf{x}_t$ with m components generated by;

$$\mathbf{x}_t = F(\mathbf{x}_{t-j}) \quad j = 1, \ldots, \rho_1$$

say, is said to have an attractor A if $\mathbf{x}_t$ tends to A as it becomes large. Thus, the distance between $\mathbf{x}_t$ and A becomes arbitrarily small as t increases, using some distance measure. The attractor may be simple, such as a point in m-space or a plane in $m - k$ space, some $k > 0$, or a set of p points if $\mathbf{x}_t$ eventually has a limit cycle of period p. The attractor may be complicated, such as those found in the theory of chaotic processes illustrate, called 'strange attractors' which may have noninteger dimension as discussed in the many books on chaos, such as Gleick (1987).

For stochastic processes this definition is of reduced relevance. Because of the continuing shocks to the system, $\mathbf{x}_t$ will usually not converge. Suppose that a signed (Euclidean) distance z_t^A from $\mathbf{x}_t$ to A can be defined, and that a point $\mathbf{x}_t^A$ on A can be found which is the nearest to $\mathbf{x}_t$ of all points on A. (The Euclidean distances of $\mathbf{x}_t$ from zero is defined as the positive square root of the sum of squares of the components of $\mathbf{x}_t$.) The length of the straight line between $\mathbf{x}_t$ and $\mathbf{x}_t^A$ determines the magnitude of z_t^A. Consider two lines, one joining $\mathbf{x}_t$ to $\mathbf{x}_t^A$ and the other joining $\mathbf{x}_t^A$ to the origin, and let the angle between these two lines be θ, i.e. $-\pi/2 \leq \theta < \pi/2$. Give z_t^A a negative sign, if the direction of the first line is away from the origin, and otherwise let z_t^A have a positive sign. This distribution of signs is clearly rather arbitrary and will change if the origin is changed, but it is nevertheless useful.

Whether or not A, some part of the full space, is an attractor can be determined from the properties of the univariate series z_t^A, which will be assumed to be unique. (If there are two points on A equidistant from $\mathbf{x}_t$, some method of choosing one has to be used, but this is considered to be a zero-probability event.) Even if this does occur z_t^A may still be uniquely determined, unless the rule to determine its sign gives different values.

Definition: A can be called an attractor if z_t^A is short-memory in mean with zero mean. This definition has no impact if the components of $\mathbf{x}_t$ are all short-memory in mean as any part of the space will produce a z_t series which is short-memory in mean. However, the definition is relevant if all components are long-memory in mean, as it implies that there is a function of $\mathbf{x}_t$, which is a signed distance, that produces a short-memory in mean series. The implication is that if the components of $\mathbf{x}_t$ are long-memory in mean and unbounded (in at least one direction) then without an attractor, the plot of $\mathbf{x}_t$ through time in R^m, the R real space of dimension m, will be wide-ranging, but with an attractor, their plot will stay 'near' A, in a precisely defined way. Note that R^1, the real line, z_t^A will have $A = 0$ as an attractor. A univariate series that is not short-memory in mean need not have an attractor, an example being a random walk without drift, although it can be argued that A is the whole line R^1. Similarly, a series with an upward trend can be thought of as having plus infinity as an attractor, but using a different distance measure (for example the Euclidean distance on $f(x_t)$ where $f()$ is the logistic function). However, those extensions of the basic attractor idea have less practical value.

An example of an attractor is for a pair of $I(1)$ series x_{1t}, x_{2t} which have a linear combination

$$w_t = x_{1t} - \alpha x_{2t} - c$$

where c is a constant, such that w_t is $I(0)$ with zero mean. The attractor is:

$$A : x_1 = \alpha x_2 + c.$$

Note that $z_t^A = w_t \cos \psi$ for an angle ψ, so if w_t is $I(0)$ with zero mean so will be z_t^A. This linear attractor is the basis of the concept of cointegration, discussed in Granger (1986), Engle and Granger (1987), and elsewhere. The approach discussed here allows for nonlinear generalizations of cointegration.

If z_t^A (henceforth z_t) has an AR(1) generating mechanism of the form:

$$z_t = \rho z_{t-1} + e_t \qquad (5.3.1)$$

where e_t is zero mean i.i.d. and denoting the squared Euclidean distance of z_t from zero by $d_A(z_t)$, that is $d_A(z_t) = z_t^2$ with $A = 0$ in this simple case, then:

$$\Delta = d_A[E[z_{t+1}]] - d_A(z_t) < 0. \qquad (5.3.2)$$

Thus, the distance of the expected value of the next value of the series from the attractor is less than this distance for the current value. This can also be taken to be a characterizing property of an attractor, although a different way of measuring this distance has to be for non-AR(1) models, as discussed below. A plausible measure of the 'strength of attraction' of A for a particular value of the series, is:

$$S(z_t) = 1 - \frac{d_A[E[z_t+1]]}{d_A(z_t)},$$

which for the AR(1) model (5.3.1) is just:

$$S(z_t) = 1 - \frac{(\rho z_t)^2}{z_t^2} \qquad (5.3.3)$$
$$= 1 - \rho^2.$$

For a NLAR(1) model of the form:

$$z_t = \rho(z_{t-1})z_{t-1} + e_t,$$

it is seen that:

$$S(z_t) = 1 - \rho^2(z_{t-1}), \qquad (5.3.4)$$

so that here the strength of attraction can depend on the size of the series. This is likely to occur in economics if the attractor exists because of the actions of a government or of a market. For example, consider the market for tomatoes in two parts of a country, the north and south, with prices P_{nt}, P_{st} respectively. If these prices are equal, the market will be in equilibrium. So $P_n = P_s$ is an attractor. If the prices are unequal it will be possible to make a profit by buying tomatoes in one region and selling them in the other. This trading mechanism will be inclined to equate prices again, raising prices in the buying region and lowering them in the selling region. The greater the difference in the prices, the higher will be the profit motive and thus also the trading level, so that the strength of attraction will depend on the distance of the actual prices from the attractor.

If z_t is stationary $AR(p)$ with $p > 1$, and with zero mean, it can be written in a state-space form:

$$z_t = \boldsymbol{\beta}' \mathbf{w}_t$$

where

$$\mathbf{w}_t = \mathbf{R}\mathbf{w}_{t-1} + \mathbf{e}_t$$

with $\mathbf{e}_t$ a vector white noise, each component having zero mean, $\mathbf{w}_t$ is the state vector with p components, and $\mathbf{R}$ is a matrix with all eigenvalues less than one in modulus. All the $\mathbf{w}_t$ components are $I(0)$ and zero mean, and so its attractor is the p vector of zeros $\mathbf{O}_p$.

The squared distance of $\mathbf{z}_t$ from its attractor is then:

$$d_A(\mathbf{w}_t) = \sum_{j=1}^{p} w_{jt}^2 = \mathbf{w}_t' \mathbf{w}_t.$$

With the constraints on $\mathbf{R}$ given above, it can be shown that the inequality (5.3.2) still holds, i.e.

$$\Delta = d_A[E[\mathbf{w}_{t+1}]] - d_A(\mathbf{w}_t) < 0.$$

This is seen by noting that:

$$-\Delta = \mathbf{w}_t'\mathbf{w}_t - \mathbf{w}_t'\mathbf{R}'\mathbf{R}\mathbf{w}_t.$$

As $\mathbf{R}'\mathbf{R}$ is a symmetric matrix, with eigenvalues $\lambda_j = |\mu_j|^2$, if μ_j is an eigenvalue of $\mathbf{R}$, and so can be written as:

$$\mathbf{R}'\mathbf{R} = \mathbf{T}' \begin{bmatrix} \lambda_1 & \cdot & 0 \\ & \ddots & \\ 0 & & \lambda_p \end{bmatrix} \mathbf{T} \equiv T'DT$$

where $\mathbf{T}'\mathbf{T} = I$ and $\mathbf{D}$ is the diagonal matrix shown. Thus:

$$-\Delta = \mathbf{w}_t'\mathbf{T}'[\mathbf{I} - \mathbf{D}]\mathbf{T}\mathbf{w}_t$$

and the result follows by noting that $\mathbf{I} - \mathbf{D}$ is a diagonal matrix with all diagonal terms positive, so $\mathbf{T}'[\mathbf{I} - \mathbf{D}]\mathbf{T}$ is a positive definite matrix. Thus, if nearness to an attractor of a general $I(0)$ process is defined in terms of nearness to zero of the state-space vector, the expected value is nearer than the current value of the process. The result can be generalized to $I(0)$ ARMA processes.

The definition discussed here, that of the signed distance z_t being $I(0)$ with zero mean is related to an early idea of an attractor, called the 'centre of gravity' equilibrium. Suppose that z_t is a univariate short-memory in mean zero mean process and generated by a nonlinear autoregressive model:

$$z_t = f(z_{t-j}, j = 1 \ldots, p) + e_t.$$

One can ask what would happen to this if $e_t = 0$ for all $t > t_0$, so that the process becomes deterministic. If it is assumed that this deterministic process is not chaotic, then $z_t \rightarrow z^* = 0$ where z^* is the equilibrium value. It follows that a system $\mathbf{x}_t$ with m components, each of which is long-memory in mean but with a z_t^A that is short-memory in mean and with zero mean, will tend to lie on the attractor if it becomes deterministic at $t = t_0$, as z_t^A will tend to zero and so the distance of the system from the attractor will go to zero.

Attractors are discussed in Granger and Hallman (1991b). They discuss methods of estimation and testing for attractors and this discussion forms the basis, together with Hallman's Ph.D. thesis (1990), for the next section.

5.4 Estimation and Testing for Attractors

Consideration will just be given to a pair of LMM series (y_t, x_t) and only possible attractors of the form

$$A : \theta(y) - \phi(x)$$

leading to the distance measure:

$$z_t = \theta(y_t) - \phi(x_t) - \text{constant}$$

where z_t is SMM with zero mean. This is clearly not the most general possible set of attractors but it is a sensible plan to start consideration of estimation here, especially as there exist useful algorithms for this set. One of these algorithms is the alternating conditional expectations (ACE) procedure proposed by Breiman and Friedman (1985). Suppose one considers a class of function C, whose properties are discussed below. The aim of the ACE algorithm is to find instantaneous transforms $\theta(y)$, $\phi(x)$ such that corr$(\theta(y), \phi(x))$ is maximized, which is equivalent to minimizing

$$e^2(\theta, \phi) = \frac{E\{[\theta(y) - \phi(x)]^2\}}{E\theta^2(y)}. \qquad (5.4.1)$$

In the first stage of the iteration, take

$$\theta_1(y) \equiv \frac{y}{|y|}$$

and then search over the class C to find $\phi(x)$ so that $e^2(\theta, \phi)$ is minimized. Let this ϕ be ϕ_1. Now search over C to find θ such that $e^2(\theta, \phi_1)$ is minimized. This alternating process continues until $e^2(\theta, \phi)$ changes by less than some small predetermined quantity S.

A modification of this procedure has been proposed by Tibshirani (1988) called AVAS (additivity and variance stabilization) which aims to find transformations θ, ϕ such that

$$E(\theta(y_t)|x_t = x) = \phi(x)$$

and with $\text{var}(\theta(y_t)|\phi(x_t)) = \text{constant}$. The sequence is as follows.

(i) Put $\theta(y) = (y - E(y))/[\text{var}(y)]^{1/2}$ and search over C to get $\phi(x_t)$ such that $e^2(\theta_1, \phi)$ is minimized, producing $\phi_1(x)$

(ii) Estimate the variance function

$$v(u) = \text{var}(\theta(y)|\phi_1(x) = u)$$

and compute;

$$h_1(y) = \int_0^y [v(u)]^{-1/2} \, du;$$

(iii) Set

$$\tilde{\theta}_2(y) = h_1(\theta_1(y))$$

and

$$\tilde{\theta}_2(y) = \frac{\tilde{\theta}_2(y) - E[\tilde{\theta}_2(y)]}{[\text{var}(\tilde{\theta}_2(y))]^{1/2}};$$

(iv) Return to step (i) and repeat the sequence. Stop when $e^2(\theta, \phi)$ stabilizes.

In practice, it is suggested that $v(u)$ is estimated by using a smoothed estimate of the log of (the sample version of) the squared residual $r^2 = E(\hat{\theta}(y) - \hat{\phi}(x))^2$ against $u = \phi(x)$. The class of functions C could be a parametric class such as polynomials or Fourier functions or logistics, but is usually taken to be some class of nonparametric functions, such as smoothers or cubic splines. C is generally taken to be a class of smooth functions and can be well approximated by any of the many parametric or nonparametric forms. A smoother is some running moving average on ordered data, corresponding to the use of a window, or it could use a nearest neighbour procedure, as discussed in Section 7.1.

Examples of the use of these techniques can be found in Granger and Hallman (1991b) and in Hallman (1990). A few examples were found for pairs of series which were not cointegrated in levels but appeared to be after ACE or AVAS transformations. The distance series z_t were tested for SMM by a standard Dickey–Fuller test but with an allowance in degrees of freedom because the transformations were estimated. An alternative test using ranks is also proposed in Granger and Hallman (1991a), and was found to be more stable because ranks are not affected by positive monotonic transformations. Experience from a small number of simulations and from analysis of real data suggested that both algorithms were useful but that AVAS produced better and more interpretable results. In particular, the result that US log non-durable consumption and log income were cointegrated was found by AVAS but not by ACE. It is also true that it is not easy to find good examples.

The procedures discussed here can be generalized to consider an attractor between y_t and $x_{1t}, x_{2t} \ldots, x_{pt}$, but not for any subset of x. For a pair of series y_t, x_t there may be an attractor between y_t, x_t, and x_{t-1}, but not between y_t and x_t; an example is when x_t is $I(2)$, y_t is $I(1)$ but Δx_t, y_t are linearly cointegrated.

5.5 Nonlinear Error-Correction Models

If y_t, x_t are a pair of $I(1)$ series, so that their differences are SMM and if they are (linearly) cointegrated, with $z_t = x_t - Ay_t$ being SMM, then there will exist a (linear) error-correction model of the form

$$\left. \begin{aligned} \Delta x_t &= \rho_1 z_{t-1} + \text{lags } \Delta x_t, \Delta y_t + e_{xt} \\ \Delta y_t &= \rho_2 z_{t-1} + \text{lags } \Delta x_t, \Delta y_t + e_{yt} \end{aligned} \right\} \tag{5.5.1}$$

with at least one of ρ_1, ρ_2 non-zero. If the attractor $x = Ay$ is thought of as equilibrium, then the error-correction model may be thought of as the disequilibrium mechanism that leads to the particular equilibrium. However, as a function of a SMM process is generally also SMM, an alternative error-correction model has z_{t-1} in (5.5.1) replaced by $g(z_{t-1})$ where $g(z)$ is a function such that $g(0) = 0$ and $E[g(z_t)]$ exists. The function $g(\,)$ can be estimated nonparametrically or by assuming a particular parametric form. Escribano (1986, 1987) used a cubic function of z_t in a UK money demand equation and achieved a parsimonious model. A particularly easy to use function is to include z^+ and z^- separately into the error correction model, where

$$z^+ \left\{ \begin{aligned} &= 1 \text{ if } z > 0 \\ &= 0 \text{ otherwise} \end{aligned} \right\} \quad \text{and } z^- = z - z^+.$$

Granger and Lee (1989) using US sales, production, and inventory data for several industrial groupings found that both z^+ and z^- often entered significantly but with quite different coefficients, resulting in better-fitting and better-forecasting models. The type of nonlinearity discussed here is concerned with a varying strength of attraction to a linear attractor. For example, the attractor may be stronger on one side than on the other, so that z^+ may have a larger coefficient than z^-.

The theory of error-correction models for nonlinear attractors is still incomplete. A difficulty is that if a series is LMM then its difference is not necessarily SMM. A possible procedure is to define an operator

$$\square_d x_t = x_t - \psi(x_{t-j}, j = 1 \ldots, d)$$

where d is the minimum integer such that the truncation ψ exists and $\square_d x_t$ is SMM. Clearly, if x_t is SMM, one can take $d = 0$. Similarly, if x_t is LMM and generated by the NLAR(1) system

$$x_t = \psi(x_{t-1}) + e_t$$

where e_t is white noise and $|\psi(x)| > |x|$ for $|x_0|$ say, then $d = 1$ for this series. The possible form of the error-correction model is

$$\square_d x_t = \rho_1 z_{t-1} + \text{lagged } \square_d x_t, \square'_d y_t + e_{mt}$$

and a similar equation for $\square'_d y_t$, with at least one ρ_1, $\rho_2 \neq 0$ and with

$$z_t = \theta(y_t) - \phi(x_t)$$

being SMM, if the attractor has the form

$$\theta(y) = \phi(x).$$

The equations balance, as all terms are SMM but no theory or practical experience with these models is available.

In the definition of $\square_d$, the function ψ can be estimated using the techniques discussed in the previous section, being generalized to cover the many input, single output case.

5.6 Modelling Implications

The models that have been considered in theory in previous chapters and will be considered in practice in the next two chapters are often of the form

$$y_t = \alpha_0 + \alpha'_1 \mathbf{x}_t + \Sigma \beta_j \phi_j(\gamma'_j \mathbf{x}_t) + \varepsilon_t. \tag{5.6.1}$$

For example $\phi(\ )$ will be sine and cosine functions in flexible Fourier-form parametric models, it will be the logistic function in a neural network function, or a smooth nonparametric form in projection pursuit, all of which are discussed in Chapter 7. In the first two cases the ϕ functions are bounded and so the linear component is essential if y_t is LMM and unbounded. Clearly the explanatory variables $\mathbf{x}$ need to include some LMM (or at least LMD) variables in this case, but this occurs automatically if $\mathbf{x}_t$ includes lagged y_t. It seems that a pure flexible Fourier-form model involving just trigonometric functions is the least appropriate with long-memory processes as $\sin x_t$ and $\cos x_t$ are both SMM even if x_t is LMM, as shown in Granger and Hallman (1991*a*). Thus, unless there is linear cointegration, (5.6.1) will be inclined not to capture nonlinear long-memory properties of the relationship between x_t and y_t. If y_t is LMM but not bounded, there could also be difficulties with the use of a logistic function for ϕ. If x_t has a monotonic trend, then $\phi(x)$ will be near one for higher t values and so will add little to the explanation of y_t. This is particularly true if the linear component in (5.6.1) is missing.

If y_t and $\mathbf{x}_t$ are (linearly) cointegrated then in (5.6.1) the terms $\phi_j(\gamma_j' \mathbf{x}_t)$ need to be SMM and this implies that in most cases γ is limited so that $\gamma' \mathbf{x}$ is SMM, and any cointegration between the x is utilized. Otherwise, the balance of the equation (5.6.1) would be incorrect, in that the two sides of the equation would have different long-run properties. It thus seems appropriate to start any analysis that involves these models by determining the long-run properties of the individual series and then finding if there is any linear cointegration between them.

The model that is often used in analysis is the simple one

$$y_t = f(x_t) + \text{residual}. \qquad (5.6.2)$$

It is worth noting that if the residual is SMM but y_t and x_t are LMM, so consequentially is $f(x_t)$, then this is equivalent to finding that $y = f(x)$ is an attractor for this system. It follows that the techniques of Section 5.4 are particularly relevant for analysis in LMM situations.

6

Linearity Testing

Many parametric nonlinear models discussed in this book have a linear model nested in the nonlinear structure. Before building a nonlinear model it is advisable to find out if indeed a linear model would adequately characterize the economic relationships under analysis. If this were the case, there would be more statistical theory available for building a reasonable model than if a nonlinear model were appropriate. Furthermore, obtaining optimal forecasts for more than one period ahead would be much simpler if the model were linear. It may happen, at least when the time-series are short, that the investigator successfully estimates a nonlinear model although the true relationship between the variables in question is linear. The danger of unnecessarily complicating the model-building is therefore real, but can be diminished by linearity testing. Sometimes linearity tests are also useful in specifying a nonlinear model, but this may be the case only if the set of conceivable nonlinear families of models can be assumed to be rather small. Examples of this will be discussed later. Another occasion in which linearity testing may be useful is after specifying and estimating a nonlinear model. The residuals of the model may be subjected to linearity tests to see if the nonlinear features in the original data have been adequately captured by the estimated nonlinear specification. If linearity is still rejected, the model obviously has to be respecified and re-estimated.

The linearity tests may be divided into two broad categories. One contains all the tests derived without a specific nonlinear alternative in mind. The other category consists of tests against a specific nonlinear model. Nevertheless, a few tests in the former category may also be interpreted as score or Lagrange multiplier (LM) tests against a nonlinear alternative. Such an interpretation, if available, is instructive because it reveals against which types of nonlinearities the general test in question has the best power. The tests against a specific nonlinear alternative are usually formulated as LM or LM-type tests. This is natural, because the estimation of the nonlinear model is then not necessary. Pagan's (1978) paper was the first to point that out. In a few cases there is also a particular objection against the two other classical tests, the likelihood ratio (LR) and Wald tests. These tests require that the model be estimated under the alternative. However, many of the nonlinear models discussed in Chapter 2 are not identified under the assumption of linearity. Attempts to estimate the nonlinear alternative when the null hypothesis is in fact true may, and should, therefore fail (although sometimes they may succeed, as discussed above). On the other hand, it turns out that in at least some of those cases it is still possible to derive an LM-type test for linearity. However, it is worth pointing out that the application of the LM principle is not always necessary. Many linearity tests considered in this chapter may also be formulated as diagnostic tests based on residuals of a linear model and their distribution. Pagan and Hall (1983) contains a thorough discussion of this approach.

There are yet other tests for which an LM test interpretation simply does not exist. An example is the BDS test (Brock *et al.* 1987) originally designed to test if a process generating the data is deterministic or not. A multivariate version of the test will be discussed later.

The focus of the chapter will be on testing linearity in the conditional mean, although conditional heteroskedasticity will also receive some attention. General guidelines for testing linearity in the presence of heteroskedasticity and conditional heteroskedasticity will be discussed. Many LM-type linearity tests may be made robust against conditional heteroskedasticity. If enough is known about conditional heteroskedasticity to parameterize it, linearity tests may be carried out under specific assumptions of the parametric structure of heteroskedasticity. This alternative will be discussed. Testing the hypothesis of constant conditional error variance against conditional heteroskedasticity will also be touched upon in the chapter.

6.1 Lagrange Multiplier Tests

6.1.1 Tests with parameterized conditional variance

Before considering individual tests it is useful to pay attention to some general features of Lagrange multiplier tests. For this purpose, consider the following multivariate nonlinear model

$$y_t = \boldsymbol{\beta}' \mathbf{z}_t + f(\mathbf{z}_t; \boldsymbol{\psi}) + u_t, \ t = 1, \ldots, T \qquad (6.1.1)$$

where $\boldsymbol{\beta} = (\beta_0, \beta_1, \ldots, \beta_{p+k})'$, $\mathbf{z}_t = (1, y_{t-1}, \ldots, y_{t-p}; x_{t1} \ldots, x_{tk})'$, $\boldsymbol{\psi} = (\psi_1, \ldots, \psi_m)'$, and $f(\mathbf{z}_t; \boldsymbol{\psi})$ is an at least twice continuously differentiable function of $\boldsymbol{\psi}$ such that $f(\mathbf{z}_t; \mathbf{0}) = 0$. Function f is also generally a continuous function of $\mathbf{z}_t$ but limiting cases with a finite number of discontinuities may occur.

Furthermore, let $Eu_t = 0$, $Eu_t u_s = 0$, $s \neq t$, $Eu_t \mathbf{z}_t = 0$ and

$$\text{var}(u_t | I_t) = g(\mathbf{z}_t; \boldsymbol{\beta}, \boldsymbol{\psi}, \boldsymbol{\eta}) = g_t > 0 \qquad (6.1.2)$$

where I_t is the information set containing all the information up until t except y_t, and $\boldsymbol{\eta} = (\eta_0, \ldots, \eta_q)'$. Function g_t is assumed to be at least twice continuously differentiable with respect to the parameters. It is also assumed that $\boldsymbol{\beta}$ and $\boldsymbol{\psi}$ are not functions of $\boldsymbol{\eta}$. Because the distributional results are asymptotic, $y_0, y_{-1}, \ldots, y_{-(p-1)}$ may be treated as fixed. Assuming independence of errors and conditional normality, the conditional logarithmic likelihood for observation t is thus

$$l_t = -(1/2)\ln 2\pi - (1/2)\ln g_t - (1/2g_t)u_t^2. \qquad (6.1.3)$$

To derive LM tests for testing hypotheses concerning (6.1.1) we need the first partial derivatives of (6.1.3). The hypothesis of interest is $H_0: \boldsymbol{\psi} = 0$ and the partial derivatives are:

$$\frac{\partial l_t}{\partial \boldsymbol{\beta}} = g_t^{-1}\left\{ u_t \mathbf{z}_t + (1/2)(u_t^2/g_t - 1)\frac{\partial g_t}{\partial \boldsymbol{\beta}} \right\} \qquad (6.1.4)$$

$$\frac{\partial l_t}{\partial \boldsymbol{\psi}} = g_t^{-1}\left\{ u_t \frac{\partial f_t}{\partial \boldsymbol{\psi}} + (1/2)(u_t^2/g_t - 1)\frac{\partial g_t}{\partial \boldsymbol{\psi}} \right\} \qquad (6.1.5)$$

where $f_t = f(\mathbf{z}_t; \boldsymbol{\psi})$, and

$$\frac{\partial l_t}{\partial \boldsymbol{\eta}} = -(1/2g_t)(u_t^2/g_t - 1)\frac{\partial g_t}{\partial \boldsymbol{\eta}}. \qquad (6.1.6)$$

Furthermore, the expectations of the blocks of the Hessian matrix $\bar{H}$ (multiplied by -1) are

$$-E\sum_{t=1}^{T} \frac{\partial^2 l_t}{\partial \boldsymbol{\beta} \partial \boldsymbol{\beta}'} = \sum_{t=1}^{T} Eg_t^{-1}\mathbf{z}_t\mathbf{z}_t' + (1/2)\sum_{t=1}^{T} Eg_t^{-2}\frac{\partial g_t}{\partial \boldsymbol{\beta}}\frac{\partial g_t}{\partial \boldsymbol{\beta}'} \qquad (6.1.7)$$

$$-E\sum_{t=1}^{T} \frac{\partial^2 l_t}{\partial \boldsymbol{\beta} \partial \boldsymbol{\psi}'} = \sum_{t=1}^{T} Eg_t^{-1}\mathbf{z}_t \frac{\partial f_t}{\partial \boldsymbol{\psi}'} + (1/2)\sum_{t=1}^{T} Eg_t^{-2}\frac{\partial g_t}{\partial \boldsymbol{\beta}}\frac{\partial g_t}{\partial \boldsymbol{\psi}'} \qquad (6.1.8)$$

$$-E\sum_{t=1}^{T} \frac{\partial^2 l_t}{\partial \boldsymbol{\beta} \partial \boldsymbol{\eta}'} = -(1/2)\sum_{t=1}^{T} Eg_t^{-2}\frac{\partial g_t}{\partial \boldsymbol{\beta}}\frac{\partial g_t}{\partial \boldsymbol{\eta}'} = \mathbf{0} \qquad (6.1.9)$$

$$-E\sum_{t=1}^{T} \frac{\partial^2 l_t}{\partial \boldsymbol{\psi} \partial \boldsymbol{\psi}'} = \sum_{t=1}^{T} Eg_t^{-1}\frac{\partial f_t}{\partial \boldsymbol{\psi}}\frac{\partial f_t}{\partial \boldsymbol{\psi}'} + (1/2)\sum_{t=1}^{T} Eg_t^{-2}\frac{\partial g_t}{\partial \boldsymbol{\psi}}\frac{\partial g_t}{\partial \boldsymbol{\psi}'}$$

$$(6.1.10)$$

$$-E\sum_{t=1}^{T} \frac{\partial^2 l_t}{\partial \boldsymbol{\psi} \partial \boldsymbol{\eta}'} = -(1/2)\sum_{t=1}^{T} Eg_t^{-2}\frac{\partial g_t}{\partial \boldsymbol{\psi}}\frac{\partial g_t}{\partial \boldsymbol{\eta}'} = \mathbf{0} \qquad (6.1.11)$$

and

$$-E\sum_{t=1}^{T} \frac{\partial^2 l_t}{\partial \boldsymbol{\eta} \partial \boldsymbol{\eta}'} = (1/2)\sum_{t=1}^{T} Eg_t^{-2}\frac{\partial g_t}{\partial \boldsymbol{\eta}}\frac{\partial g_t}{\partial \boldsymbol{\eta}'}. \qquad (6.1.12)$$

Results (6.1.9) and (6.1.11) follow from Theorem 4 in Engle (1982) and imply that the sample information matrix is block diagonal. This has important implications to testing linearity in the presence of ARCH.

To define the LM statistic, let

$$\mathbf{s}_t = \left(\frac{\partial l_t}{\partial \boldsymbol{\psi}'}, \frac{\partial l_t}{\partial \boldsymbol{\beta}'}, \frac{\partial l_t}{\partial \boldsymbol{\eta}'} \right),$$

$$\mathbf{m} \equiv T^{-1}(\mathbf{m}'_\psi, \mathbf{m}'_\beta, \mathbf{m}'_\eta)' = T^{-1} \sum_{t=1}^{T} \mathbf{s}_t,$$

and

$$M = T^{-1} \sum (E \mathbf{s}_t \mathbf{s}_t') = [\mathbf{M}_{ij}]. \tag{6.1.13}$$

Under $H_0: \boldsymbol{\psi} = 0$, $E\mathbf{s}_t = 0$ and matrices (6.1.7–12) scaled and evaluated under H_0 form the blocks of (6.1.13) as $\mathbf{M} = -T^{-1}\bar{\mathbf{H}}$. The general form of the LM test for testing $H_0: \boldsymbol{\psi} = 0$, i.e. linearity of (6.1.1) against $H_1: \boldsymbol{\psi} \neq 0$, is then

$$LM_\psi = \hat{\mathbf{m}}'_\psi \operatorname{cov}(\hat{\mathbf{m}}_\psi)^{-1} \hat{\mathbf{m}}_\psi = \hat{\mathbf{m}}'_\psi (\hat{\mathbf{M}}_{\psi\psi} - \hat{\mathbf{M}}_{\psi\beta} \hat{\mathbf{M}}_{\beta\beta}^{-1} \hat{\mathbf{M}}_{\beta\psi})^{-1} \hat{\mathbf{m}}_\psi,$$

$$\tag{6.1.14}$$

where $\hat{\mathbf{m}}'_\psi$, $\hat{\mathbf{M}}_{\psi\psi}$, $\hat{\mathbf{M}}_{\psi\beta}$, and $\hat{\mathbf{M}}_{\beta\beta}$ are consistent estimators of $\mathbf{m}'_\psi$, $\mathbf{M}_{\psi\psi}$, $\mathbf{M}_{\psi\beta}$, and $\mathbf{M}_{\beta\beta}$ respectively, under the null hypothesis. When H_0 is valid, LM_ψ has an asymptotic χ^2 distribution with m degrees of freedom if the rather general assumptions given in White (1984, Theorem 4.25) are satisfied. They are essentially conditions for the existence of moments implied by (6.1.13) and do not include the assumption of normality of errors. If normality is not assumed, (6.1.3) has to be interpreted as a pseudo-log-likelihood.

This theory is rather general and it is illuminating to consider some special cases. If in (6.1.2)

$$g_t = g(\mathbf{z}_t; \boldsymbol{\beta}, \boldsymbol{\psi}, \boldsymbol{\eta}) = g_1(\mathbf{z}_t, \boldsymbol{\eta}),$$

so that g_t does not depend on $\boldsymbol{\beta}$ or $\boldsymbol{\psi}$, we have

$$\frac{\partial g_t}{\partial \boldsymbol{\beta}} = \mathbf{0} \quad \text{and} \quad \frac{\partial g_t}{\partial \boldsymbol{\psi}} = \mathbf{0}.$$

As a result, (6.1.7), (6.1.8), and (6.1.10) simplify further. Let $\mathbf{h}_t = \partial f(\mathbf{z}_t, 0)/\partial \boldsymbol{\psi}$. From (6.1.14) it is seen that the test may be carried out in stages as follows:

(i) Estimate $\boldsymbol{\beta}$ and $\boldsymbol{\eta}$ consistently from $y_t = \boldsymbol{\beta}'\mathbf{z}_t + u_t$, $E(u_t|I_t) = 0$, $\operatorname{var}(u_t|I_t) = g(\mathbf{z}_t, \boldsymbol{\eta})$ and compute $\tilde{u}_t = y_t - \tilde{\boldsymbol{\beta}}'\mathbf{x}_t$ and $\text{SSR}_0 = \sum \tilde{u}_t^2$.

(ii) Standardize the residuals, $\mathbf{z}_t$ and $\hat{\mathbf{h}}_t$:

$$\tilde{u}_t^* = \tilde{u}_t \tilde{g}_t^{-1/2}, \ \mathbf{z}_t^* = \mathbf{z}_t \tilde{g}_t^{-1/2}, \ \hat{\mathbf{h}}_t^* = \hat{\mathbf{h}}_t \tilde{g}_t^{-1/2}$$

where $\tilde{g}_t = g_1(\mathbf{z}_t, \tilde{\boldsymbol{\eta}})$. Estimate the parameters of $\tilde{u}_t^* = \boldsymbol{\delta}' \mathbf{z}_t^* + \boldsymbol{\psi}' \hat{\mathbf{h}}_t^* + e_t$ by ordinary least squares and compute $\mathrm{SSR} = \sum \hat{e}_t^2$.

(iii) Compute the test statistic $LM_\psi^* = \dfrac{\mathrm{SSR}_0 - \mathrm{SSR}}{\mathrm{SSR}_0/T}$.

The third stage may be replaced by an F version of the test:

(iii)' Compute the test statistic $LM_\psi^{**} = \dfrac{(\mathrm{SSR}_0 - \mathrm{SSR})/m}{\mathrm{SSR}/(T - p - k - m - 1)}$.

The null distribution of LM_ψ^{**} is approximated by an F distribution. In small samples and if m is large the size of the F approximation may be closer to the nominal size than the size of the $\chi^2(m)$ approximation; see, for example, Harvey (1990: 174–5) for discussion. If $g_t \equiv \eta_0 = \sigma^2$ the situation is simplified further. The first stage consists of ordinary least-squares estimation of $\boldsymbol{\beta}$ and σ^2 while the second stage proceeds without any standardization.

Consider the next case where

$$g(\mathbf{z}_t; \boldsymbol{\beta}, \boldsymbol{\psi}, \boldsymbol{\eta}) = \eta_0 + \sum_{j=1}^{q} \eta_j u_{t-j}^2,$$

i.e. (6.1.1) has $\mathrm{ARCH}(q)$ errors. In that case

$$\frac{\partial g_t}{\partial \boldsymbol{\beta}} = -2 \sum_{j=1}^{q} \eta_j u_{t-j} \mathbf{z}_{t-j} \tag{6.1.15}$$

and

$$\frac{\partial g_t}{\partial \boldsymbol{\psi}} = -2 \sum_{j=1}^{q} \eta_j u_{t-j} \frac{\partial f_t}{\partial \boldsymbol{\psi}}. \tag{6.1.16}$$

From (6.1.15) and (6.1.16) it follows that

$$(1/2) \sum_{t=1}^{T} E g_t^{-2} \mathbf{a}_t \mathbf{a}_t' = 2 \sum_{t=1}^{T} E g_t^{-2} \sum_{j=1}^{q} \eta_j^2 u_{t-j}^2 \mathbf{b}_{t-j} \mathbf{b}_{t-j}' \tag{6.1.17}$$

where

$$\mathbf{a}_t = \left(\frac{\partial g_t}{\partial \boldsymbol{\beta}'}, \frac{\partial g_t}{\partial \boldsymbol{\psi}'} \right)' \quad \text{and} \quad b_t = \left(\mathbf{z}_t', \frac{\partial g_t}{\partial \boldsymbol{\psi}'} \right)'.$$

Following Engle (1982), (6.1.7), (6.1.8), and (6.1.10) may be estimated by

$$- \sum_{t=1}^{T} \frac{\partial^2 \hat{l}_t}{\partial \mathbf{w} \partial \mathbf{w}'} = \sum_{t=1}^{T} (\tilde{g}_t^{-1} + 2\tilde{u}_t^2 \sum_j \tilde{\eta}_j^2 \tilde{g}_{t+j}^{-2}) \tilde{\mathbf{b}}_t \tilde{\mathbf{b}}_t' = \sum_t p_t \tilde{\mathbf{b}}_t \tilde{\mathbf{b}}_t'$$

$$\tag{6.1.18}$$

where $\mathbf{w} = (\boldsymbol{\beta}', \boldsymbol{\psi}')'$, and the end effects are ignored. Likewise,

$$\frac{\partial \sum_t \hat{l}_t}{\partial \mathbf{w}} = \sum_t \left\{ g_t^{-1} \tilde{u}_t \tilde{\mathbf{b}}_t - (2g_t)^{-1}(\tilde{u}_t^2/\tilde{g}_t - 1) \sum_{j=1}^q \tilde{\eta}_j \tilde{u}_{t-j} \tilde{\mathbf{b}}_{t-j} \right\}$$

$$= \sum_t \left\{ \tilde{g}_t^{-1} - \sum_{j=1}^q (2\tilde{g}_{t+j})^{-1}(\tilde{u}_{t+j}^2/\tilde{g}_{t+j} - 1)\tilde{\eta}_j \right\} \tilde{u}_t \tilde{\mathbf{b}}_t$$

$$= \sum_t q_t \tilde{u}_t \tilde{\mathbf{b}}_t. \tag{6.1.19}$$

Estimators (6.1.18) and (6.1.19) are the ones needed to compute the test statistic (6.1.14).

As an example, consider the following dynamic model

$$y_t = \beta_1 y_{t-1} + \beta_2 x_t + \psi u_{t-1} y_{t-1} + u_t \tag{6.1.20}$$

where $u_t \sim \text{ARCH}(q)$, $Eu_t x_t = 0$ and $\{x_t\}$ is stationary. The model is bilinear, and the linearity hypothesis is $H_0:\psi = 0$. In (6.1.18) and (6.1.19), $\tilde{\mathbf{b}}_t = (\mathbf{z}_t', \tilde{u}_{t-1} y_{t-1})'$ where $\mathbf{z}_t = (y_{t-1}, x_t)'$, and $\tilde{u}_t$ is a consistent estimator of u_t under the assumption of $\text{ARCH}(q)$ errors and $\psi = 0$ in (6.1.20).

In economics there are few examples of situations where ARCH can be safely assumed while the theory leaves the issue of nonlinearity of the conditional mean open. Note, however, that testing the *linear* specification when ARCH is present may be of some interest, although apparent ARCH may often be just a consequence of misspecification of the conditional mean. The testing may then simply be done by replacing $f(\mathbf{z}_t, \boldsymbol{\psi})$ in (6.1.1) by a linear combination $\boldsymbol{\psi}' \bar{\mathbf{z}}_t$ where $\bar{\mathbf{z}}_t$ is a vector of variables not included in $\mathbf{z}_t$, and the above considerations apply.

Joint testing of linearity and constant conditional variance is also uncomplicated. The null hypothesis is

$$H_0:\boldsymbol{\psi} = 0 \quad \& \quad \bar{\boldsymbol{\eta}} = 0 \tag{6.1.21}$$

where $\bar{\boldsymbol{\eta}} = (\eta_1, \ldots, \eta_q)'$. Under (6.1.21),

$$\left. \frac{\partial g_t}{\partial \boldsymbol{\psi}} \right|_{H_0} = 0 \quad \text{and} \quad \left. \frac{\partial g_t}{\partial \boldsymbol{\beta}} \right|_{H_0} = 0,$$

so that the information matrix is again block diagonal, the off-diagonal blocks (6.1.9) and (6.1.11) being null matrices. Thus the LM test statistic of (6.1.21) may be written as

$$LM_{\psi\eta} = \hat{\mathbf{m}}_\psi'(\hat{\mathbf{M}}_{\psi\psi} - \hat{\mathbf{M}}_{\psi\beta}\hat{\mathbf{M}}_{\beta\beta}^{-1}\hat{\mathbf{M}}_{\beta\psi})^{-1}\hat{\mathbf{m}}_\psi$$

$$+ \hat{\mathbf{m}}_{\bar{\eta}}'(\hat{\mathbf{M}}_{\bar{\eta}\bar{\eta}} - \hat{\mathbf{M}}_{\bar{\eta}0}\hat{\mathbf{M}}_{00}^{-1}\hat{\mathbf{M}}_{0\bar{\eta}})^{-1}\hat{\mathbf{m}}_{\bar{\eta}}$$

$$= LM_\psi + LM_{\bar{\eta}} \tag{6.1.22}$$

where $LM_{\bar{\eta}}$ is the LM test for $H_0 : \bar{\eta} = 0$ given $\psi = 0$, the sub-index 0 represents η_0, and the necessary estimators in (6.1.22) are OLS estimators from $y_t = \beta' z_t + u_t$. Higgins and Bera (1989) made use of this block diagonality in constructing a joint test against bilinearity and ARCH in a linear model. However, although (6.1.22) is an attractive factorization in that it makes joint testing easy, performing the joint test may not be very useful in practice. This is because a rejection of the joint null hypothesis as such does not give much information about causes of a possible rejection: nonlinear conditional mean, nonlinear conditional variance, or both. Considering the values of LM_ψ and $LM_{\bar{\eta}}$ separately is generally more useful, although Higgins and Bera (1989) did provide a counter example.

The above block diagonality is also an important result in the following case. Consider testing $H_0 : \psi_T = 0 | \bar{\eta} = 0$ against $H_\psi^T : \psi_T = \delta T^{-1/2} | \bar{\eta} = 0$, $\delta \neq 0$, and $\bar{H}_0 : \bar{\eta} = 0 | \psi_T = 0$ against $H_{\bar{\eta}} : \bar{\eta} \neq 0 | \psi_T = 0$, and assume that the data are generated according to H_ψ^T. The null models defined by H_0 and $\bar{H}_0$ are identical and $H_{\bar{\eta}}$ is an inappropriate alternative. Luukkonen et al. (1988a) and Teräsvirta (1990a) recently considered this situation in the univariate time-series context. The block diagonality under the joint null hypothesis implies that $LM_{\bar{\eta}}$ has zero asymptotic relative efficiency with respect to LM_ψ^T, $T \rightarrow \infty$, against $H_\psi^T (T \rightarrow \infty)$. In other words, the asymptotic power of $LM_{\bar{\eta}}$ against a sequence of local alternative models (6.1.1) with $\psi_T = \delta T^{-1/2}$ and $\bar{\eta} = 0$ does not exceed the size of the test. This local asymptotic result does not imply that $LM_{\bar{\eta}}$ has no power against inappropriate global alternatives. Nevertheless, it indicates that the LM tests against ARCH like the one by McLeod and Li (1983) are, in small samples, usually much less powerful in detecting nonlinearity in conditional mean than the appropriate LM test. There are simulation results demonstrating this, see for example Luukkonen et al. (1988a) and Lee et al. (1993). The asymptotic relative efficiency of a linearity test with respect to another will be discussed in more detail in Section 6.6.

Finally, a remark about the LM tests is in order. In a few cases, the nonlinear function in (6.1.1) with the parameter vector $\psi = (\gamma', \theta')'$ factors so that

$$f(z_t, \psi) = f_1(z_t, \gamma) \theta' z_t \qquad (6.1.23)$$

where $f_1(z_t, 0) = 0$. Thus the linearity hypothesis can be expressed as $H_0 : \gamma = 0$. It is immediately seen from (6.1.23) that (6.1.1) is only identified under $H_1 : \gamma \neq 0$ because, if the null hypothesis is true, θ can take any value. Davies (1977, 1987) discussed this testing problem, and his general solution was first to derive a test statistic assuming θ fixed: let this statistic be $S_\gamma(\theta)$. Assuming that large values of S_γ are critical, the recommended (conservative) final statistic is

$$\bar{S}_\gamma = \sup_\theta S_\gamma(\theta). \tag{6.1.24}$$

It turns out that in testing linearity against many models of interest in this book this solution has the desirable property that the asymptotic distribution of (6.1.24) under $H_0{:}\gamma = 0$ is a chi-squared distribution. This is not a standard outcome, because usually the asymptotic distribution is not known and has to be approximated. The solution is based on an approximation and a subsequent reparameterization of (6.1.23) in such a way that the identification problem disappears. Godfrey (1988: 86–7) provided another example in specification testing in which the null distribution is known; for examples in univariate time-series linearity testing see Saikkonen and Luukkonen (1988) and Luukkonen *et al.* (1988*b*).

6.1.2 Testing in the presence of unspecified heteroskedasticity

In the previous section it was assumed that the conditional variance of the errors was parameterized. If there is not enough information about the data-generating process to do that but heteroskedasticity is still suspected, linearity tests may be made robust against unspecified heteroskedasticity. Davidson and MacKinnon (1985) considered ways of doing that. Take model (6.1.1) and the null hypothesis $\psi = 0$. In (6.1.2), assume that

$$g_t = \mathrm{var}\,(u_t | I_t) = \sigma_t^2, \tag{6.1.25}$$

and let $\boldsymbol{\Omega} = \mathrm{diag}\,(\sigma_1^2, \ldots, \sigma_T^2)$. Furthermore, assume that (6.1.25) is ignored by erroneously assuming $\sigma_t^2 \equiv \sigma^2$. In this case, treating σ^2 as fixed,

$$\hat{\mathbf{m}}_\psi = \sigma^{-2} T^{-1} \sum_{t=1}^{T} \tilde{u}_t \, \frac{\partial \hat{f}_t}{\partial \psi} = \sigma^{-2} T^{-1} \mathbf{H}' \mathbf{M}_x \hat{\mathbf{u}}$$

where

$$\mathbf{H}' = \left[\frac{\partial \hat{f}_1}{\partial \psi} \, \frac{\partial \hat{f}_2}{\partial \psi} \, \cdots \, \frac{\partial \hat{f}_T}{\partial \psi}\right] = (\hat{\mathbf{h}}_1' \hat{\mathbf{h}}_2' \, \ldots \, \hat{\mathbf{h}}_T')',$$

$$\mathbf{M}_x = (\mathbf{I} - \mathbf{X}(\mathbf{X}'\mathbf{X})^{-1}\mathbf{X}'); \quad \mathbf{X}' = (\mathbf{z}_1', \mathbf{z}_2' \, \ldots \, \mathbf{z}_T'),$$

and

$$\hat{\mathbf{u}} = (\hat{u}_1, \ldots, \hat{u}_T)'.$$

Furthermore, $\hat{\mathbf{h}}_t'$, $t = 1, \ldots, T$, is a consistent estimator of $\partial f_t / \partial \psi$ under

H_0. However, generally

$$\text{cov}(\hat{\mathbf{m}}_\psi) = \sigma^{-4} T^{-2} \mathbf{H}' \mathbf{M}_x \mathbf{\Omega} \mathbf{M}_x \mathbf{H} \neq \sigma^{-2} T^{-2} \mathbf{H}' \mathbf{M}_x \mathbf{H}$$

where the rightmost expression holds for $\mathbf{\Omega} = \sigma^2 \mathbf{I}$. Thus in principle

$$LM_\psi = \hat{\mathbf{u}}' \mathbf{M}_x \mathbf{H} (\mathbf{H}' \mathbf{M}_x \mathbf{\Omega} \mathbf{M}_x \mathbf{H})^{-1} \mathbf{H}' \mathbf{M}_x \hat{\mathbf{u}}. \tag{6.1.26}$$

To make (6.1.26) operational, $\mathbf{\Omega}$ has to be approximated by observable quantities, so write

$$LM_\psi^* = \mathbf{1}' \hat{\mathbf{U}} \mathbf{M}_x \mathbf{H} (\mathbf{H}' \mathbf{M}_x \hat{\mathbf{U}} \hat{\mathbf{U}} \mathbf{M}_x \mathbf{H})^{-1} \mathbf{H}' \mathbf{M}_x \hat{\mathbf{U}} \mathbf{1} \tag{6.1.27}$$

where $\hat{\mathbf{U}} = \text{diag}(\hat{u}_1, \ldots, \hat{u}_T)$ and $\mathbf{1} = (1, \ldots, 1)'$, and $\mathbf{\Omega}$ has been approximated by $\text{diag}(\hat{u}_1^2, \ldots, \hat{u}_T^2)$. Davidson and MacKinnon (1985) suggested the use of (6.1.27) as a statistic which is robust against heteroskedasticity. The test may also be formulated as an auxiliary regression type of test as follows:

(i) Regress y_t on $\mathbf{z}_t$ and compute the residuals $\hat{u}_t$, $t = 1, \ldots, T$.

(ii) Regress the elements of $\mathbf{z}_t$ on $\hat{\mathbf{h}}_t$ and compute the residuals (residual matrix is $\mathbf{M}_x \mathbf{H}$).

(iii) Weight the residuals by $\hat{\mathbf{u}}$ and regress $\mathbf{1}$ on the weighted residuals $\hat{\mathbf{U}} \mathbf{M}_x \mathbf{H}$. The explained sum of squares from this regression is (6.1.27).

Davidson and MacKinnon (1985) also discussed several other robust test statistics, but their Monte Carlo experiments indicated that (6.1.27) may have the best small sample properties. Since their study was concentrated on testing linear hypotheses in linear models, they issued a warning that heteroskedasticity-robust tests based on unrestricted residuals (obtained by estimating the model under H_1) are often unreliable in small samples. On the other hand, linearity tests like the LM tests discussed here are usually based on restricted residuals because restricted estimation does not involve estimating a nonlinear model. Davidson and MacKinnon (1985) found that tests based on restricted residuals performed better than those based on unrestricted ones. This raises the hopes that (6.1.27) would be a feasible linearity test in the presence of unspecified heteroskedasticity. However, it has to be added that the existing small sample evidence is hardly sufficient to fully justify these hopes yet. A more general treatment of heteroskedasticity-robust specification tests can be found in Wooldridge (1990).

6.2 Applications of Lagrange Multiplier Tests

6.2.1 Testing linearity against LSTR

Sometimes a model builder may have economic theory indicating the type of nonlinearity he may want to consider. In such a situation it may be possible to derive a LM test for linearity which is optimal in terms of power against that nonlinearity. In this section, some examples of this kind will be considered. Assume first that the nonlinear model is a LSTR model

$$y_t = \boldsymbol{\pi}'\mathbf{z}_t + F(\tilde{\mathbf{z}}_t)\boldsymbol{\theta}'\mathbf{z}_t + u_t, \ t = 1, \ldots, T \tag{6.2.1}$$

where $\mathbf{z}_t = (1, \tilde{\mathbf{z}}_t')'$, $\tilde{\mathbf{z}}_t = (y_{t-1}, \ldots, y_{t-p}, x_{t1}, \ldots, x_{tk})'$, $\boldsymbol{\pi} = (\pi_0, \pi_1, \ldots, \pi_m)'$, $\boldsymbol{\theta} = (\theta_0, \tilde{\boldsymbol{\theta}}')'$ with $\tilde{\boldsymbol{\theta}} = (\theta_1, \ldots, \theta_m)'$, $m = p + k$; $u_t \sim \text{nid}(0, \sigma^2)$, $Eu_t\mathbf{z}_t = 0$, and

$$F(\tilde{\mathbf{z}}_t) = (1 + \exp\{-\gamma(\mathbf{a}'\tilde{\mathbf{z}}_t - c)\})^{-1} - 1/2, \ \gamma > 0 \tag{6.2.2}$$

with $\mathbf{a} = (0, \ldots, 0, 1, 0, \ldots, 0)'$. The $m \times 1$ vector $\mathbf{a}$ represents the fact that the transition variable is not known. Often this is somewhat too general an assumption. For instance, the researcher may know that the transition variable is a lag of the dependent variable but does not know which one. In that case $\mathbf{a}$ and $\tilde{\mathbf{z}}_t$ are modified accordingly. It may also be assumed that $\tilde{\mathbf{z}}_t = x_{t,k+1}$, $Ex_{t,k+1}u_t = 0$, i.e. a variable not among the elements of $\mathbf{z}_t$, so that $\mathbf{a} = 1$.

The null hypothesis of linearity is $H_0: \gamma = 0$, and $H_1: \gamma > 0$. It is seen from (6.2.1) and (6.2.2) that the model is only identified under the alternative. When the null hypothesis is true, $\boldsymbol{\theta}$, $\mathbf{a}$, and c can take any value. To derive a test for linearity consider the conditional log likelihood for observation t:

$$l_t = -\tfrac{1}{2}\ln 2\pi - \tfrac{1}{2}\ln \sigma^2 - \frac{u_t^2}{2\sigma^2}. \tag{6.2.3}$$

Following Davies (1977) by keeping $\boldsymbol{\theta}$, $\mathbf{a}$, and c fixed one obtains

$$\left.\frac{\partial l_t}{\partial \boldsymbol{\pi}}\right|_{\gamma=0} = (1/\sigma^2)\tilde{u}_t\mathbf{z}_t \tag{6.2.4}$$

where

$$\tilde{u}_t = y_t - \boldsymbol{\pi}'\mathbf{z}_t$$

and

$$\left.\frac{\partial l_t}{\partial \gamma}\right|_{\gamma=0} = (1/4\sigma^2)\tilde{u}_t\left[\sum_{i \geqslant j} \varphi_{ij}^*\tilde{z}_{ti}\tilde{z}_{tj} + \varphi_0^* + \sum_j \varphi_j^*\tilde{z}_{tj}\right] \tag{6.2.5}$$

where

$$\varphi_{ij}^* = a_i\theta_j + a_j\theta_i, \quad i = 1, \ldots, m; \ j = i, \ldots, m \tag{6.2.6}$$

$$\varphi_0^* = -c\theta_0, \quad \varphi_j^* = \theta_0 a_j - c\theta_j, \quad j = 1, \ldots, m. \tag{6.2.7}$$

This suggests the following LM test.

(i) Regress y_t on $\mathbf{z}_t$, compute residuals $\hat{u}_t = y_t - \hat{\boldsymbol{\pi}}'\mathbf{z}_t$ and $\text{SSR}_0 = \sum \hat{u}_t^2$.

(ii) Estimate $\boldsymbol{\psi}_1 = (\psi_{01}, \ldots, \psi_{m1})'$ and ψ_2 from the model (note that all φ_{ij}^* and φ_i^* are fixed)

$$\hat{u}_t = \boldsymbol{\psi}_1'\mathbf{z}_t + \psi_2\left\{\sum_{i \geq j}\varphi_{ij}^*\tilde{z}_{ti}\tilde{z}_{tj} + \varphi_0^* + \sum_j \varphi_i^*\tilde{z}_{tj}\right\} + v_t^* \qquad (6.2.8)$$

and compute $\text{SSR}(\boldsymbol{\theta}, \mathbf{a}, c) = \sum \hat{v}_t^{*2}$.

(iii) Compute the test statistic

$$\text{LM}(\boldsymbol{\theta}, \mathbf{a}, c) = T(\text{SSR}_0 - \text{SSR}(\boldsymbol{\theta}, \mathbf{a}, c))/\text{SSR}_0 \qquad (6.2.9)$$

or its F version. Statistic (6.2.9) has an asymptotic $\chi^2(1)$ distribution when the null hypothesis is valid.

However, (6.2.9) is not an applicable statistic because it depends on $\boldsymbol{\theta}$, $\mathbf{a}$, and c. Fortunately, in this case obtaining (6.1.14) is simple. Let $\varphi_{ij} = \psi_2\varphi_{ij}^*$ and $\varphi_j = \psi_{j1} + \psi_2\varphi_j^*$. For each triplet $(\boldsymbol{\theta}, \mathbf{a}, c)$ there exist φ_{ij} and φ_j. Rearranging terms in (6.2.8) yields

(ii') $$\hat{u}_t = (\boldsymbol{\psi}_1 + \psi_2\boldsymbol{\varphi})'\mathbf{z}_t + \sum_{i \geq j}\varphi_{ij}\tilde{z}_{ti}\tilde{z}_{tj} + v_t \qquad (6.2.10)$$

where $\boldsymbol{\varphi} = (\varphi_0, \varphi_1, \ldots, \varphi_m)'$. From (6.2.10) it is seen that

$$\text{SSR} = \inf_{\boldsymbol{\theta},\mathbf{a},c}\text{SSR}(\boldsymbol{\theta}, \mathbf{a}, c) = \sum \hat{v}_t^2$$

where $\hat{v}_t$ are the OLS residuals from regressing $\hat{u}_t$ on $\mathbf{z}_t$ and $\tilde{z}_{ti}\tilde{z}_{tj}$, $i = 1, \ldots, m$; $j = i, \ldots, m$. Under the usual regularity conditions discussed in Section 6.1 the test statistic

$$LM = T(\text{SSR}_0 - \text{SSR})/\text{SSR}_0 \qquad (6.2.11)$$

has an asymptotic $\chi^2(m(m + 1)/2)$ distribution, when $H_0: \varphi_{ij} = 0$, $i = 1, \ldots, m$; $j = i, \ldots, m$, is valid. An F approximation to (6.2.11) is recommended in small samples.

Two things can be noticed from (6.2.6), (6.2.7), and (6.2.10). First, in the univariate case $\tilde{\mathbf{z}}_t = (y_{t-1}, \ldots, y_{t-m})'$ the test based on (6.2.11) is equivalent to a linearity test based on a quadratic dual of the Volterra expansion of y_t, i.e. the linearity test of Tsay (1986). The present test is thus a generalization of the Tsay test. Tsay (1986) considered his test a general linearity test, but this treatment demonstrates that it is also an LM-type test against a specific nonlinear model. Second, none of the parameters φ_{ij} included in H_0 is a function of θ_0. Thus (6.2.11) can be expected to have little power against alternatives in which $\tilde{\boldsymbol{\theta}}$ is close to a null vector.

Luukkonen *et al.* (1988b) discussed a remedy to this deficiency in a univariate case, and it generalizes to the present situation. The idea is to use a cubic approximation of $F(\tilde{\mathbf{z}}_t)$ about $\gamma = 0$, i.e. to replace $F(\tilde{\mathbf{z}}_t) = (1 + \exp\{-h_t\})^{-1} - 1/2$ by

$$T(\tilde{z}_t) = g_1 h_t + (g_3/6)h_t^3 \tag{6.2.12}$$

where $h_t = \gamma(\mathbf{a}'\tilde{\mathbf{z}}_t - c)$, and $g_1 = \partial F(0)/\partial\gamma$, $g_3 = \partial^3 F(0)/\partial\gamma^3$. Proceeding as above and combining terms yields an auxiliary regression with quadratic, cubic, and fourth-order terms; note that $(\mathbf{a}'\tilde{\mathbf{z}}_t)^j = \sum_{i=1}^m a_i \tilde{z}_{ti}^j$. However, not all these terms contain information about θ_0; see Luukkonen *et al.* (1988b) and Teräsvirta (1990b) for discussion. An obvious idea is to reduce the number of terms and thus increase the power of the test under H_1 by augmenting (6.2.10) only by the terms whose regression coefficients in the auxiliary regression are functions of θ_0. This yields

(ii″) $$\hat{u}_t = \boldsymbol{\beta}'\mathbf{z}_t + \sum_{i \geq j} \varphi_{ij}\tilde{z}_{ti}\tilde{z}_{tj} + \sum_{j=1}^m \psi_j \tilde{z}_{tj}^3 + \eta_t. \tag{6.2.13}$$

Thus the procedure consists of testing $H_0: \varphi_{ij} = 0$, $i = 1, \ldots, m$; $j = i$, $\ldots, m$; $\psi_j = 0$, $j = 1, \ldots, m$, in (6.2.13). Under H_0, the test statistic has an asymptotic $\chi^2(m(m+1)/2 + m)$ distribution.

If the transition variable $\tilde{z}_{td}$ is known, the above tests simplify considerably. In testing against logistic STR, (6.2.10) is replaced by

$$\hat{u}_t = \boldsymbol{\beta}'\mathbf{z}_t + \sum_{j=1}^m \varphi_{dj}\tilde{z}_{td}\tilde{z}_{tj} + v_t.$$

The null hypothesis $H_0: \varphi_{dj} = 0$, $j = 1, \ldots, m$, contains m parameters, and when it is valid, the test statistic (6.2.11) has an asymptotic $\chi^2(m)$ distribution. The full test based on (6.2.12) has the auxiliary regression

$$\hat{u}_t = \boldsymbol{\beta}'\mathbf{z}_t + \sum_{j=1}^m (\varphi_{dj}\tilde{z}_{td}\tilde{z}_{tj} + \psi_{dj}\tilde{z}_{td}^2\tilde{z}_{tj} + \kappa_{dj}\tilde{z}_{td}^3\tilde{z}_{tj}) + v_t, \tag{6.2.14}$$

so that $H_0: \varphi_{dj} = \psi_{dj} = \kappa_{dj} = 0$, $j = 1, \ldots, m$, and the corresponding LM-type test statistic has an asymptotic $\chi^2(3m)$ distribution. The test based on (6.2.14) is useful in STR model specification when the transition variable has to be specified from the data. This will be discussed in Chapter 7.

It is important to note that these tests retain their power as $\gamma \to \infty$, i.e. as the smooth transition regression model becomes a switching regression model; Luukkonen *et al.* (1988b) provided an example of this in the univariate case for which Petruccelli (1990) contributed additional small sample simulation results. The tests are thus readily available for testing linearity against switching regression either with an unknown or known switching variable, should the underlying economic theory demand such an alternative to linearity.

6.2.2 Testing linearity against ESTR

The exponential STR differs radically from the logistic one in that, while in the LSTR model the parameters change monotonically with the transition variable, the change is nonmonotonic in the ESTR model. In fact, the change is symmetric about a value of the transition variable. This difference is reflected in the appropriate test statistics when linearity is tested against ESTR. The ESTR model is (6.2.1) where

$$F(\tilde{\mathbf{z}}_t) = 1 - \exp\{-\gamma(\mathbf{a}'\tilde{\mathbf{z}}_t - c)^2\}, \gamma > 0. \qquad (6.2.15)$$

Being a STR model, the ESTR model resembles the LSTR model in that it is only identified when it is assumed that $\gamma > 0$ (or $\gamma < 0$). In testing linearity against (6.2.1) with (6.2.15), the null hypothesis is $\gamma = 0$. To construct an LM-type test one can begin with (6.2.3) which leads to (6.2.4) and

$$\left.\frac{\partial l_t}{\partial \gamma}\right|_{\gamma=0} = (1/\sigma^2)\tilde{u}_t\left[\sum_i\sum_j\psi_{ij}\tilde{z}_{ti}\tilde{z}_{tj}^2 + \sum_{i\geq j}\varphi_{ij}\tilde{z}_{ti}\tilde{z}_{tj} + \sum_{j=0}^m\varphi_j z_{tj}\right] + v_t$$

$$(6.2.16)$$

where

$$\psi_{ij} = a_i\theta_j, \ i, j = 1, \ldots, m \qquad (6.2.17)$$

$$\varphi_{ij} = \delta_{ij}\theta_0 a_j - 2c(a_i\theta_j + a_j\theta_i); \ \delta_{ij} = 1, \ i = j, \text{ zero otherwise,}$$

$$j = 1, \ldots, m; \ i = j, \ldots, m \qquad (6.2.18)$$

$$\varphi_0 = c^2\theta_0, \ \varphi_j = c(c\theta_j - 2a_j), \quad j = 1, \ldots, m. \qquad (6.2.19)$$

Using the same arguments as in the previous section one obtains a LM-type test for linearity. The auxiliary regression corresponding to (6.2.10) now becomes

$$\hat{u}_t = \boldsymbol{\beta}'\mathbf{z}_t + \sum_i\sum_j\psi_{ij}\tilde{z}_{ti}\tilde{z}_{tj}^2 + \sum_{i\geq j}\varphi_{ij}\tilde{z}_{ti}\tilde{z}_{tj} + v_t \qquad (6.2.20)$$

and the LM-type statistic (6.2.11) has an asymptotic χ^2 distribution with $m^2 + m(m+1)/2$ degrees of freedom under the null hypothesis

$$H_0: \psi_{ij} = 0, \ i, j = 1, \ldots, m; \ \varphi_{ij} = 0, \ j = 1, \ldots, m; \ i = j, \ldots, m.$$

$$(6.2.21)$$

If the transition variable is known to be $\tilde{z}_{td}$, (6.2.21) reduces to

$$\hat{u}_t = \boldsymbol{\beta}'\mathbf{z}_t + \sum_{i=1}^m(\psi_{id}\tilde{z}_{ti}\tilde{z}_{td}^2 + \varphi_{id}\tilde{z}_{ti}\tilde{z}_{td}) + v_t \qquad (6.2.22)$$

while the degrees of freedom in the asymptotic χ^2 distribution under the null hypothesis decreases to $2m$. The difference between (6.2.14) and (6.2.22) is that the latter regression does not contain any fourth-order terms, and this fact may be used for discriminating between LSTR and ESTR models. This will be discussed in more detail in Chapter 7.

The test is sensitive to $\theta_0 \neq 0$ as is seen from (6.2.18). If one knows that both $c = 0$ and $\theta_0 = 0$, then $\varphi_{ij} = 0$ for all i and j, and the auxiliary regressions (6.2.20) and (6.2.22) do not contain the quadratic terms. In the univariate case assuming that the transition variable is y_{t-1}, (6.2.22) without the quadratic terms is the same as in the LM-type linearity test of Saikkonen and Luukkonen (1988) against exponential autoregression. This is because in the original univariate EAR model (Haggan and Ozaki, 1981), $c = \theta_0 = 0$.

6.2.3 Testing linearity against STR-D

The STR-D models are another class of STR models. In STR models, the nonlinearity is determined by values of the transition variable deviating from a fixed value. In STR-D, it is due to the deviation of a previous value or values of the dependent variable from a linear path. Consider first the LSTR-D model which is (6.2.1) with $\theta_0 = 0$ and

$$F(\tilde{\boldsymbol{v}}_{t-1}) = (1 + \exp\{-\gamma(\mathbf{a}'\tilde{\boldsymbol{v}}_{t-1})\})^{-1} - 1/2, \ \gamma > 0 \qquad (6.2.23)$$

where $\mathbf{a}$ is as before, $\tilde{\boldsymbol{v}}_t = (\tilde{u}_t, \tilde{u}_{t-1}, \ldots, \tilde{u}_{t-h+1})'$, $\tilde{u}_t = y_t - \boldsymbol{\pi}'\mathbf{z}_t$. In this case, differentiating (6.2.3) yields

$$\frac{\partial l_t}{\partial \boldsymbol{\pi}} =$$

$$(1/\sigma^2)u_t[\mathbf{z}_t - \gamma(1 + \exp\{-\gamma(\mathbf{a}'\tilde{\boldsymbol{v}}_{t-1})\})^{-2}\exp\{-\gamma(\mathbf{a}'\tilde{\boldsymbol{v}}_{t-1})\}\mathbf{Z}_{t-1}\mathbf{a}(\boldsymbol{\theta}'\mathbf{z}_t)]$$

where $\mathbf{Z}_{t-1} = (\mathbf{z}_{t-1}\mathbf{z}_{t-2}\ldots\mathbf{z}_{t-m})$ so that

$$\left.\frac{\partial l_t}{\partial \boldsymbol{\pi}}\right|_{\gamma=0} = (1/\sigma^2)\tilde{u}_t\mathbf{z}_t \qquad (6.2.24)$$

as before. Furthermore,

$$\left.\frac{\partial l_t}{\partial \gamma}\right|_{\gamma=0} = (1/\sigma^2)\tilde{u}_t\left[\sum_{i=1}^{m}\sum_{j=1}^{h}\varphi_{ij}\tilde{z}_{ti}\tilde{u}_{t-j} + \sum_{j=1}^{h}\varphi_j\tilde{u}_{t-j}\right] \qquad (6.2.25)$$

where

$$\varphi_{ij} = \theta_i a_j, \quad i = 1, \ldots, m; \ j = 1, \ldots, h$$

$$\varphi_j = \theta_0 a_j = 0, \quad j = 1, \ldots, h,$$

because we assumed $\theta_0 = 0$. Combining (6.2.25) and the arguments of the preceding section results in an LM-type test for $\gamma = 0$. It is a test for

$$H_0: \varphi_{ij} = 0, \quad i = 1, \ldots, m; \, j = 1, \ldots, h, \qquad (6.2.26)$$

in the following auxiliary regression

$$\hat{u}_t = \boldsymbol{\beta}' \mathbf{z}_t + \sum_{i=1}^{m} \sum_{j=1}^{h} \varphi_{ij} \tilde{z}_{ti} \hat{u}_{t-j} + v_t. \qquad (6.2.27)$$

When (6.2.26) is valid, statistic (6.2.11) has an asymptotic $\chi^2(mh)$ distribution. The LM-type test based on (6.2.27) is equivalent to the LM linearity test of the hypothesis $H_0: \delta_{ij} = 0$, $i = 1, \ldots, m; \, j = 1, \ldots, h$, in

$$y_t = \boldsymbol{\pi}' \mathbf{z}_t + \sum_{i=1}^{m} \sum_{j=1}^{h} \delta_{ij} \tilde{z}_{ti} u_{t-j} + u_t. \qquad (6.2.28)$$

When (6.2.28) is univariate, i.e. $\tilde{\mathbf{z}}_t = (y_{t-1}, \ldots, y_{t-m})'$, it is a univariate bilinear model, and testing the above null hypothesis within (6.2.27) amounts to testing linearity against bilinearity. Weiss (1986) and Saik-konen and Luukkonen (1988) discussed testing linearity against univari-ate bilinear models. The test remains unchanged if instead of $\mathbf{a} = (0, \ldots, 0, 1, 0, \ldots, 0)'$, one assumes $\mathbf{a} = (a_1, \ldots, a_h)'$ with one standard-izing restriction, $\sum_{j=1}^{h} a_j = 1$ (say). Thus the relationship between testing linearity against bilinearity of type (6.2.28) and STR-D is not due to assuming the lag d in $\tilde{u}_{t-d}$ is unknown as in (6.2.23). However, if there is only a single lag in the exponent and it is known, (6.2.27) simplifies to

$$\hat{u}_t = \boldsymbol{\beta}' \mathbf{z}_t + \sum_{i=1}^{m} \varphi_{id} \tilde{z}_{ti} \hat{u}_{t-d} + v_t. \qquad (6.2.29)$$

The test statistic (6.2.11) now has an asymptotic χ^2 distribution with only m degrees of freedom when $\varphi_{id} = 0$, $i = 1, \ldots, m$. If the model is an ESTR-D model with the nonlinearity symmetric about the deviation from the linear path, the above results hold when $\hat{u}_{t-j}$, $j = 1, \ldots, h$, is replaced by $\hat{u}_{t-j}^2$ in (6.2.27) and (6.2.29).

6.3 Testing Linearity against an Unspecified Alternative

6.3.1 RESET

In this section, linearity tests against general model misspecification are discussed. These include the Regression Error Specification Test (RESET; Ramsey 1969), tests based on duals of Volterra expansions (Tsay 1986) or Kolmogorov–Gabor polynomials (Spanos 1986), and the neural network test (Lee *et al.* 1993). The RESET has certainly been one of the most popular tests against misspecification of functional form. It may be carried out in three stages as follows:

(i) Assume the linear part of the model is

$$y_t = \boldsymbol{\beta}'\mathbf{z}_t + u_t, \, t = 1, \ldots, T$$

where $\mathbf{z}_t = (1, y_{t-1}, \ldots, y_{t-p}, x_{t1}, \ldots, x_{tk})'$. Estimate $\boldsymbol{\beta}$ by OLS and compute $\hat{u}_t = y_t - \hat{y}_t$ where $\hat{y}_t = \hat{\boldsymbol{\beta}}'\mathbf{z}_t$, and $\text{SSR}_0 = \sum \hat{u}_t^2$.

(ii) Estimate the parameters of

$$\hat{u}_t = \boldsymbol{\delta}'\mathbf{z}_t + \sum_{j=2}^{h} \psi_j \hat{y}_t^j + v_t \tag{6.3.1}$$

by OLS and compute $\text{SSR} = \sum \hat{v}_t^2$.

(iii) Compute the test statistic

$$F = \frac{(\text{SSR}_0 - \text{SSR})/(h-1)}{\text{SSR}/(T-m-h)} \tag{6.3.2}$$

where $m = p + k$. If $E\mathbf{z}_t u_{t-s} = 0$ for all s, (6.3.2) is exactly $F(h-1, T-m-h)$ distributed under $H_0: \psi_j = 0$, $j = 2, \ldots, h$. If $E\mathbf{x}_t u_{t-s} = 0$ for all s but $\mathbf{z}_t$ contains lags of y_t, then $(h-1)F$ has an asymptotic χ^2 distribution under the null of linearity. To illustrate the potential power of the RESET it is useful to regard the test as an LM-type test. We may think of several models for which the RESET is an LM-type linearity test. Take for instance the following LSTR model

$$y_t = \boldsymbol{\pi}'\mathbf{z}_t + \psi\left[\left(1 + \exp\left\{-\left(\sum_{j=1}^{h-1} \gamma_j(\boldsymbol{\phi}'\mathbf{z}_t)^j\right)\right\}\right)^{-1} - 1/2\right]\boldsymbol{\theta}'\mathbf{z}_t + u_t$$

$$\tag{6.3.3}$$

where $\psi = 1$, $\gamma_j > 0$ (say), $j = 1, \ldots, h-1$; $\boldsymbol{\phi} = (\phi_0, \phi_1, \ldots, \phi_m)'$, $\sum \phi_j = 1$ (say), and $u_t \sim \text{nid}(0, \sigma^2)$. Setting $\boldsymbol{\gamma} = (\gamma_1, \ldots, \gamma_{h-1})'$, the null hypothesis of linearity is

$$H_0: \boldsymbol{\gamma} = 0 \tag{6.3.4}$$

and H_1: at least one $\gamma_j > 0$. The log-likelihood function for observation t equals (6.2.3), so that

$$\left.\frac{\partial l_t}{\partial \boldsymbol{\pi}}\right|_{\gamma=0} = (1/\sigma^2)\tilde{u}_t\mathbf{z}_t \tag{6.3.5}$$

as before, and

$$\frac{\partial l_t}{\partial \gamma_j}$$

$$= (1/\sigma^2)u_t \exp\left\{-\sum \gamma_j(\boldsymbol{\theta}'\mathbf{z}_t)^j\right\}\left(1 + \exp\left\{-\sum \gamma_j(\boldsymbol{\theta}'\mathbf{z}_t)^j\right\}\right)^2 (\boldsymbol{\phi}'\mathbf{z}_t)^j(\boldsymbol{\theta}'\mathbf{z}_t).$$

This yields

$$\frac{\partial l_t}{\partial \gamma_j}\bigg|_{\gamma=0} = (1/4\sigma^2)\tilde{u}_t(\boldsymbol{\phi}'\mathbf{z}_t)^j(\boldsymbol{\theta}'\mathbf{z}_t), \quad j = 1, \ldots, h - 1. \quad (6.3.6)$$

The partial derivatives (6.3.5) and (6.3.6) and the considerations in the previous section suggest an LM-type test. However, let $\boldsymbol{\theta} = \boldsymbol{\phi} = \boldsymbol{\pi}$ and drop $\sum \varphi_j = 1$. This does not affect (6.3.5), but the model is now identified even under the null hypothesis (6.3.4). Furthermore, the subsequent test is an LM test. More specifically, as $\hat{y}_t = \hat{\boldsymbol{\pi}}'\mathbf{z}_t$ it is a RESET, testing linearity against the STR model in which the vector of 'linear parameters' changes from $\pi/2$ to $3\pi/2$ as the exponent $-\sum \gamma_j(\boldsymbol{\pi}'\mathbf{z}_t)^j$ increases from $-\infty$ to ∞. Teräsvirta (1990a) presented another model which gives rise to the RESET and is thus locally asymptotically equivalent to (6.3.3) with $\boldsymbol{\theta} = \boldsymbol{\phi} = \boldsymbol{\pi}$. Also if (6.3.3) is univariate, $\mathbf{z}_t = (1, y_{t-1}, \ldots, y_{t-p})'$, and $h = 2$, the RESET is identical to Keenan's (1985) univariate linearity test.

Model (6.3.3) with $\boldsymbol{\theta} = \boldsymbol{\phi} = \boldsymbol{\pi}$ gives an example of a nonlinear model against which the RESET has good power. However, the model is also rather restrictive because all 'linear parameters' are changing at the same rate with $\mathbf{z}_t$ and the rate itself is dependent on $\boldsymbol{\pi}'\mathbf{z}_t$. The test may therefore be expected to have rather mediocre power properties against a wide range of interesting nonlinear alternatives. This becomes even clearer if one considers a modified RESET which Thursby and Schmidt (1977) found to be superior to the original RESET. The auxiliary regression in that test is

$$\hat{u}_t = \boldsymbol{\delta}'\mathbf{z}_t + \sum_{j=2}^{h} \boldsymbol{\psi}_j'\tilde{\mathbf{z}}_t^{(j)} + v_t \quad (6.3.7)$$

where $\tilde{z}_t^{(j)} = (y_{t-1}^j, \ldots, y_{t-p}^j, x_{t1}^j, \ldots, x_{tk}^j)$, $j = 2, \ldots, h$. The authors suggested using $h = 4$ for the best results. This modified test fits into the same framework as the original RESET. An LM-type test with the auxiliary regression (6.3.7) can be obtained from (6.3.3) by assuming $\boldsymbol{\psi} \neq 0$ is unknown and setting $\boldsymbol{\theta} = \boldsymbol{\phi} = \mathbf{a} = (0, 0, \ldots, 0, 1, 0, \ldots, 0)'$ where the first element a_0 corresponding to the intercept cannot equal unity. This follows because $(\mathbf{a}'\mathbf{z}_t)^j = \mathbf{a}'\mathbf{z}_t^{(j)}$. Thus the modified test is an LM-type test against an LSTR model in which only one 'linear parameter' changes but the investigator does not know which one. The transition variable is the same as the one whose coefficient is changing. As before, vector $\mathbf{a}$ is a notational convention making explicit the assumption that the transition variable is not known to the investigator.

Model (6.3.3) with $\boldsymbol{\theta} = \boldsymbol{\phi} = \mathbf{a}$ and $\boldsymbol{\psi} \neq 0$ is thus rather narrow in that if more than one variable has a 'changing linear parameter' the auxiliary regression (6.3.7) no longer covers that possibility. In such a situation cross-products of independent variables are needed. These missing cross-products in the auxiliary regression then translate into lack of power in the modified RESET.

6.3.2 Tests based on expansions

Another way of discovering functional misspecification of unknown form in a linear model is through the use of the 'dual' of the Volterra expansion (Priestley 1980) of the nonlinear function, i.e. the Taylor expansion of the function, see (2.1.2), or Kolmogorov–Gabor polynomials. The corresponding auxiliary regression becomes

$$\hat{u}_t = \boldsymbol{\beta}'\mathbf{z}_t + \sum_{i=1}^{m}\sum_{j=i}^{m}\varphi_{ij}\tilde{z}_{ti}\tilde{z}_{tj} + \sum_{i=1}^{m}\sum_{j=i}^{m}\sum_{k=j}^{m}\varphi_{ijk}\tilde{z}_{ti}\tilde{z}_{tj}\tilde{z}_{tk} + \ldots + v_t.$$

(6.3.8)

If the quadratic approximation to (6.3.8) is considered, the null hypothesis is

$$H_0 : \varphi_{ij} = 0, \quad i = 1, \ldots, m; \ j = i, \ldots, m. \qquad (6.3.9)$$

The alternative is that at least one $\varphi_{ij} \neq 0$. The higher-order terms are ignored. The resulting test has already been shown to be an LM-type test against an LSTR model when the transition variable is not known. For the cubic expansion, the linearity hypothesis equals

$$H_0 : \psi_{ijk} = 0, \quad i = 1, \ldots, m; \ j = i, \ldots, m; \ k = j, \ldots, m,$$

$$\varphi_{ij} = 0, \quad i = 1, \ldots, m; \ j = i, \ldots, m. \qquad (6.3.10)$$

Again, the higher-order coefficients are ignored. The test of (6.3.10) can also be represented as an LM-type test. A possible model, a generalization of which will be of some interest later, is the following variant of the LSTR model

$$y_t = \boldsymbol{\pi}'\mathbf{z}_t + \theta_0[(1 + \exp\{-\gamma(\mathbf{a}'\mathbf{z}_t)\})^{-1} - 1/2] + u_t \qquad (6.3.11)$$

where $\mathbf{a} = (a_0, a_1, \ldots, a_m)'$, $\sum a_j = 1$, $\gamma > 0$, and $u_t \sim \text{nid}(0, \sigma^2)$, i.e. i.i.d. and normally distributed. Model (6.3.11) is more general than (6.2.1) with (6.2.2) in that the exponent is a linear combination of all z_{tj}, not only a single one. On the other hand it is less general because the only 'linear parameter' changing with $\gamma(\mathbf{a}'\mathbf{z}_t)$ is the intercept $\pi_0 + \theta_0 F(\mathbf{z}_t)$. The model is called a logistic smooth transition intercept (LSTI) model. When $\gamma = 0$ or $\theta_0 = 0$ which imply linearity, the model is not identified.

Consider an LM-type test for testing linearity of the LSTI model: $H_0: \gamma = 0$ against $H_1: \gamma > 0$. Differentiating the log-likelihood for observation t yields

$$\left.\frac{\partial l_t}{\partial \boldsymbol{\pi}}\right|_{\gamma=0} = (1/\sigma^2)\tilde{u}_t \mathbf{z}_t \tag{6.3.12}$$

and

$$\frac{\partial l_t}{\partial \gamma} = (\theta_0/\sigma^2)u_t(1 + \exp\{-\gamma(\mathbf{a}'\mathbf{z}_t)\})^{-2}\exp\{-\gamma(\mathbf{a}'\mathbf{z}_t)\}(\mathbf{a}'\mathbf{z}_t),$$

so that

$$\left.\frac{\partial l_t}{\partial \gamma}\right|_{\gamma=0} = (\theta_0/4\sigma^2)\tilde{u}_t \mathbf{a}'\mathbf{z}_t. \tag{6.3.13}$$

Note that (6.3.13) is just a linear combination of the elements of (6.3.12). This is one way of seeing that an LM-type linearity test based directly on previous arguments is not available. The situation is in some way analogous to that in which only the intercept of an LSTR model changes with the value of the transition function and which was discussed in Section 6.2.1. It may again be mitigated by replacing the logistic function by its cubic approximation (6.2.12), which also solves the identification problem. If this is done then it can be shown that the approximated (6.3.11) has the form

$$y_t = \tilde{\boldsymbol{\pi}}'\mathbf{z}_t + \sum_{i=0}^{m}\sum_{j=0}^{m}\sum_{k=0}^{m}\tilde{\psi}_{ijk}z_{ti}z_{tj}z_{tk}$$

$$= \tilde{\boldsymbol{\pi}}'\mathbf{z}_t + \sum_{i=1}^{m}\sum_{j=i}^{m}\sum_{k=j}^{m}\psi_{ijk}\tilde{z}_{ti}\tilde{z}_{tj}\tilde{z}_{tk} + \sum_{i=1}^{m}\sum_{j=1}^{m}\varphi_{ij}\tilde{z}_{ti}\tilde{z}_{tj} + \tilde{u}_t \tag{6.3.14}$$

where

$$\psi_{ijk} = (\gamma^3\theta_0 g_3/6)a_i a_j a_k, \quad i = 1, \ldots, m; \ j = i, \ldots, m; \ k = j, \ldots, m \tag{6.3.15}$$

$$\varphi_{ij} = (\gamma^3\theta_0 g_3/6)a_i a_j a_0, \quad i = 1, \ldots, m; \ j = i, \ldots, m. \tag{6.3.16}$$

Definitions (6.3.15) and (6.3.16) indicate that the linearity hypothesis is now

$$H_0': \psi_{ijk} = 0, \quad i = 1, \ldots, m; \ j = i, \ldots, m; \ k = j, \ldots, m$$

$$\varphi_{ij} = 0, \quad i = 1, \ldots, m; \ j = i, \ldots, m. \tag{6.3.17}$$

As before, the model (6.3.11) is only identified when (6.3.17) is not valid, but an LM-type test can be derived using previous arguments; see also Luukkonen *et al.* (1988*b*).

6.3.3 Neural network test

White (1989*a*) recently proposed another linearity test for discovering 'neglected nonlinearity' called the neural network test; see also Lee *et al.* (1993). The neural network models are inspired by features of the way information is thought to be processed in the brain. In the single-layer feed-forward model, inputs z_{tj}, $j = 0, 1, \ldots, m$, to the processor are sent to a 'hidden', i.e. unobserved processing unit i and amplified or attenuated by a factor γ_{ij}; in total there are q such units. The units sum up the $(m + 1)$ amplified or attenuated signals and generate an output activation or squashing function $\tilde{\psi}(\gamma_j' z_t)$ where $\gamma_j = (\gamma_{0j}, \gamma_{ij}, \ldots, \gamma_{mj})'$. The output is

$$y_t = \theta_0 + \sum_{j=1}^{q} \theta_j \tilde{\psi}(\gamma_j' z_t).$$

In deriving the linearity test it is assumed that direct links also exist from input to output, so that the total network output is

$$y_t = \pi' z_t + \sum_{j=1}^{q} \theta_j \tilde{\psi}(\gamma_j' z_t). \tag{6.3.18}$$

The linearity hypothesis is

$$Pr\{E(y_t | z_t) = \tilde{\pi}' z_t\} = 1 \tag{6.3.19}$$

for some $\tilde{\pi}$. To move this theory to a more familiar ground, assume that the output also contains noise, so that

$$y_t = \pi' z_t + \sum_{j=1}^{q} \theta_j \tilde{\psi}(\gamma_j' z_t) + u_t \tag{6.3.20}$$

where $Ez_t u_t = 0$, $u_t \sim \text{nid}(0, \sigma^2)$. Now the test of (6.3.19) may also be interpreted as testing $H_0 : \theta_1 = \ldots = \theta_q = 0$ in (6.3.20). The squashing function $\tilde{\psi}$ is commonly assumed bounded and monotonically increasing like, say, a cumulative distribution function. Lee *et al.* (1993) chose the c.d.f. of the logistic distribution: $\tilde{\psi}(\gamma_j' z_t) = (1 + \exp\{-\gamma_j' z_t\})^{-1}$. This makes (6.3.20) a generalization of the LSTI model (6.3.11). The test is carried out by drawing the direction vectors γ_j, $j = 1, \ldots, q$, at random from a feasible distribution; Lee *et al.* (1993) used a uniform distribution. Because q may be large and the observed components $\tilde{\psi}(\gamma_j' z_t)$, $j = 1, \ldots, q$, heavily correlated, the authors recommended using a small number of principal components instead of the q original variables in testing linearity of (6.3.20).

However, it is useful to look at the testing problem from another angle. Note that without losing any generality one can substitute

$$\psi(\gamma_j' z_t) = \tilde{\psi}(\gamma_j' z_t) - 1/2 = (1 + \exp\{-\gamma_j' z_t\})^{-1} - 1/2$$

for $\tilde{\psi}$ in (6.3.20). Then it becomes clear that the null hypothesis can also be formulated simply as $H_0: \gamma = 0$ by setting $\gamma_j = \gamma a_j$, $j = 1, \ldots, q$ and assuming $\sum a_{jk} = 1$, $\gamma \geqslant 0$, $\mathbf{a}_j = (a_{0j}, \ldots, a_{mj})'$. The interpretation is obvious: when this null hypothesis is true, the hidden processing units are inactive. The only output is generated through $\boldsymbol{\beta}'\mathbf{z}_t$ and contaminated by additive white noise. This of course resembles testing linearity against (6.3.11), and replacing ψ again by its cubic approximation yields (6.3.14) where now

$$\psi_{ijk} = (\gamma^3 g_3/6) \sum_{h=1}^{q} \theta_h a_{ih} a_{jh} a_{kh}, \quad i = 1, \ldots, m; \, j = i, \ldots, m;$$

$$k = j, \ldots, m \quad (6.3.21)$$

$$\varphi_{ij} = (\gamma^3 g_3/6) \sum_{h=1}^{q} \theta_h a_{ih} a_{jh} a_{0h}, \quad i = 1, \ldots, m; \, j = i, \ldots, m.$$

$$(6.3.22)$$

The null hypothesis is again (6.3.14), and the q-component sums in (6.3.21) and (6.3.22) reflect the fact that (6.3.20) is not identified even under the alternative, if γ_j are interpreted as completely unknown parameter vectors as has been done here. The test obtained in this manner is the one based on the dual of the cubic Volterra expansion and considered in the previous section. Drawing the values of γ_j randomly and testing $H_0: \theta_h = 0$, $h = 1, \ldots, q$, may therefore be seen as another way of bypassing the identification problem. A crucial question is how much inferior this procedure is to the LM-type solution based on the cubic approximation of the squashing function. At least some loss of power may be expected through the random drawings. Another interesting question is the role of the intercept in the test. Suppose the linear model does not contain the intercept, i.e. $\pi_0 = 0$ in (6.3.20). It may be reasonable to augment $\hat{\mathbf{z}}_t$ anyway to contain the intercept when using the test. Otherwise $a_{0h} = 0$, $h = 1, \ldots, q$, in (6.3.22), and this is equivalent to omitting the quadratic terms from the expansion. This may cause a serious loss of power against some types of nonlinearity. Unfortunately, including the intercept when it is not needed may have a similar effect.

Teräsvirta *et al.* (1993) conducted a simulation study to consider these two questions. The results indicate that testing $H_0: \theta_h = 0$, $h = 1, \ldots, q$, and drawing the values of γ_j randomly is not an adequate substitute for the LM-type test of $\gamma_j = \mathbf{0}$, $j = 1, \ldots, q$, based on the cubic approximation of the output activating functions. As an example, take the following bivariate neural network model

$$y_t = -1 + (1 + \exp\{-100(y_{t-1} + x_t)\})^{-1}$$

$$+ (1 + \exp\{-100(y_{t-1} - x_t)\})^{-1} + u_t \quad (6.3.23)$$

where $x_t = 0.8x_{t-1} + v_t$, $u_t \sim \text{nid}(0, 0.05^2)$, $v_t \sim \text{nid}(0, 0.05^2)$, $\text{cov}(u_t, v_s)$

= 0 for all s, t. Generating 1000 data sets with 100 observations each from (6.3.23) and testing linearity gave the results in Table 6.1. The two tests based on the cubic dual of the Volterra expansion, V3 and V23, have the best power. The neural network tests are clearly weaker than those two. In this case, there is no intercept in this exponent, and including one there when applying the neural network test causes a remarkable loss of power. This limited experiment already shows that the test is clearly sensitive to the presence or absence of the intercept. Other experiments reported in Teräsvirta *et al.* (1993) are in accord with these findings.

6.3.4 Tests based on rearranged observations

The problem of parameter changes has received a lot of attention in the statistical and econometric literature. In the former it is often called a change-point problem and in the latter the structural change or structural break problem. Many techniques developed for testing parameter constancy against structural change are applicable to testing linearity against nonlinearity of switching type. For instance, a switching regression model with two regimes is piecewise linear in the same way as a linear model whose parameters change once at a given point of time. The available observation vectors (assuming i.i.d. errors or a martingale difference error process) may be rearranged in the ascending or descending order according to the switching variables. If this is done, linearity tests may be obtained using ideas previously applied to detecting structural change.

A common feature for many test statistics for testing parameter constancy is that they can be represented using stochastic processes defined on the interval $[0, 1]$. Let α be the probability of the process to exceed a given value s; α is often called a crossing probability. Then s is

TABLE 6.1.   Empirical power of some linearity tests against the alternative model (6.3.23) at sample size 100 and significance levels 0.05 and 0.01, based on 1000 replications

| Significance | Test | | | |
level	V3	V23	NNPC	NNIPC
0.05	.917	.862	.648	.377
0.01	.762	.630	.470	.207

Note: V3 is the test based on the cubic dual of the Volterra expansion without quadratic terms, V23 is the same with quadratic terms, NNPC is the neural network test (Lee *et al.* 1993) without the intercept in the exponent (principal components used), NNIPC is the same with the intercept in the exponent.
Source: Teräsvirta *et al.* (1993).

the critical value of the test corresponding to the significance level α. The limiting null distributions of these test statistics are nonstandard, and results from the theory of Wiener processes are needed to characterize them. For an overview of the necessary theory see, for example, Banerjee *et al.* (1993). As a first example of this kind, Petruccelli and Davies (1986) considered the cumulative sums of recursive residuals from recursive estimation of parameters of an AR model with rearranged observations. Ertel and Fowlkes (1976) suggested this in order to test linearity against switching regression. Petruccelli and Davies (1986) were interested in testing linearity against threshold autoregression with known delay parameter d. This implies ordering the observation vectors according to y_{t-d} instead of t. The corresponding test of parameter constancy is the CUSUM test of Brown *et al.* (1975).

To consider the test, let $T(i)$ be the ith reordered observation and $r = T(i)/T$ (i is dropped from the notation). The ordered linear model is

$$y_{rT} = \mathbf{z}'_{rT}\boldsymbol{\pi}(r) + u_{rT}, \quad r = 1/T, \ldots, 1 \tag{6.3.24}$$

where $\mathbf{z}'_{rT} = (1, y_{rT-1}, \ldots, y_{rT-p}; x_{rT,1}, \ldots, x_{rT,k})$ is the ith observation vector when the observations are rearranged according to transition variable z_{tj} and $\boldsymbol{\pi}(r) = (\pi_1(r), \ldots \pi_m(r))'$, $m = p + k + 1$, is the parameter vector at rT. The null hypothesis $H_0:\boldsymbol{\pi}(r) = \boldsymbol{\pi}$, $\forall r$ in (6.3.24) and the alternative is simply that H_0 is not valid. Consider now the original observations $\mathbf{z}_t = (z_{t1}, \ldots, z_{tm})'$ and errors u_t. The following assumptions are needed:

(A1) $\displaystyle\limsup_{T\to\infty} (1/T)\sum_{t=1}^{T} \|\mathbf{z}_t\|^{2+\delta} < \infty$ a.s., for some $\delta > 0$;

(A2) $\displaystyle\plim_{T\to\infty} (1/T)\sum_{t=1}^{T} \mathbf{z}_t\mathbf{z}'_t = \plim_{T\to\infty} (1/T)\mathbf{Z}'_T\mathbf{Z}_T = \mathbf{Q}$;

   $\mathbf{Q}$ is a positive definite nonstochastic matrix;

(A3)   The errors u_t form a martingale difference sequence:

$$E(u_s|I_t) = 0, \quad E(u_t^2|I_t) = \sigma^2$$

where I_t is the information set

$$I_t = \{y_{t-j}, x_{t-i,h}|h = 1, \ldots, k; i \geqslant 0, j \geqslant 1\}.$$

The OLS estimator of π based on i ordered observations is $T(1), \ldots,$ $rT - 1$, rT, is $\hat{\boldsymbol{\pi}}_{rT} = (\mathbf{Z}'_{rT}\mathbf{Z}_{rT})^{-1}\mathbf{Z}'_{rT}\bar{\mathbf{y}}_{rT}$, where $\bar{\mathbf{y}}_{rT} = (y_{T(1)}, \ldots, y_{rT})$. The recursive residual is

$$w_{rT} = (y_{rT} - \mathbf{z}'_{rT}\hat{\boldsymbol{\pi}}_{rT-1})/f_{rT}$$

where

$$f_{rT} = (1 + \mathbf{z}'_{rT}(\mathbf{Z}'_{rT-1}\mathbf{Z}_{rT-1})^{-1}\mathbf{z}_{rT}).$$

Assume now that $u_{rT} \sim \text{nid}(0, \sigma^2)$, $\mathbf{z}_{rT}$ do not contain lagged values of the dependent variable and that $x_{T(i),1}, \ldots, x_{T(i),k}$ are fixed regressors. Under these more restrictive conditions Brown *et al.* (1975) showed that w_{rT}, $r_0 \leqslant r \leqslant 1$, are normal variables. The CUSUM quantity is

$$W_{rT} = \hat{\sigma}^{-1} \sum_{j=r_0+1}^{r} w_{jT} \tag{6.3.25}$$

where $\hat{\sigma}$ is a consistent estimator of σ. If σ is known,

$$EW_{rT} = 0, \quad EW_{rT}^2 = (r - r_0)T, \quad [EW_{jT}W_{kT}] = \{\min(j, k) - r_0\}T. \tag{6.3.26}$$

The test statistic is

$$S_T = \max_{r_0+1 \leqslant r \leqslant 1} \left| \frac{W_{rT}}{\sqrt{(1 - r_0)T}} \right| \bigg/ \left(1 + 2\frac{r - r_0}{1 - r_0}\right) \tag{6.3.27}$$

and the critical value a for the significance level α may be computed from

$$Pr\left\{\max_{r_0+1 \leqslant r \leqslant 1} \left| \frac{W_T(r)}{\sqrt{(1 - r_0)T}} \right| \bigg/ \left(1 + 2\frac{r - r_0}{1 - r_0}\right) \geqslant a\right\} = \alpha/2$$

where $W_T(r)$ is a continuous Gaussian process, $r \in [0.1]$, with mean and autocovariances as in (6.3.26), i.e. a Brownian motion starting from zero at r_0. Brown *et al.* (1975) gave the following pairs of values:

$$\alpha = 0.01, \; a = 1.143$$

$$\alpha = 0.05, \; a = 0.948$$

$$\alpha = 0.10, \; a = 0.850.$$

Note that the application of (6.3.27) corresponds to rejecting the null hypothesis of parameter constancy 'on-line' when W_{rT} crosses either one of the lines

$$\pm a(\sqrt{(1 - r_0)T} + 2(r - r_0)T/\sqrt{(1 - r_0)T}).$$

Recently, Krämer *et al.* (1988) showed that including lags of y_{rT} in $\mathbf{z}_{rT}$ and retaining the assumptions A1–A3 does not change the asymptotic distribution of the CUSUM statistic Brown *et al.* (1975) had derived. In the present notation their result is that

$$\lim_{T \to \infty} Pr\{S_T \geqslant a\} = \alpha/2$$

when the assumptions A1–A3 hold.

Petruccelli and Davies (1986) obtained their linearity test by considering the asymptotic crossing probability of $W_T(r)$ as discussed above. Asymptotically,

$$Pr\{\sup_{r\in[0,1]} |W_T(r)/\sqrt{(1-r_0)T}| \leqslant s\}$$

$$= 4\pi^{-1}\sum_{k=0}^{\infty}(-1)^k(2k+1)^{-1}\exp\{-(2k+1)^2\pi^2/(8s^2)$$

$$= 1 - p(s),\qquad\qquad (6.3.28)$$

see for example Billingsley (1968: 79–80). Thus, for fixed T, one computes

$$\tilde{S}_T = \max_{r_0\leqslant r\leqslant 1}|W_{rT}|/\sqrt{(1-r_0)T}$$

and sets $s = \tilde{S}_T$ in (6.3.28). Then $p(\tilde{S}_T)$ is the p-value of the CUSUM test, and the null of parameter constancy is rejected at significance level α whenever the p-value is less than α.

The CUSUM tests are known to have low power when the parameter change or switch from one regime to the other occurs late in the rearranged series. Then the amount of evidence about the switch remains too small to cause a rejection of the null hypothesis of constant coefficients. Of course the ordering of the observations may be reversed so that a late change becomes an early one. Petruccelli (1990) suggested reversing the cumulative sums so that instead of W_{rT} one would consider $M_{rT} = \hat{\sigma}^{-1}\sum_{j=r+1}^{1}w_{jT}$ and argued that the test based on M_{rT} is an improvement over (6.3.27) based on W_{rT}.

It may also be that the CUSUM tests often have low power against ESTR or a three-regime switching regression in which the outer regimes are identical. This is because the accumulated evidence about a parameter change is weakened when the parameters either change back to their early values (switching regression) or start moving back towards them (ESTR) when the value of the transition variable increases.

The disadvantage of low power against late parameter changes may be alleviated by basing the CUSUM test directly on OLS residuals. Ploberger and Krämer (1992) recently considered this possibility. The cumulative sums are now

$$B_{rT} = \hat{\sigma}^{-1}\sum_{j=1/T}^{r}\hat{u}_{jT}\qquad\qquad (6.3.29)$$

where $\hat{u}_{jT}$ is the OLS residual and the suggested test statistic

$$U_T = \max_{1/T\leqslant r\leqslant 1}|T^{-1/2}B_{rT}|.$$

The partial sum process $T^{-1/2}B_{rT}$ converges to the standard Brownian Bridge $T^{-1/2}B_T(r)$, $r \in [0, 1]$, or 'tied-down' $(B_T(1) \equiv 0)$ Brownian motion as $T \to \infty$. As a result,

$$\lim_{T \to \infty} Pr\{U_T > u\} = 2 \sum_{k=1}^{\infty} (-1)^{k+1} \exp\{-2k^2 u^2\} = 1 - p(u),$$

(6.3.30)

see for example Billingsley (1968: 85). The test is carried out by computing the right-hand side of (6.3.30) for $u = U_T$. If $p(U_T) < \alpha$, the null hypothesis is rejected at significance level α. This can be called the CUSUM-O test. Ploberger and Krämer (1992) give the following pairs of critical values and significance levels

$$\alpha = 0.01, u = 1.63$$

$$\alpha = 0.05, u = 1.36$$

$$\alpha = 0.10, u = 1.22.$$

The test statistic (6.3.30) has the property that its power is symmetric about the midpoint of the sample. Used as a linearity test the CUSUM-O test possesses a computational advantage over the CUSUM test based on recursive residuals (CUSUM-R). Suppose the test is repeated for different transition variables if the transition variable is not known in advance. For the CUSUM-O test it then suffices to rearrange the OLS residuals according to the transition variable and compute the partial sums and the test. If the CUSUM-R test is applied, a recursive parameter estimation routine is needed for each transition variable to recompute the recursive residuals before calculating the partial sums and the values of the test statistic.

Although the CUSUM tests are not designed for any particular nonlinear alternative they can be expected to be relatively powerful against switching regression with two regimes. However, it has to be pointed out that the LM-type tests against STR discussed in Section 6.2 very often have good power even in cases in which the true alternative is a switching regression model. For the univariate case, simulation experiments in Luukkonen *et al.* (1988*a*) and Petruccelli (1990) contain ample evidence of this. The evidence is limited to CUSUM-R tests, however. The available small sample experiments with CUSUM-O only concern comparisons with CUSUM-R when time is the transition variable and there is a single structural break in the series. In these comparisons reported in Ploberger and Krämer (1992) neither test dominates the other but overall CUSUM-O appears a more powerful test than CUSUM-R.

It may also be mentioned that Tsay (1989) suggested testing the linearity of (6.3.24) using rearranged observations and recursive residuals f_{rT}. The test was intended for use in the specification of univariate

TAR models along the lines in Tsay (1989). Generalized to the multivariate case, it consists of running a regression

$$f_{rT} = \mathbf{z}'_{rT}\boldsymbol{\delta} + \eta_i, \ i = h + 1, \ldots, T \qquad (6.3.31)$$

and testing $H_0 : \boldsymbol{\delta} = 0$ in (6.3.31). It can be shown that, if Assumptions A1–A3 hold, the usual test statistic based on the OLS estimation of $\boldsymbol{\delta}$ has an asymptotic $\chi^2(m)$ distribution under H_0. In univariate simulations of Petruccelli (1990) where the nonlinear model was a TAR model, this test did not perform as well on the average as for instance the LM-type test of Section 6.2 or the 'reverse CUSUM' test briefly mentioned above.

Another possibility for testing linearity when ordering the observations according to the transition variable is to use the recursive parameter estimators $\hat{\boldsymbol{\pi}}(r)$ themselves. They cannot be compared to the unknown true parameter vector under the null hypothesis of linearity, $\boldsymbol{\pi} = \boldsymbol{\pi}(r)$, $\forall r$, but they may be compared to its estimate from the full sample, $\hat{\boldsymbol{\pi}}(1)$. Ploberger $et\ al.$ (1989) proposed considering the largest deviation among components; $\|\hat{\boldsymbol{\pi}}(r) - \hat{\boldsymbol{\pi}}(1)\|_{\infty} = \max_{k=1,\ldots,m} |\hat{\pi}_k(r) - \hat{\pi}_k(1)|$, and the largest deviation of the maximum over $\hat{\boldsymbol{\pi}}(m/T), \ldots, \hat{\boldsymbol{\pi}}(1)$. To obtain a tractable asymptotic null distribution, $\max_{T(m),\ldots,T} \|\hat{\boldsymbol{\pi}}(r) - \hat{\boldsymbol{\pi}}(1)\|_{\infty}$ has to be appropriately standardized. Let $G_{rT} = \|(\mathbf{Z}'_T\mathbf{Z}_T)^{1/2}(\hat{\boldsymbol{\pi}}(r) - \hat{\boldsymbol{\pi}}(1)))\|_{\infty}$ where $\mathbf{Z}'_T\mathbf{Z}_T = \sum_{t=1}^{T}\mathbf{z}_t\mathbf{z}'_t$. Furthermore, $(\mathbf{Z}'_T\mathbf{Z}_T)^{1/2} = \boldsymbol{\Lambda}^{1/2}\mathbf{C}'$ using the spectral decomposition $\mathbf{Z}'_T\mathbf{Z}_T = \mathbf{C}\boldsymbol{\Lambda}\mathbf{C}'$ where $\boldsymbol{\Lambda}$ is the diagonal matrix of eigenvalues so that $\boldsymbol{\Lambda}^{1/2} = \mathrm{diag}(\lambda_1^{1/2}, \ldots, \lambda_m^{1/2})$. Define

$$F_{rT} = (r/\hat{\sigma})G_{rT} \qquad (6.3.32)$$

where $\sigma^2 = \sum_{t=m+1}^{T}\hat{u}_t^2 / \{(1 - m/T)T\}$ with $\hat{u}_t = y_t - \mathbf{z}'_t\hat{\boldsymbol{\pi}}(1)$. Again, F_{rT} is a stochastic process with a known limiting process $F_T(r) = \lim_{T\to\infty} F_{rT}$, $r \in [0, 1]$, which, in this case, is an m-dimensional Brownian bridge ($F_T(1) = 0$). The linearity test is based on $\max_{m/T \leqslant r \leqslant 1} F_{rT}$. The crossing probability of this process is

$$Pr\{F_T(r) > s\} = 1 - \left[1 + 2\sum_{k=1}^{\infty}(-1)^k \exp\{-2k^2s^2\}\right]^m \qquad (6.3.33)$$

(Ploberger $et\ al.$ 1989, Krämer and Sonnberger 1986) so that the right-hand side provides the asymptotic significance level for (6.3.32) given the critical value s. Note that for $m = 1$, (6.3.33) equals (6.3.30). The CUSUM-O test is thus identical to the fluctuation test for testing $\boldsymbol{\pi}(r) = \boldsymbol{\pi}$, $\forall r$, in a model with a single regressor.

If the alternative to linearity is a switching regression with two regimes, another possibility of using rearranged observations for testing linearity opens up. The rearranged observations in (6.3.24) may be divided into two sets and the parameters of the model estimated assuming that $\pi(j) = \pi_1$, $j = 1/T, \ldots, r$, and $\pi(j) = \pi_2$, $j = r + 1/T$, $\ldots, 1$; rT is called the cut-off point. The null hypothesis is $H_0 : \pi_1 = \pi_2$. Because the switching value of the transition variable is unknown, Quandt (1960) proposed carrying out the likelihood ratio $(F-)$ test varying r and using the maximum value of these tests as the final statistic. Let $\hat{\pi}_j$, $j = 1, 2$, be the OLS estimators of π in (6.3.24) based on observations $\{T(1), \ldots, T(i_0)\}$ and $\{T(i_0 + 1), \ldots, T(T)\}$, respectively, let $(\mathbf{y}_1, \mathbf{Z}_1)$ and $(\mathbf{y}_2, \mathbf{Z}_2)$ be the corresponding observation matrices and $\hat{\mathbf{u}}^{(j)} = \mathbf{y}_j - \mathbf{Z}_j \hat{\pi}_j$, $j = 1, 2$. Then the 'sup F'-test statistic is

$$\sup F_{T(j)} = \sup \frac{(\hat{\mathbf{u}}'\hat{\mathbf{u}} - \hat{\mathbf{u}}^{(1)'}\hat{\mathbf{u}}^{(1)} - \hat{\mathbf{u}}^{(2)'}\hat{\mathbf{u}}^{(2)})/m}{(\hat{\mathbf{u}}^{(1)'}\hat{\mathbf{u}}^{(1)} + \hat{\mathbf{u}}^{(2)'}\hat{\mathbf{u}}^{(2)})/(T - 2m)} \qquad (6.3.34)$$

where $\hat{\mathbf{u}}$ is the vector of OLS residuals from the OLS estimation of the model using all the observations $\{T(1), \ldots, T(T)\}$. After some matrix algebra (6.3.34) can be written as

$$\sup F_{rT} = \sup \frac{\left\{\sum_{j=1}^{2} (\hat{\pi}(1) - \hat{\pi}_j)'\mathbf{Z}_j'\mathbf{Z}_j(\hat{\pi}(1) - \hat{\pi}_j)\right\}/m}{(\hat{\mathbf{u}}^{(1)'}\hat{\mathbf{u}}^{(1)} + \hat{\mathbf{u}}^{(2)'}\hat{\mathbf{u}}^{(2)})/(T - 2m)}. \qquad (6.3.35)$$

From (6.3.35) it is seen that the sup F-test may be regarded as a symmetric variant of the fluctuation test. It is symmetric in the sense that the power of the test is similar against a regime switch early and late in the ordered sample. This is intuitively clear from (6.3.35) where it is seen that the fluctuations are measured 'in both directions', i.e. coefficient estimates based on the first as well as the last observations of the ordered sample are considered simultaneously.

Quandt (1960) did not yet know the null distribution of (6.3.35). However, even here a stochastic process related to F_{rT} with a known limiting distribution under H_0 may be derived. Andrews (1990) derived this distribution for a more general situation than the switching regression model discussed here. Assumptions A1–A3 are sufficient to obtain the required results. The distribution is based on a convergence result analogous to the one applied in the fluctuation test. Let $F_T(r) = \lim_{T \to \infty} \{mT/(T - 2m)\} F_{rT}$, $r \in [0, 1]$. Then $F_T(r)$ is a standardized m-dimensional Brownian bridge, and the probability of $\sup F_T(r)$ exceeding a given value can be computed. This probability depends not only on m but also on the earliest cut-off point $r_0 T$. (It is assumed that the regressions are computed for cut-off points $[r_0 T, \ldots, (1 - r_0)T]$.) Andrews (1990) tabulated the asymptotic critical values for $r_0 = 0.15$ and significance levels $\alpha = 0.01, 0.025, 0.05$, and 0.1, respectively.

In simulations of Andrews, in which the alternative to linearity is a switching regression with a single switch-point in time, the sup F-test compared very favourably to both the CUSUM-R and the fluctuation test.

Chan and Tong (1990) and Chan (1990, 1991) (see also Tong 1990, sect. 5.3.5), considered the same problem as Andrews in a univariate piecewise linear context. The null model was a stationary $AR(p)$ model with i.i.d. errors and the alternative a TAR(2; p, p) model. Chan (1991) used an approximation different from that in Andrews (1990) to obtain critical values for this likelihood ratio test. These values, of course, also depend on p and the range $[r_0, 1 - r_0]$. While Andrews tabulated the values for $r_0 = 0.15$, as mentioned above, Chan used $r_0 = 0.10$ and 0.25, respectively.

A common feature for all these tests is that they are generally powerful against switching regression with two regimes. They may be less powerful against smooth transition regression and in some cases against switching regression with more than two regimes.

6.3.5 The BDS test

Brock *et al.* (1987), henceforth BDS, developed a test based on concepts that arise in the theory of chaotic processes. A chaotic process is produced by a deterministic generator but may have the appearance of a stochastic process, and similar autocorrelation properties, as mentioned in Section 3.3. A useful summary statistic of such processes is called the correlation exponent and this is defined as follows. Let $\mathbf{X}_{t,m}$ denote a set of consecutive terms from a series x_t, so that $\mathbf{X}_{t,m} = (x_t, x_{t+1}, \ldots, x_{t+m-1})$. A pair of such vectors are said to be ε apart if this is true for each pair of corresponding terms. Thus $\mathbf{X}_{t,m}$ and $\mathbf{X}_{s,m}$ are no more than ε apart if

$$|x_{t+j} - x_{s+j}| \leq \varepsilon, \quad j = 0, 1, \ldots, m - 1.$$

Define the correlation integral $C_m(\varepsilon)$ as in (3.3.1) as the limit of T^{-2} times the number of ε-close pairs (s, t). Now let

$$v_m = \lim_{\varepsilon \to 0} \frac{\partial \log (C_m(\varepsilon))}{\partial \log \varepsilon}.$$

If a process is truly chaotic, then

$$C_m(\varepsilon) \simeq \varepsilon^v \tag{6.3.36}$$

for $m > d$, v being the correlation exponent, and is independent of m. If a process is truly stochastic, then v will increase linearly with m. The lower bound for m for which (6.3.36) holds is the dimension of the chaotic process and need not be an integer. If d is large the chaotic process will be indistinguishable from a stochastic one unless extremely large data sets are available, examples being the random number series produced on computers.

The BDS test uses the test statistic

$$S(m, \varepsilon) = \hat{C}_m(\varepsilon) - [\hat{C}_1(\varepsilon)]^m$$

for some single choice of m and ε. Under the null hypothesis $H_0 : x_t$ is i.i.d., $\sqrt{T} S(m, \varepsilon)$ will have a normal distribution with mean zero and variance that is a complicated function of m and ε, and is given in BDS or Brock and Potter (1992). Some simulations in Liu (1990) suggest that the choice of m is less critical than that of ε on the power of the test.

For a particular series, y_t, one first fits a linear model, such as an AR(p) using a suitable model selection criterion, and the BDS test is applied to the residuals of this linear model. The asymptotic distribution of the test statistic is the same when the time series under consideration is observed white noise and when it consists of estimated white noise residuals. In the multivariate case, the test is applied to the residuals of the multiple regression model. If the null hypothesis is rejected, one can conclude that there is nonlinearity present, but its form is not determined. It can be chaos or a nonlinear stochastic process.

The test statistic is seen to be very different in form from the other tests considered in this chapter. For that reason, there is no LM-type interpretation available for the test. It is based on results for the speed of divergence of a pair of chaotic series with slightly different starting-values, as this is quite different for chaotic and stochastic processes. Lee *et al.* (1993) included the BDS test in their simulations in which the alternative to linearity was a stochastic nonlinear model. The test often seemed to have reasonable power, but in those cases even tests with zero asymptotic relative efficiency with respect to the appropriate LM test had high power. The results were thus rather inconclusive, but it appears that at least in small samples up to 200 observations the BDS test may not be an ideal choice.

6.4 Testing Constant Conditional Variance against Conditional Heteroskedasticity

Joint testing of linearity of the conditional mean and constant conditional variance was already mentioned in Section 6.1. In this section we discuss testing the latter hypothesis only, assuming that the conditional mean is linear. To make the discussion more specific we assume, following Engle (1982), that (6.1.2) has the form

$$\text{var}(u_t | \mathscr{F}_t) = g(\mathbf{w}_t' \boldsymbol{\eta}) = g_t \tag{6.4.1}$$

where $\mathbf{w}_t = (1, w_{t1}, \ldots, w_{tq})'$, $w_{tj} \in \mathscr{F}_t$, $j = 1, \ldots, q$. Let $\boldsymbol{\eta} = (\eta_0, \bar{\boldsymbol{\eta}}')'$. If $\bar{\boldsymbol{\eta}} = \mathbf{0}$, we assume that $g_t \equiv \sigma^2$ (constant). The null hypothesis is

$$H_0 : \bar{\boldsymbol{\eta}} = \mathbf{0} \text{ or } g(\mathbf{w}_t' \boldsymbol{\eta}) \equiv \sigma^2. \tag{6.4.2}$$

To test (6.4.2) we make use of the block diagonality of the information matrix of (6.1.1). The partial derivatives needed to construct an LM test for (6.4.2) are thus

$$\frac{\partial l_t}{\partial \boldsymbol{\eta}} = \frac{1}{2g_t}\left(\frac{u_t^2}{g_t} - 1\right)\frac{\partial g_t}{\partial(\mathbf{w}_t'\boldsymbol{\eta})}\,\mathbf{w}_t$$

so that

$$\frac{\partial l_t}{\partial \boldsymbol{\eta}}\bigg|_{H_0} = \frac{h^0}{2\sigma^2}\left(\frac{u_t^2}{\sigma^2} - 1\right)\mathbf{w}_t$$

where $h^0 = \dfrac{\partial g_t}{\partial(\mathbf{w}_t'\boldsymbol{\eta})}\bigg|_{H_0}$. Furthermore,

$$\frac{\partial^2 l_t}{\partial \boldsymbol{\eta}\partial \boldsymbol{\eta}'} = \frac{1}{2g_t^2}\left(\frac{u_t^2}{g_t} - 1\right)\left(\frac{\partial g_t}{\partial(\mathbf{w}_t'\boldsymbol{\eta})}\right)^2\mathbf{w}_t\mathbf{w}_t' - \frac{1}{2g_t}\left(\frac{u_t^2}{g_t^2}\right)\left(\frac{\partial g_t}{\partial(\mathbf{w}_t'\boldsymbol{\eta})}\right)^2\mathbf{w}_t\mathbf{w}_t'$$
$$+ \frac{1}{2g_t}\left(\frac{u_t^2}{g_t} - 1\right)\frac{\partial^2 g_t}{\partial(\mathbf{w}_t'\boldsymbol{\eta})^2}\,\mathbf{w}_t\mathbf{w}_t'$$

and

$$-E\sum_{t=1}^{T}\frac{\partial^2 l_t}{\partial \boldsymbol{\eta}\partial \boldsymbol{\eta}'}\bigg|_{H_0} = \frac{1}{2}\left(\frac{h^0}{\sigma^2}\right)^2\sum_{t=1}^{T}E\mathbf{w}_t\mathbf{w}_t'.$$

Let $\mathbf{w}_t = (1, \bar{\mathbf{w}}_t')$. Then the LM statistic $LM_{\bar{\eta}}$ in (6.1.22) which is a test of (6.4.2) has the form

$$LM_{\bar{\eta}} = \frac{1}{2}\left\{\sum_{t=1}^{T}\left(\frac{\tilde{u}_t^2}{\tilde{\sigma}^2} - 1\right)\bar{\mathbf{w}}_t'\right\}\left\{\sum_{t=1}^{T}\bar{\mathbf{w}}_t\bar{\mathbf{w}}_t' - T^{-1}\left(\sum_{t=1}^{T}\bar{\mathbf{w}}_t\right)\left(\sum_{t=1}^{T}\bar{\mathbf{w}}_t'\right)\right\}^{-1}$$
$$\times \left\{\sum_{t=1}^{T}\left(\frac{\tilde{u}_t^2}{\tilde{\sigma}^2} - 1\right)\bar{\mathbf{w}}_t\right\}$$
$$= \frac{1}{2}\left\{\sum_{t=1}^{T}\left(\frac{\tilde{u}_t^2}{\tilde{\sigma}^2} - 1\right)\bar{\mathbf{w}}_t'\right\}\left\{\sum_{t=1}^{T}(\bar{\mathbf{w}}_t - \bar{\mathbf{w}})(\bar{\mathbf{w}}_t - \bar{\mathbf{w}})'\right\}^{-1}$$
$$\times \left\{\sum_{t=1}^{T}\left(\frac{\tilde{u}_t^2}{\tilde{\sigma}^2} - 1\right)\bar{\mathbf{w}}_t\right\} \tag{6.4.3}$$

where $\bar{\mathbf{w}} = T^{-1}\sum_1^T\bar{\mathbf{w}}_t$, $\tilde{\sigma}^2 = T^{-1}\sum_1^T\tilde{u}_t^2$ and $\tilde{u}_t$ is a consistent estimator of u_t under H_0. Note that

$$\operatorname*{plim}_{T\to\infty} T^{-1}\sum_{t=1}^{T}\left(\frac{\tilde{u}_t^2}{\tilde{\sigma}^2} - 1\right)^2 = 2. \tag{6.4.4}$$

This suggests the following test procedure:

(i) Estimate the parameters of (6.1.1) consistently under H_0 (note that $\boldsymbol{\psi} = \mathbf{0}$) and compute the residual sum of squares $\text{SSR}_0 = \sum \tilde{u}_t^2$.

(ii) Regress $\tilde{u}_t^2$ on $\mathbf{w}_t$ and compute the residual sum of squares SSR.

(iii) Compute the test statistic

$$LM_{\tilde{\eta}} = \frac{(\text{SSR}_0 - \text{SSR})/q}{\text{SSR}/(T - m - q - 1)} \tag{6.4.5}$$

which has an approximate $F(q, T - m - q - 1)$ distribution under (6.4.2).

If $\mathbf{w}_t = (1, u_{t-1}^2, \ldots, u_{t-q}^2)'$ then $\mathbf{w}_t$ has to be replaced by its consistent estimator $\tilde{\mathbf{w}}_t = (1, \tilde{u}_{t-1}^2, \ldots, \tilde{u}_{t-q}^2)'$ under H_0, and (6.4.5) is a test statistic of constant conditional variance against the conditional variance obeying an ARCH(q) model.

As Engle (1982) pointed out, (6.4.3) does not contain h^0, so that many different functional forms of ARCH, like the linear or exponential ones as alternatives, all lead to the same test.

Another interesting case is the one in which

$$\mathbf{w}_t = (1, y_{t-1}^2, \ldots, y_{t-p}^2, x_{t1}^2, \ldots, x_{tk}^2)'.$$

Then (6.4.5) is a test of (6.1.1) with $f(\mathbf{z}_t; \boldsymbol{\psi}) \equiv 0$ against the alternative that the model is

$$y_t = \beta_0 + \boldsymbol{\beta}(t)'\tilde{\mathbf{z}}_t + u_t, \quad t = 1, 2, \ldots, T$$

where $\boldsymbol{\beta}(t)$ is a $m \times 1$ vector of stochastic parameters, $m = p + k$, $\mathbf{z}_t = (1, \tilde{\mathbf{z}}_t')'$ as before,

$$E\boldsymbol{\beta}(t) = \boldsymbol{\beta}, \quad \text{cov}(\boldsymbol{\beta}(t)) = \text{diag}(\eta_1, \ldots, \eta_m), \quad \eta_j > 0, \quad j = 1, \ldots, m.$$

If (6.1.1) as such is the null model then applying the test requires the estimation of a nonlinear model. If $f(\mathbf{z}_t; \boldsymbol{\psi}) \equiv 0$ in (6.1.1), the residuals $\tilde{u}_t$ are just OLS residuals of a linear model. This is no doubt the most frequent case in practice. Nevertheless, testing the constancy of conditional variance against ARCH after estimating a nonlinear model is a useful diagnostic check. A rejection does not necessarily mean that the true model is the specified nonlinear one with ARCH errors. It may as well be taken as a symptom of a misspecification of the conditional mean and could lead to a respecification of the model.

Consider for a moment (6.4.3) and rewrite it as

$$LM_{\tilde{\eta}}^* = T \frac{\left\{\frac{1}{T}\sum(\tilde{u}_t^2 - \hat{\sigma}^2)(\tilde{\mathbf{w}}_t - \bar{\mathbf{w}})'\right\}\left\{\frac{1}{T}\sum(\tilde{\mathbf{w}}_t - \bar{\mathbf{w}})(\tilde{\mathbf{w}}_t - \bar{\mathbf{w}})'\right\}^{-1}\left\{\frac{1}{T}\sum(\tilde{u}_t^2 - \hat{\sigma}^2)(\tilde{\mathbf{w}}_t - \bar{\mathbf{w}})\right\}}{\frac{1}{T}\left(\sum \tilde{u}_t^2 - \hat{\sigma}^2\right)^2}.$$

This uses (6.4.4) and the fact that $\text{plim}_{T\to\infty} T^{-1}\sum(\tilde{u}_t^2 - \sigma^2) = 0$. Under (6.4.2), approximately,

$$\left[\frac{1}{T}\sum(\tilde{u}_t^2 - \sigma^2)(\bar{\mathbf{w}}_t - \bar{\mathbf{w}})\right]_j = \frac{1}{T}\sum(\tilde{u}_t^2 - \tilde{\sigma}^2)(\tilde{u}_{t-j}^2 - \tilde{\sigma}^2), \; j \neq 0.$$

(6.4.6)

Likewise,

$$\left[\frac{1}{T}\sum(\bar{\mathbf{w}}_t - \bar{\mathbf{w}})(\bar{\mathbf{w}}_t - \bar{\mathbf{w}})'\right]_{ij} = \frac{1}{T}\sum(\tilde{u}_{t-i}^2 - \tilde{\sigma}^2)(\tilde{u}_{t-j}^2 - \tilde{\sigma}^2).$$

(6.4.7)

Because asymptotically $\text{plim}_{T\to\infty} T^{-1}\sum(\tilde{u}_{t-i}^2 - \sigma^2)(\tilde{u}_{t-j}^2 - \sigma^2) = 0$ for $i \neq j$ under (6.4.2), the covariance matrix in (6.4.3) may be replaced by another consistent estimator of $T^{-1}\mathbf{M} = T^{-1}(\mathbf{M}_{\bar{\eta}\bar{\eta}} - \mathbf{M}_{\bar{\eta}0}\mathbf{M}_{00}^{-1}\mathbf{M}_{0\bar{\eta}})$, which is

$$T^{-1}\tilde{\mathbf{M}} = \left\{T^{-1}\sum_1^T(\tilde{u}_t^2 - \tilde{\sigma}^2)^2\right\}\mathbf{I}_q.$$

(6.4.8)

Doing that and making use of (6.4.6) yields

$$LM_{\bar{\eta}}^{**} = T\sum_{j=1}^q r_j^2(\tilde{u}_t^2)$$

(6.4.9)

where

$$r_j(\hat{u}_t^2) = \frac{\dfrac{1}{T}\sum(\tilde{u}_t^2 - \tilde{\sigma}^2)(\tilde{u}_{t-j}^2 - \tilde{\sigma}^2)}{\dfrac{1}{T}\sum(\tilde{u}_t^2 - \tilde{\sigma}^2)^2}$$

is the sample autocorrelation between $\tilde{u}_t^2$ and $\tilde{u}_{t-j}^2$. A slight modification of (6.4.9) in the spirit of Ljung and Box (1978) yields an asymptotically equivalent statistic

$$LM_{\bar{\eta}}^{ML} = T(T+2)\sum_{j=1}^q r_j^2(\hat{u}_t^2)/(T-j).$$

(6.4.10)

McLeod and Li (1983) suggested (6.4.10) as a general test statistic of linearity against unspecified nonlinearity. It is seen from above that it is in fact an LM statistic against ARCH.

6.5. Locally Equivalent Alternatives

In this section we shall discuss nonlinear models that are in some sense locally close to each other. In order to do that we need a definition for this closeness. A useful definition is obtained using the concept of local equivalence, see, for example, Godfrey (1988) and Gouriéroux and Monfort (1990). Consider two nonlinear models

$$y_t = f_1(\boldsymbol{\alpha}, \boldsymbol{\beta}; \mathbf{x}_t) + u_t, \quad u_t \sim \text{i.i.d.}(0, \sigma^2) \tag{6.5.1}$$

and

$$y_t = f_2(\boldsymbol{\alpha}, \boldsymbol{\phi}; \mathbf{x}_t) + v_t, \quad v_t \sim \text{i.i.d.}(0, \sigma^2). \tag{6.5.2}$$

Assume that f_1 and f_2 are at least twice continuously differentiable. Parameter vector $\boldsymbol{\alpha}$ is assumed to relate to the 'linear part' of the models whereas $\boldsymbol{\beta}$ and $\boldsymbol{\phi}$ that have the same dimension are 'nonlinear' parameters. Consider these models in the neighbourhood of linearity. Local equivalence of these models is defined as follows.

Definition (Gouriéroux and Monfort, 1990). Models (6.5.1) and (6.5.2) are locally equivalent in a neighbourhood of $H_{01}:\boldsymbol{\beta} = \mathbf{0}$, $H_{02}:\boldsymbol{\phi} = \mathbf{0}$, if the following two conditions are satisfied:

  (i) $f_1(\boldsymbol{\alpha}, \mathbf{0}; \mathbf{x}_t) = f_2(\boldsymbol{\alpha}, \mathbf{0}; \mathbf{x}_t)$
  (ii) $\partial f_1^0/\partial \boldsymbol{\beta} = \mathbf{A}(\partial f_2^0/\partial \boldsymbol{\phi})$ where $f_j^0 = f_j(\boldsymbol{\alpha}, \mathbf{0}; \mathbf{x}_t)$, $j = 1, 2$, and $\mathbf{A}$ is nonsingular.

The first condition means that both alternatives have the same null model. Condition (ii) says that the two partial derivatives are linearly dependent. It follows from (ii) that the LM tests derived for testing H_{01} and H_{02} are identical. If this is the case, a rejection of the null hypothesis does not contain any more evidence in favour of (6.5.1) than (6.5.2).

From the definition it follows that it is always possible to find a locally equivalent alternative to (6.5.1), i.e. given f_1 we can find f_2. Expand f_1 into a Taylor series about the null hypothesis H_{01}. This gives

$$f_1(\boldsymbol{\alpha}, \boldsymbol{\beta}; \mathbf{x}_t) = f_1(\boldsymbol{\alpha}, \mathbf{0}; \mathbf{x}_t) + \left(\frac{\partial f_1^0}{\partial \boldsymbol{\beta}}\right)' \boldsymbol{\beta} + R_2(\mathbf{x}_t).$$

Define

$$f_2(\boldsymbol{\alpha}, \boldsymbol{\beta}; \mathbf{x}_t) = f_1^0 + \left(\frac{\partial f_1^0}{\partial \boldsymbol{\beta}}\right)' \boldsymbol{\beta}. \tag{6.5.3}$$

It is seen that f_2 satisfies conditions (i) and (ii); note that $\boldsymbol{\phi} = \boldsymbol{\beta}$. It should be pointed out that in cases where (6.5.1) is stable, its locally equivalent counterpart based on (6.5.3) may be explosive. However, equation (6.5.3) offers an alternative way of deriving LM tests based on transforming the model into a locally equivalent one and then constructing the test. As an example, consider the LSTR model (6.3.3) and select $\psi = 1$, $h = 2$, $\pi = \varphi = \boldsymbol{\theta}$. As mentioned before (6.3.3) is one of the possible models behind RESET for $h = 2$. It can be written as

$y_t = f_1 + v_t$ where

$$f_1 = \boldsymbol{\pi}'\mathbf{z}_t + [(1 + \exp\{-\gamma_1(\boldsymbol{\pi}'\mathbf{z}_t)\})^{-1} - 1/2]\boldsymbol{\pi}'\mathbf{z}_t. \qquad (6.5.4)$$

The linearity hypothesis is $\gamma_1 = 0$, and from (6.5.3)

$$f_2 = \boldsymbol{\pi}'\mathbf{z}_t + \delta(\boldsymbol{\pi}'\mathbf{z}_t)^2, \qquad (6.5.5)$$

where $\delta = \gamma_1/4$. The idea of RESET appears perhaps more transparent in f_2 than in f_1 but the LM test of $\gamma_1 = 0$ within $y_t = f_1 + u_t$ is the same as that of $\delta = 0$ within $y_t = f_2 + u_t^*$.

6.6 Comparing Linearity Tests using Asymptotic Relative Efficiency

Several tests considered in this chapter have been tests against a specific nonlinear alternative, including tests originally claimed to be general, i.e. aimed at discovering various types of nonlinearity. Often economic theory does not give enough guidance to allow an accurate dynamic specification of the nonlinear model. There exists the possibility, often a strong one, that linearity is tested against an inappropriate alternative instead of the data-generating process. An interesting question then is how much power an inappropriate test may have relative to the appropriate one. This has sometimes been investigated by simulation, but generalizing the results is a problem. Asymptotic relative efficiency offers an alternative strategy for studying this question in cases where the alternative to the null hypothesis is well specified.

To define this concept, consider testing linearity of (6.1.1), and assume that $u_t \sim \text{nid}(0, \sigma_u^2)$. Suppose, however, that the data-generating process is

$$y_t = \boldsymbol{\beta}'\mathbf{z}_t + h(\mathbf{z}_t; \boldsymbol{\sigma}) + u_t, \quad t = 1, 2, \ldots, T \qquad (6.6.1)$$

where $u_t \sim \text{nid}(0, \sigma_u^2)$ and h is at least twice a continuously differentiable function of σ such that $h(\mathbf{z}_t; \mathbf{0}) = 0$. Let

$$L_{1T}(\boldsymbol{\beta}, \boldsymbol{\psi}; \mathbf{Z}_T) = \sum_{t=1}^{T} l_{1t}(\boldsymbol{\beta}, \boldsymbol{\psi}; \mathbf{Z}_T) \qquad (6.6.2)$$

and

$$L_{2T}(\boldsymbol{\beta}, \boldsymbol{\sigma}; \mathbf{Z}_T) = \sum_{t=1}^{T} l_{2t}(\boldsymbol{\beta}, \boldsymbol{\sigma}; \mathbf{Z}_T) \qquad (6.6.3)$$

be the logarithmic (pseudo) likelihood functions of (6.1.1) with $u_t \sim \text{nid}(0, \sigma_u^2)$ and (6.6.1), respectively. The null hypothesis to be tested is

$$H_{01} : \boldsymbol{\psi} = \mathbf{0} \text{ in } (6.6.2)$$

and the alternative is $H_{11}:\psi \neq 0$. Let LM_ψ be the corresponding LM test. The linearity hypothesis for the true model is

$$H_{02}:\sigma = 0 \text{ in (6.6.3)}$$

the alternative is $H_{12}:\sigma \neq 0$, and the corresponding LM test is called LM_σ.

Note that $L_{1T}(\beta, 0; Z_T) = L_{2T}(\beta, 0; Z_T)$. In order to derive an asymptotic distribution of LM_ψ under H_{12} consider a sequence of Pitman's local alternatives $\sigma_T = \delta/T^{1/2}$, $\delta \neq 0$. This is a technical device without a proper physical meaning, and its sole purpose is to obtain the appropriate asymptotic distribution. Assume that large values of the test statistic are critical. If the test statistic is consistent so that its value increases beyond any fixed bound with the number of observations when the fixed alternative hypothesis is true, it is not possible to define its asymptotic distribution. Considering local alternatives moderates this rate of growth and thus offers a way of comparing asymptotic distributions of different test statistics. Davidson and MacKinnon (1987) provided a very general discussion of these ideas. Saikkonen (1989) contains a more specific treatment of the concept of asymptotic relative efficiency (ARE) and some extensions.

As a starting-point, define a combined model with likelihood function $L_T(\beta, \psi, \sigma; Z_T)$. The null hypothesis is

$$H_{03}:\sigma = 0 \quad \text{in } L_T(\beta, \psi, \sigma, Z_T) \qquad (6.6.4)$$

and the corresponding alternative is $H_{13}:\sigma \neq 0$. Assume that the true value of σ is $\sigma_0 = \delta/T^{1/2}$, $\delta \neq 0$, and let $\theta_0 = (\beta_0', 0', \sigma_0')'$ be the true value of $\theta = (\beta', \psi', \sigma')'$, respectively. Also define $\theta_0^* = (\beta_0', 0', 0')$, the value of θ for which is $L_{1T} = L_{2T} = L_T$. Next define the information matrix of θ as

$$\mathbf{J}(\theta) = -\plim_{T\to\infty}(T^{-1}\partial^2 L_T(\theta)/\partial\theta\partial\theta')$$

and assume that the corresponding matrices obtained from L_{1T} and L_{2T} are positive definite at $\theta = \theta_0^*$. Define block ab as

$$\mathbf{J}_{ab} = [\mathbf{J}(\theta_0^*)]_{ab} = -\plim_{T\to\infty}[T^{-1}\partial^2 L_T(\theta_0^*)/\partial\mathbf{a}\partial\mathbf{b}']$$

where $\mathbf{a}$, $\mathbf{b} = \beta$, ψ, σ. It can be shown that under $H_{1\sigma}:\sigma = \delta/T^{1/2}$, asymptotically, LM_ψ has a non-central χ^2 distribution with $r = \dim(\psi)$ degrees of freedom and non-centrality parameter

$$\lambda_\psi(\delta) = \delta' J_{\sigma\psi\cdot\beta} J_{\psi\psi\cdot\beta}^{-1} J_{\psi\sigma\cdot\beta}\delta \qquad (6.6.5)$$

where $\mathbf{J}_{ab\cdot c} = \mathbf{J}_{ab} - \mathbf{J}_{ac}\mathbf{J}_{cc}^{-1}\mathbf{J}_{cb}$. The appropriate test, LM_σ, has a non-central χ^2 distribution with $s = \dim(\sigma)$ degrees of freedom and non-centrality parameter $\lambda_\sigma(\delta) = \delta' \mathbf{J}_{\sigma\sigma\cdot\beta}\delta$. This is also true for the other classical test statistics, the likelihood ratio, and the Wald statistics, if they are available, because they are asymptotically equivalent to the LM statistic.

Because we are able to compute the noncentrality parameters $\lambda_\psi(\delta)$ and $\lambda_\sigma(\delta)$, comparing the asymptotic distributions by comparing their non-centrality parameters is an attractive idea. We may form the ratio

$$e_{\psi\sigma}(\delta) = \lambda_\psi(\delta)/\lambda_\sigma(\delta). \tag{6.6.6}$$

It turns out that for $r = s$, the inverse of (6.6.6) is approximately (in large samples) the ratio of the sample size $T_\psi(\delta)$ needed to obtain a certain power p_α against $H_{1\sigma}$ using LM_ψ to the sample size $T_\sigma(\delta)$ giving the same power using LM_σ. The limit of this ratio as the sample size grows to infinity is the ARE of LM_ψ with respect to LM_σ. However, for $r \neq s$, Saikkonen (1989) showed that a plausible definition of ARE is

$$e_{\varphi\sigma}(\delta) = \frac{\lambda_\psi(\delta)d(s, \alpha, P_\alpha)}{\lambda_\sigma(\delta)d(r, \alpha, P_\alpha)} \tag{6.6.7}$$

where $d(k, \alpha, p_\alpha)$ is the non-centrality parameter such that the $1 - p_\alpha$ fractile of the $\chi_k^2(d(k, \alpha, p_\alpha))$ distribution and the $1 - \alpha$ fractile of the χ_k^2 distribution coincide. Tabulated values of $d(k, \alpha, p_\alpha)$ can be found for example in Pearson and Hartley (1972).

It is seen that the ARE is generally a function of δ. This may be considered a disadvantage as a scalar would be a more concise measure. However, it is possible to obtain an upper and a lower bound for ARE that are independent of δ. For $r = s = 1$, (6.6.6) is indeed a scalar. A necessary condition for the lower bound to be positive is that rank $(\mathbf{J}_{\psi\sigma\cdot\beta}) = s$. If rank $(\mathbf{J}_{\psi\sigma\cdot\beta}) < s$, there exists a nonzero δ such that $\mathbf{J}_{\psi\sigma\cdot\beta}\delta = 0$. Thus if the inappropriate alternative contains less parameters than the appropriate one would, then there are points in the parameter space defined by the alternative model that belong to the implicit null hypothesis of the test (Davidson and MacKinnon, 1987). They are points such that the power of the test against them does not exceed the size of the test.

As an example, consider the following LSTR model

$$y_t = \beta x_t + [\theta(1 + \exp\{-\gamma x_t\})^{-1} - 1/2]x_t + u_t \tag{6.6.8}$$

where

$$x_t = \sum_{j=1}^{p} \pi_j x_{t-j} + v_t, \tag{6.6.9}$$

say, such that all the roots of $1 - \sum_{j=1}^{p}\pi_j z^j = 0$ are outside the unit circle, with $(u_t, v_t) \sim \text{nid}(0, \text{diag}(\sigma_u^2, \sigma_v^2))$, and (β, θ, γ) and

$(\pi_1, \ldots, \pi_p)$ are variation-free. Assume further that there is a sequence of data-generating bilinear models

$$y_t = \beta x_t + \sigma_T x_t u_{t-1} + u_t \tag{6.6.10}$$

where $\sigma_T = \delta/T^{1/2}$, $\delta \neq 0$, and where x_t is generated by (6.6.9). Suppose we want to test

$$H_{0\gamma}: \gamma = 0 \text{ in } (6.6.8) \tag{6.6.11}$$

against $H_{1\gamma}: \gamma > 0$, whereas the true model is a member of the sequence (6.6.10). The appropriate alternative would then be $H_{1\sigma}: \sigma_T \neq 0$. To compute the ARE of the LM-type test of (6.6.11) replace (6.6.8) by the 'locally equivalent' model, see Section 6.5,

$$y_t = \beta x_t + \psi x_t^2 + u_t \tag{6.6.12}$$

and consider testing $H_{0\psi}: \psi = 0$ instead of (6.6.11) as in Section 6.2.1. (Note that the definition of local equivalence is not strictly applicable here because (6.6.8) and (6.6.10) do not have the same number of nonlinear parameters. Nevertheless, as one of the two nonlinear parameters is not identified under the null hypothesis the application of (6.5.3) gives the linear form (6.6.12).) The conditional likelihood function L_T of the composite model is

$$L_T(\beta, \psi, \sigma, \mathbf{Z}_T) = -(T/2)\ln 2\pi - (T/2)\ln \sigma_u^2$$

$$- (1/2\sigma^2)\sum_1^T (y_t - \beta x_t - \psi x_t^2 - \sigma_T x_t u_{t-1})^2$$

$$\tag{6.6.13}$$

assuming u_0 fixed. From (6.6.13) and the definition of σ_T it follows that

$$\mathbf{J}_{\sigma\psi} = \operatorname*{plim}_{T\to\infty} \frac{\partial^2 L_T}{\partial \sigma_T \partial \psi}\bigg|_{H_{0\psi}} = -\operatorname*{plim}_{T\to\infty}(1/\sigma_u^2 T)\sum_1^T x_t^3 \tilde{u}_{t-1} = 0$$

where $\tilde{u}_t = y_t - \beta x_t - \sigma_T x_t \tilde{u}_{t-1}$. Likewise $\mathbf{J}_{\sigma\beta} = \mathbf{J}_{\psi\beta} = 0$, it then follows that $\mathbf{J}_{\sigma\psi\cdot\beta} = 0$. Thus in this case where x_t is a strongly exogenous variable, the information matrix of the parameters of the composite model is block diagonal, and from (6.6.5) the ARE of LM_ψ equals zero. This is the same situation encountered above in testing linearity (constancy of the conditional variance) of a model against ARCH while the data-generating process is a model with a nonlinear conditional mean and no ARCH. There the information matrix is block diagonal, and nonlinearity in the mean may be difficult to detect by the McLeod and Li (1983) linearity test, the test being an LM test against ARCH with zero ARE with respect to the appropriate LM test.

Next modify the example by substituting y_{t-1} for x_t in (6.6.8), (6.6.10), and (6.6.12) assuming $|\beta| < 1$. (Definition (6.6.9) is dropped.) The accordingly modified (6.6.13) yields

$$\mathbf{J}_{\sigma\psi} = \plim_{T\to\infty} \frac{\partial^2 L_T}{\partial\sigma_T\partial\psi}\bigg|_{H_{0\psi}} = -\plim_{T\to\infty}(1/\sigma_u^2 T)\sum y_{t-1}^3 \tilde{u}_{t-1} = 3\sigma_u^2(1-\beta^2)^{-1}$$

(6.6.14)

where $\tilde{u}_t = y_t - \beta y_{t-1} - \sigma_T y_{t-1}\tilde{u}_{t-1}$. Straightforward computation also yields

$$\mathbf{J}_{\psi\psi} = 3\sigma_u^2(1-\beta^2)^{-2} \quad \text{and} \quad \mathbf{J}_{\sigma\sigma} = \sigma_u^2(3-2\beta^2)(1-\beta^2)^{-1}.$$

(6.6.15)

Furthermore, $\mathbf{J}_{\sigma\beta} = \mathbf{J}_{\psi\beta} = 0$ that $\mathbf{J}_{ab\cdot\beta} = \mathbf{J}_{ab}$ for a, $b = \sigma$, ψ. Combining (6.6.6), (6.6.14), and (6.6.15) yields the ARE:

$$e_{\psi\sigma}(\delta) = 3(1-\beta^2)/(3-2\beta^2).$$

(6.6.16)

It is seen from Fig. 6.1 that (6.6.16) is a monotonically decreasing function of $|\beta|$ for $0 \leqslant |\beta| < 1$. If $\beta = 0$, $e_{\psi\sigma}(\delta) = 1$, so that LM_ψ and LM_σ are asymptotically equivalent. Intuitively, this may also be guessed by comparing modified (6.6.10) and (6.6.12). If $H_{1\sigma}$ holds and $\beta = 0$,

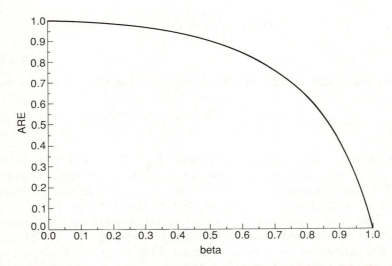

FIG. 6.1. Asymptotic relative efficiency of the LM-type linearity test against univariate STAR model (6.6.8) with $x_t = y_{t-1}$ with respect to the LM test against the univariate bilinear model (6.6.10) with $x_t = y_{t-1}$ and a fixed bilinear coefficient

then by ignoring the term of order T^{-2},

$$y_t = \sigma_T y_{t-1} u_{t-1} + u_t = \sigma_T(\sigma_T y_{t-2} u_{t-2} + u_{t-1})u_{t-1} + u_t \approx \sigma_T u_{t-1}^2 + u_t,$$

which approximates modified (6.6.12) in the neighbourhood of $y_{t-1} = u_{t-1}$. More generally, assume that the true model is (6.6.10) with a fixed nonzero coefficient with $x_t = y_{t-1}$. Furthermore, suppose the LM test against this model rejects linearity. Then it is quite likely that a linearity test against STAR based on (6.6.12) ($x_t = y_{t-1}$) also rejects it if $|\beta| < 0.5$, say, as the ARE of the STAR test with respect to the appropriate test then exceeds 0.9.

More examples on applying ARE in univariate time-series can be found in Luukkonen *et al.* (1988*a*) and Teräsvirta (1990*a*).

6.7 Which Test to Use?

It is clear from this chapter that there is no shortage of linearity tests. A question any prospective model builder must face is which ones to apply. If there is sufficient prior information available about the alternative, then tests against a well-specified alternative are a natural choice. The LM and LM-type tests discussed in previous sections also have the advantage that they are easy to use. However, they also have power against many more alternatives than the appropriate one. Thus, if there is not enough economic theory to point out a single nonlinear alternative to the null hypothesis, rejecting the null cannot mean accepting the alternative. An additional complication is that as a rule there are several nonlinear models corresponding to the same auxiliary regression. All this does not render the parametric tests invalid in situations where there is uncertainty about the true alternative. One can perform several LM-type tests and compare their p-values or strength of rejection. The alternatives against which linearity is rejected very strongly are more likely to allow a reasonable description of nonlinearity of the data-generating process than those against which the rejection is weak. The tests can thus be used as a model selection device for finding out where to look for an appropriate nonlinear model. A model selection strategy for STR models in this spirit will be discussed in the next chapter.

If one has prior information saying that the nonlinear model is a switching regression rather than an STR model, tests based on ordered observations and discussed in Section 6.3.4 become useful. On the other hand, the small sample evidence indicates that the LM-type test against STR may still be a reasonable choice. The converse is less likely: if the transition is smooth, the tests of Section 6.3.4 may be clearly less powerful than their smooth transition counterparts.

If the ultimate aim is to build parametric nonlinear models, tests against a well-specified alternative are more useful than the ones against an unspecified alternative. However, the RESET for instance may be a very useful test if the number of variables under the linearity hypothesis is large while the time-series are short. Because the RESET uses few degrees of freedom it may then be preferred to tests with larger alternatives.

The number of observations is often a concern at least to econometricians working with relatively short macroeconomic series. A small sample rules out tests like the BDS test or the tests based on the bispectrum mentioned in Section 2.2 because a fairly large sample is needed to achieve good power. These tests are also computationally much more demanding than the ones based on auxiliary regressions. The BDS test has sometimes been used to find out if a series is chaotic. Because the null hypothesis of the test is that the observations are i.i.d., while the alternative is that they are not, it is clear that this motivation is unwarranted. The BDS test is currently very popular in the analysis of long financial time-series like relatively high-frequency stock-market or exchange-rate data where the number of observations is not an obstacle. However, it is not often followed by a parametric model building exercise. The main aim of the users seems to have been to demonstrate that the observations (often residuals from a linear model) are not i.i.d. and for this purpose BDS by definition of course is an appropriate test.

7

Building Nonlinear Models

Preamble

If a test suggests that a series is nonlinear or is part of a nonlinear relationship, the question naturally arises—how can the relationship be modelled? This chapter surveys a variety of approaches that can be considered, both parametric and nonparametric. Particular attention is paid to the specification and estimation of smooth transition regression models, including how to decide which variety of these models to use. These models were shown in Chapter 3 to arise naturally in economic theory and can also be shown to provide adequate approximations of some of the alternative models in simple cases.

7.1 Introduction

The topic of this chapter is how to construct a model relating a series Y_t to its own lags and possibly also the lags and current value of another variable X_t. Potentially, $\mathbf{X}_t$ can be a vector and such a case is considered in Section 7.3. For example, Y_t may be the total daily demand for electricity in some region and X_t may be the average temperature for the day. A test of linearity, such as those discussed in the previous chapter, may well suggest that there is a nonlinear relationship between these variables, a specially hot day will increase demand for electricity because of air-conditioning use and a very cold day will also increase demand because of pumps, blowers, and other aspects of heating that use electricity. Intermediate temperatures will lead to relatively low electricity demand. Thus a simple model has

$$Y_t = f(X_t) + u_t \qquad (7.1.1)$$

where $f(x)$ is u-shaped but not necessarily symmetrical. However, the actual form of the function is not known, there is no economic theory that provides a clear specification. Its u-shape and its expected smoothness come from general considerations rather than some utility-maximizing representative agent theory. Further, a more complicated model such as

$$Y_t = f(X_t, X_{t-1}, Y_{t-1}) + u_t \qquad (7.1.2)$$

could be superior, reflecting heat or cold build-up in a building or missing variables. The model can perhaps be further improved with the use of the time-varying coefficients, to account for household behaviour being different at weekends, say, or introducing other relevant variables such as electricity prices, appliances efficiency, or population size. All the problems of models that are faced in the linear situation are still present, of course, but are compounded by the question of how to specify the function $f(\ )$. A variety of alternative approaches is available. For ease of notation, let $\mathbf{Z}_t$ be the vector of exploratory variables used in the model, that is Y_{t-j}, $j = 1, \ldots p$, X_{t-j}, $j = 0, \ldots, p$, for some given total lag p. Some important classes of models are:

(i) linear

$$Y_t = \boldsymbol{\beta}'\mathbf{Z}_t + u_t$$

(ii) nonparametric

$$Y_t = f(\mathbf{Z}_t) + u_t$$

where, essentially, $f(\ )$ is not constrained to belong to a specific class of functions. The function is often estimated by the use of some smoothing operation, as explained in the next section.

(iii) Semiparametric (or semi nonparametric) where some variables enter the model in a specific parametric form but one, say, enters nonparametrically, such as

$$Y_t = \boldsymbol{\beta}'\bar{\mathbf{Z}}_t + f(X_t) + u_t$$

for example. Here, Y_t could be electricity demand, X_t average temperature, and $\bar{\mathbf{Z}}_t$ various other variables which affect household or industrial use of electricity.

(iv) Parametric, where a specific functional form is assumed for $f(\ )$, usually with some parameters that have to be estimated. The linear model is an example of a parametric model. Other examples are:

(a) polynomial

$$Y_t = \alpha + \boldsymbol{\beta}'\mathbf{Z}_t + \mathbf{Z}_t'\mathbf{C}\mathbf{Z}_t + u_t$$

which is the quadratic form and $\mathbf{C}$ is a symmetric matrix of parameters;

(b) the smooth transition regression (STR) model, discussed in Section 4.2,

$$Y_t = \boldsymbol{\beta}_1'\mathbf{Z}_t + F(\mathbf{Z}_t)\boldsymbol{\beta}_2'\mathbf{Z}_t + u_t$$

where $F(\ )$ is a function that captures the transitional aspect of the model, such as the logistic

$$F(\mathbf{Z}) = (1 - \exp\{-\boldsymbol{\gamma}'\mathbf{Z}\})^{-1};$$

(*c*) the flexible Fourier form

$$X_t = \delta + \boldsymbol{\beta}'\mathbf{Z}_t + \mathbf{Z}_t'\mathbf{C}\mathbf{Z}_t + \sum_{j=1}^{q} \{c_j \sin(j(\boldsymbol{\gamma}'\mathbf{Z}_t)) + d_j \cos(j(\boldsymbol{\gamma}'\mathbf{Z}_t))\} + u_t$$

which is the quadratic polynomial plus similar sine and cosine terms;

(*d*) neural networks

$$y_t = \alpha + \sum_{j=1}^{q} \beta_j \phi(\boldsymbol{\gamma}_j'\mathbf{Z}_t) + u_t \qquad (7.1.3)$$

where $\phi(\ )$ is a squashing function, such as a cumulative distribution function or a logistic. Linear and quadratic components could also be included.

There is no clear-cut distinction between these models and many combinations and interactions are possible. In this chapter we will emphasize simple, practical techniques that can be used without too much difficulty. The next section considers nonparametric and semiparametric techniques and later sections consider parametric models.

7.2 Nonparametric and Semiparametric Models

To justify these methods, consider again the example where Y_t is daily electricity demand and X_t is average temperature for the day. The data will consist of the pairs of numbers (Y_t, X_t), $t = 1, \ldots n$ which can be plotted as in Fig. 7.1. If one expects the function in (7.1.1) to be smooth, the question arises how this can be estimated. If for a given X value, such as X_0, there are several corresponding Y values, a starting-point for the estimation would be to let $\hat{f}(X_0)$ be an average over these values. However, these multiple values may not be available at all X values. One sensible estimate would be to take X values near X_0 and to

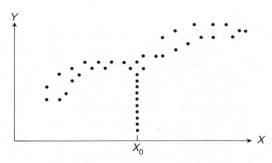

FIG. 7.1. Data plot of bivariate sample

average the Y corresponding to these X, for example, that is the k X values with smallest distance from X_0. The size of k will have to be chosen by the modeller, or can be varied with X_0 according to some criterion, based on the average distance of the neighbours for instance. If there are a pair of explanatory variables (X_{1t}, X_{2t}), then the averaging or smoothing will take place over a surface rather than a curve.

However, nearest-neighbour methods ignore any information about the curve at a point X_0 that is contained in more distant values. An alternative is to use an averaging method that gives great weight to Y values corresponding to nearby X values and smaller weights for other values.

This can be done using a kernel function $k(\omega)$ which has a bell-shape, like a Gaussian probability function with mean zero, $\phi(0, \sigma) = c \exp(-\omega^2/2\sigma^2)$. This function gives sensible weights for smoothing the curve $Y_t = f(X_t) + e_t$. Basic considerations, for instance in Ullah (1989a) or Auestad and Tjøstheim (1990), find

$$E[Y_t | X_t = x] \equiv \hat{m}(x) = c \sum_{j=1}^{T} Y_j k[(x - x_j)/h] \qquad (7.2.1)$$

where

$$c^{-1} = \sum_{j=1}^{T} k[(x - x_j)/h]$$

and where h is a parameter, called the 'band or window width', which determines the relative weights on near and distant values. Similarly, the conditional variance is given by

$$E[(Y_t - m(x))^2 | X_t = x] = \hat{V}(x) = c \sum_{j=1}^{T} Y_j^2 k[(x - x_j)/h] - \hat{m}^2(x)$$

$$(7.2.2)$$

where c^{-1} is as above.

What is interesting about these estimates is that they involve only a single parameter, h, and this can be found from an in-sample search, so that a grid of possible h-values is searched to minimize $\sum_{t=1}^{T} (Y_t - \hat{m}(X_t))^2$. The estimated conditional means can also be used to provide easy out-of-sample conditioned forecasts.

In practice, a model such as (7.1.1) is too simple and a number of explanatory variables are used. Denote these by $\mathbf{Z}_t$, with components Z_{jt}, $j = 1, \ldots, m$, which will include lagged Y_t, up to a given lag p. For convenience, suppose that each component Z_{jt} has mean zero and unconditional variance one. A natural weighting function would now be a multivariate Gaussian probability density function proportional to $\exp(\omega'A^{-1}\omega)$ where A is some covariance matrix. However, for convenience A can be taken to be diagonal and the multidimensional kernel is $\prod_{i=1}^{m}k(\omega_i/h)$ where $k(\omega)$ is the univariate Gaussian p.d.f. as used above, i.e. $k(\omega) = \exp(-\omega^2/2)$. The conditional mean is then

$$E[Y_t|\mathbf{Z}_t = \mathbf{Z}] = c\sum_{j=1}^{T}Y_j\prod_{i=1}^{m}k[(Z_j - Z_{ij})/h] \qquad (7.2.3)$$

where

$$c^{-1} = \sum_{j=1}^{T}\prod_{i=1}^{m}k[(Z_j - Z_{ij})/h].$$

A similar expression for the conditional variance is available as a direct generalization of (7.2.2). As only a single parameter h is used, the smoothing is the same in all directions (remembering that all components of $\mathbf{Z}_t$ have unit variance) and no cross-correlations are utilized. For a given kernel, such as the univariate Gaussian, the estimate is easily achieved, and some searching over h will produce a near-optimal estimate.

The only practical question that remains is that of the choice of p, the number lags of Y_t, X_t used in forming the vector $\mathbf{Z}_t$. This question is discussed in Auestad and Tjøstheim (1990, 1991) and Tjøstheim and Auestad (1991a,b) where they consider a generalization of the FPE (final prediction error) criterion that is often used in linear modelling and was proposed by Akaike (1969). Suppose that the above procedure is used for a given h and an increasing sequence of p values, $1, 2, \ldots j$, giving a sequence of error variances for the conditional means

$$\sigma_j^2 = \frac{1}{T}\sum_{j=1}^{T}(Y_j - \hat{m}(X_j))^2.$$

If the true p value is p_0, then one may expect that σ^2 is declining as j increases up to p_0 and is approximately constant hereafter. The plot of $\hat{\sigma}_j^2$ against j is therefore a possible tool for determining p_0. However, using a window width h that is determined from the data by an optimizing procedure can bias the estimates of σ_j^2, Auestad and Tjøstheim suggest incorporating a penalty for possibly overfitting by defining

$$FPE(j) = \sigma_j^2\frac{1 + c_j}{1 - c_j}$$

where

$$c_j = n^{-1}h_j^{-1}d^jA^j\left[\prod_{k=0}^{j-1}\hat{\sigma}_k\right]$$

and

$$d = \int k^2(x)\,dx$$

and A is a tuning parameter designed so that the windows cover all the data. Thus, if prob (all data in band $\pm 4\sigma$) $\simeq 1$, then $A = 8$, and $A = 6$ if the band is $\pm 3\sigma$.

Window widths h_j and p_0 are then determined by minimization of $FPE(j)$ in two steps, for fixed j, h_j is determined to minimize σ_j^2 and then p_0 is the value of j that minimizes $FPE(j)$. Auestad and Tjøstheim (1990) carried out a small simulation using just univariate models and found the suggested procedure to be satisfactory. Tjøstheim and Auestad (1991b) developed the idea further by considering other criteria like one of AIC type. Cheng and Tong (1992) proposed the use of cross-validation to find the right lags.

The kernel nonparametric estimators are easily understood and fairly easy to implement. As one ends up with a specific functional form, one-step forecasts are easily formed. There are many other types of nonparametric estimators but only two others are mentioned here: projection pursuit and cubic splines.

Projection pursuit is discussed in Friedman and Stuetzle (1981) and Huber (1985) and involves the sequential use of a non-parametric estimator combined with parameter estimator, and thus is computer intensive. If Y_t is the dependent series and $\mathbf{Z}_t$ a vector of explanatory variables, the first step is to consider a model of the form

$$Y_t = \phi_1(\gamma_1'\mathbf{Z}_t) + e_{1t}$$

where ϕ_1 is a smooth function, chosen nonparametrically to minimize the mean squared residual and γ_1 is a vector of parameters. For a predetermined nonparametric estimation procedure, γ_1 is chosen, the technique applied, and the goodness-of-fit calculated, say the sum of squared errors of e_{1t}, and then the program would search over γ_1 values to maximize the goodness-of-fit (minimize the sum of squared errors). At the second stage,

$$Y_{1t} = Y_t - \phi_1(\gamma_{10}'\mathbf{Z}_t)$$

is formed, where γ_{10}' is the optimal value found for γ_1, and then a model estimated as before of the form

$$Y_{1t} = \phi_2(\gamma_{20}'\mathbf{Z}_t) + e_{2t}$$

and so forth, until r nonlinear terms are involved, with r determined by some stopping rule, involving the size of the change in sum of squared residuals as one goes from $r - 1$ to r terms. Programs, available to perform this sequence of calculations, are computer-intensive but usable. The model can be supplemented by using linear, and possibly quadratic, terms in $\mathbf{Z}_t$.

The potential performance of projection pursuit is illustrated in the following simple experiment from Granger and Teräsvirta (1992). The model considered takes the form

$$y_t = \alpha_0 + \boldsymbol{\alpha}'\mathbf{Z}_{1t} + \sum_{j=1}^{r} \phi_j(\boldsymbol{\gamma}'_{10}\mathbf{Z}_{2t}) + u_t$$

where $\mathbf{Z}_{1t}$ is used in the linear component and is $\mathbf{Z}_{1t} = (x_{t-i}, i = 1, \ldots k_x; y_{t-i}, i = 1, \ldots k_y)$ and $\mathbf{Z}_{2t}$ is used in the nonparametric components and is $\mathbf{Z}_{2t} = (x_{t-i}, i = 1, \ldots l_x; y_{t-i}, i = 1, \ldots l_y)$. Thus, the lags used can differ in the two components. The criteria used to decide on the number of lags used was to minimize $\text{BIC} = \log \text{var}_k(u_t) + k \log T/T$ when k parameters are used in a model with a sample of size T where $\text{var}_k(u_t)$ (the sum of squared residuals/T) for a model with k parameters. The number of lags is searched over a relevant range to minimize BIC. This criterion is known to be conservative in the sense that it chooses a smaller number of parameters than most other criteria like AIC or GCV. It is dimension-consistent; if the model has a finite number of parameters, asymptotically BIC chooses this model with probability one if it is among the ones considered.

The data were generated by the bivariate STR-D model:

$$y_t = \pi x_{t-1} - 0.9x_{t-1}/[1 + \exp(-\gamma d_{t-1})] + \sigma u_t, \quad \gamma > 0 \quad (7.2.4)$$

where $d_{t-1} = y_{t-1} - \pi x_{t-2}$ is the lagged deviation from the linear path $y_t = \pi x_{t-1}$, and x_t is AR(1):

$$x_t = 0.5x_{t-1} + e_t.$$

A variety of parameter values has been tried, but the only case shown here has $\pi = 0$, $\gamma = 100$ and three values of σ, 0.5, 1.5, 3, giving different noise levels.

Three models are fitted:

(a) linear component only   (L)
(b) projection pursuit component only (PP)
(c) both parts   (LP)

The in-sample size was $T = 300$, and this was used to estimate the model, and a further 100 out-of-sample terms were used to evaluate the models. The summary statistics used in Table 7.1 are R^2, $\hat{\sigma}_I$ (the estimated in-sample standard deviation of the residual, $\hat{\sigma}_0$ (the corresponding out-of-sample standard deviation of one-step forecast errors), and the ratio $\hat{\sigma}_0/\hat{\sigma}_I$. The table shows these statistics and the lags chosen by the technique for a single set of data. For the lowest noise level, the linear model (L) fits poorly, with $\hat{\sigma}_I > 0.5$, the true value, whereas the

TABLE 7.1. Lags of y and x chosen by the projection pursuit algorithm, coefficient of determination, in-sample standard deviation, out-of-sample standard deviation of one-step forecast errors and their ratio when the data were generated from (7.2.4).

| | | In-sample | | | | | Out-sample | | |
		k_x	k_y	l_x	l_y	R^2	$\hat{\sigma}_I$	$\hat{\sigma}_0$	$\hat{\sigma}_0/\hat{\sigma}_I$
$\pi = 0$	L	1	2	–	–	.42	.66	.62	.94
$\sigma = 0.5$	PP	–	–	1	3	.68	.49	.56	1.14
	LP	1	1	3	2	.60	.55	.56	1.02
	L	1	1	–	–	.12	1.51	1.58	1.05
$\sigma = 1.5$	PP	–	2	2	1	.31	1.34	1.74	1.30
	LP	1	1	2	1	.23	1.41	1.62	1.15
	L	1	1	–	–	.05	2.92	3.08	1.05
$\sigma = 3$	PP	–	–	3	1	.27	2.56	3.20	1.25
	LP	1	2	1	3	.20	2.67	3.34	1.25

Source: Granger and Teräsvirta (1992).

models using projection pursuit fit well in-sample and also forecast better. However, for larger σ values, when the noise dominates the nonlinear component, the PP models overfit in-sample, achieving an estimate of $\hat{\sigma}_I$ lower than the true value, and then forecast less well out-of-sample. These results are found throughout our experiments: when nonlinearity is strong PP fits and forecasts very well, but when nonlinearity is weak PP data mine, overfit in-sample, and forecast poorly out-of-sample. These results suggest that one should first test linearity, if rejected then projection pursuit models can be used with some confidence, if not rejected then one should use only linear models. Linearity testing was discussed in Chapter 6.

A further class of useful nonparametric models are called cubic splines. Suppose one is interested in a model

$$y - f(x) = \text{error}$$

and further suppose that the x variable can only take certain values x_1, $x_2, \ldots x_m$, which will be called 'knots'. (In practice x can take other values but a particular subset will be designated as the knots.) The function $f(x)$ is constrained in certain ways,

(i) between the knots x_i, x_{i+1}, $f(x)$ is a cubic function of x

$$f_i(x) = \alpha_1 + \beta_i x + \gamma_i x^2 + \sigma_i x^3.$$

(ii) At each knot $f(x)$, $f'(x)$, $f''(x)$ are all assumed to be continuous, so that

$$f_i(x_i) = f_{i-1}(x_i)$$

and similarly for the first and second derivatives.

Clearly these conditions impose strong constraints on the parameters α_i, β_i, etc. and the whole function $f(x)$ which equals $f_i(x)$ between x_i and x_{i+1} etc. will be somewhat smooth. Some degrees of freedom remain in the parameters and it is assumed that these parameter values are chosen to minimize

$$\sum_{i=1}^{m}(y_i - f(x_i))^2 + \lambda \int_{x_1}^{x_m} f''(x)\, dx.$$

The first term is the usual goodness-of-fit statistic, the sum being overall y that correspond to a particular x_i, and the integral in the expression is a measure of overall smoothness of the function, so that $\lambda > 0$ measures the penalty for lack of smoothness of $f(x)$.

The actual estimation procedure can be rephrased as a linear regression, using ordinary least squares, as discussed in Härdle (1990) and Engle, Granger, Rice, and Weiss (1986) (henceforth EGRW). This fact

enables the introduction of nonparametric components into linear parametric models, such as

$$y_t = \boldsymbol{\beta}'\mathbf{x}_t + f(z_t) + \varepsilon_t \qquad (7.2.5)$$

$\mathbf{x}_t$ is a vector of explanatory variables and $f(z_t)$ is a non-parametric,
cubic spline function of a further variable z_t. As has already been
mentioned, such mixed models have been called 'semiparametric'. For a
review see Robinson (1988). For example, in EGRW, y_t is electricity
demand, z_t is temperature, which is known to have an important
nonlinear effect on this demand, and $\mathbf{x}_t$ includes electricity price,
average income for the region, and monthly dummies to account for
regular changes in customer behaviour associated with holidays, for
example. In this example, the knots were chosen to be the centre points
of twenty-five different equally long temperature ranges, dividing up the
range of 10 °F to 95 °F for the case of the Georgia utility. This means
that $f(z_t)$ is approximated by a 25×1 vector $\mathbf{h}_t$ where $\mathbf{h}_t = (0, 0, \ldots,$
$0, 1, 0, \ldots, 0)'$, and element i being unity means that the temperature at
time t belongs to range i. Model (7.2.4) becomes

$$y_t = \boldsymbol{\beta}'\mathbf{x}_t + \boldsymbol{\delta}'\mathbf{h}_t + u_t$$

where $\boldsymbol{\delta}$ is a vector of regression coefficients. The smoothness require-
ment is imposed by assuming that the vector $\mathbf{R}\boldsymbol{\delta}$ is 'small', where in the
23×25 matrix $\mathbf{R}$

$$\mathbf{R} = \begin{bmatrix} 1 & -2 & 1 & 0 & \ldots & 0 \\ 0 & 1 & -2 & 1 & \ldots & 0 \\ \cdot \cdot & & & & & \\ 0 & 0 & 0 & 0 & \ldots & 1 \end{bmatrix}.$$

The optimization problem is as follows: set $\mathbf{X} = (\mathbf{x}_1', \ldots, \mathbf{x}_T')'$ and
$\mathbf{H} = (\mathbf{h}_1', \ldots, \mathbf{h}_T')'$. Find $(\boldsymbol{\beta}', \boldsymbol{\delta}')'$ such that

$$q(\boldsymbol{\beta}, \boldsymbol{\delta}) = (\mathbf{y} - \mathbf{X}\boldsymbol{\beta} - \mathbf{H}\boldsymbol{\delta})'(\mathbf{y} - \mathbf{X}\boldsymbol{\beta} - \mathbf{H}\boldsymbol{\delta}) + \lambda\boldsymbol{\delta}'\mathbf{R}'\mathbf{R}\boldsymbol{\delta}$$

is minimized. The non-negative scalar λ indicates the proportional
weight of the sample and prior ('$\mathbf{R}\boldsymbol{\delta}$ small') information and thus
determines the degree of smoothness. The choice of λ using generalized
model-selection criteria is discussed in EGRW, where a form of FPE or
the generalized cross-validation (GCV) is suggested, and more generally
in Mellin and Teräsvirta (1992). The resulting curve consisting of the
elements of $\hat{\boldsymbol{\delta}}$, which is a function of the temperature, is shown in Fig.
7.2. The smoother curve is aesthetically more pleasing and can be
interpreted with greater confidence than the less-smooth functions. If
the temperature ranges are not equally wide, matrix $\mathbf{R}$ must be modified
as discussed in Shiller (1984).

Good acounts of non and semiparametric modelling methods are

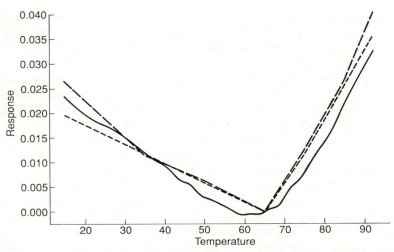

FIG. 7.2. Temperature response function for Georgia. The nonparametric estimate is given by the solid curve and two parametric estimates by the dashed curve.
Printed with the permission of the *Journal of the American Statistical Association*.

provided by Härdle (1990), Hastie and Tibshirani (1990), Delgado and Robinson (1994), Teräsvirta, Tjøstheim, and Granger (1994) and Tjøstheim (1993). For more applications to economic data, see Delgado and Robinson (1992). Although these methods can be recommended for use, they are more appropriate with long series as they can produce biased estimates if used with shorter series. The next section discusses some parametric modelling methods.

7.3 Specification of Parametric (STR) Models

The use of nonparametric and semiparametric techniques offers a rather general way of specifying nonlinear time-series models. If the model builder is willing to sufficiently restrict the set of possible nonlinear models under consideration, techniques for specifying parametric models may be available. The idea behind all these techniques is to avoid the estimation of a possibly large number of nonlinear models by first narrowing the choice down to a single family or even to a single model. Most of them are aimed at specifying univariate time-series models. Haggan *et al.* (1984) and Priestley (1988, ch. 5) discussed a technique for specifying state-dependent autoregressive models discussed in Chapter 2. It is based on recursive estimation of parameters of a linear autoregression or ARMA model assuming that the parameters depend on the past values of the process. After estimation using the Kalman Filter, the inspection of smoothed surfaces of parameter estimates or, in the one-dimensional case, a smoothed curve of parameter estimates as a function of the state leads to a choice of a model from the family of state-dependent models. This technique is likely to be difficult to apply in particular if the number of nonlinear parameters is not small, and it has not been much used in practice yet. Even in a one-dimensional case, interpreting the curve may not be easy for a non-expert as the examples in Priestley (1988, sect. 5.3) show. Besides, the sampling properties of the graphs are at this stage not well known. The method of Auestad and Tjøstheim (1990) also relies on graphs. They suggested the use of nonparametric estimates of the conditional mean and conditional variance for choosing a first-order nonlinear model from the family of state-dependent first-order models and demonstrated the applicability of the technique by simulation for various nonlinear autoregressive models. Auestad and Tjøstheim (1991) and Tjøstheim and Auestad (1991a) developed the idea further by replacing the one-dimensional conditional means and variances by projections which are particularly useful if the model is additive and of higher order than one.

Tsay (1989) presented a technique for specifying threshold autoregressive models. Perhaps because the choice is restricted to a single family of models, the method is relatively easy to apply. It consists of determining the lag length and the delay parameter using a specific linearity test and locating the threshold values and thus also determining the number of regimes by using scatterplots of various statistics. Teräsvirta (1994) developed a specification technique for smooth transition autoregressive models, and we shall next discuss its modification to multivariate STR models. As was seen in Section 4.2, the STR family of models is fairly general in the sense that it contains models capable of characterizing rather different types of nonlinear behaviour. A smooth transition regression model with $m = p + k + 1$ independent variables can be written as

$$y_t = \boldsymbol{\beta}' \mathbf{x}_t + (\boldsymbol{\theta}' \mathbf{x}_t) F(z_t) + u_t \qquad (7.3.1)$$

where $u_t \sim$ i.i.d.$(0, \sigma^2)$, $E\mathbf{x}_t u_t = 0$, $E\mathbf{z}_t u_t = 0$, $\boldsymbol{\beta} = (\beta_0, \beta_1, \ldots, \beta_m)'$, $\boldsymbol{\theta} = (\theta_0, \boldsymbol{\theta}_1')' = (\theta_0, \theta_1, \ldots, \theta_m)'$, and $\mathbf{x}_t = (1, y_{t-1}, \ldots, y_{t-p}; x_{1t}, \ldots, x_{kt})'$.

In Chapter 4 some definitions of $F(z_t)$ were discussed. Choosing $F(z_t) = (1 + \exp\{-\gamma(z_t - c)\})^{-1}$ in (7.3.1) yields the logistic STR model, whereas $F(z_t) = 1 - \exp\{-\gamma(z_t - c)^2\}$ defines the exponential STR model. Furthermore, $F(z_t) = (1 + \exp\{-\gamma(\mathbf{a}'\tilde{\boldsymbol{v}}_{t-1})\})^{-1} - 1/2$ where $\sum a_j = 1$, and $\tilde{\boldsymbol{v}}_t = (\tilde{u}_t, \tilde{u}_{t-1}, \ldots, \tilde{u}_{t-h+1})'$, $\tilde{u}_t = y_t - \boldsymbol{\beta}' \mathbf{x}_t$, characterizes the logistic STR-D model, and an exponential STR-D model is obtained by assuming $F(z_t) = 1 - \exp\{-\gamma(\mathbf{a}'\tilde{\boldsymbol{v}}_{t-1}^2)\}$, $\tilde{\boldsymbol{v}}_t^2 = (\tilde{u}_t^2, \tilde{u}_{t-1}^2, \ldots, \tilde{u}_{t-h+1}^2)'$.

Part of the specification problem consists of selecting the model family, when the choices are LSTR, ESTR, LSTR-D, and ESTR-D. Choosing z_t forms another part if the model is an LSTR or an ESTR model. Variable z_t may be a lagged y_t, any element x_{jt}, $j = 1, \ldots, k$, or another variable z_{tj} not included in $\mathbf{x}_t$.

The specification procedure for STR models consists of three steps:

(i) Specify a linear model to form a starting-point for further analysis.

(ii) Test linearity against STR using the linear model specified in (i) as the null model. If it is rejected, determine the transition variable (or a linear combination of them) from the data. At this stage it is also decided whether the model giving the best description of the data is an STR or STR-D model.

(iii) Choose between the LSTR and ESTR or LSTR-D and ESTR-D models, respectively.

The first step requires a complete specification of a (dynamic) linear model. The maximum lag length p for lagged y_t has to be determined from the data as well as the regressors $x_{t1}, \ldots, x_{tk}$ if economic theory is not fully explicit about them. A feasible model-selection criterion like AIC or BIC may be used to find an appropriate linear model. If the specified model is too parsimonious in the sense that its errors are autocorrelated, this may affect the outcome of linearity tests as the tests may have power against omitted serial correlation. Overspecification of dynamics may therefore be preferred to underspecification.

The second step builds upon the first one. The specified linear model serves as the null model of the linearity test. Tests against STR-type nonlinearity were discussed in Chapter 6. A test with power against both LSTR and ESTR amounts to testing $H_0 : \beta_1 = \beta_2 = \beta_3 = 0$ in the auxiliary regression

$$\hat{u}_t = \boldsymbol{\beta}_0' \mathbf{x}_t + \boldsymbol{\beta}_1' \mathbf{x}_t z_{td} + \boldsymbol{\beta}_2' \mathbf{x}_t z_{td}^2 + \boldsymbol{\beta}_3' \mathbf{x}_t z_{td}^3 + \eta_t \qquad (7.3.2)$$

where $\hat{u}_t$ is the OLS residual from the regression $y_t = \boldsymbol{\beta}' \mathbf{x}_t + u_t$.

Regression (7.3.2) may be used to select the transition variable z_t as follows. Carry out the test for $z_t = y_{t-1}, \ldots, y_{t-p}, x_{t1}, \ldots, x_{tk}$, and for any other z_t considered a possible candidate for a transition variable. If it is assumed that $\beta_3 = 0$ and $z_t = \tilde{u}_{t-d}$, $d = 1, \ldots, q$; linearity is being tested against a simple (single-lag) STR-D model. Alternatives with a linear combination of lags of $\tilde{u}_t$ may be considered as well. If the linearity is rejected for several choices of z_t, select the one with the smallest p-value to be the transition variable. The rationale of this rule is as follows. When the correct transition variable is selected, (7.3.2) is the appropriate auxiliary regression against the true nonlinear alternative. An incorrect transition variable makes (7.3.2) misspecified, and the power of the test must be less than that based on the correctly specified auxiliary regression. Because a number of not independent tests are performed, the true size of the multiple linearity test remains unknown. However, this is not necessarily a critical problem. If the linearity hypothesis is rejected when it is true, the estimation of the chosen nonlinear alternative may either fail, or may not give sensible results, which indicates overparameterization of the model. Nevertheless, reasonable-looking estimates may sometimes be obtained even if non-linearity is very weak. In those cases, evaluation of the model after estimating the parameters helps to find out if the model has really captured essential nonlinearities.

At any rate, if linearity is rejected, this step decides between STR and STR-D models and yields the transition variable (STR) or a linear combination of lagged residuals (STR-D).

The remaining step is needed to choose between LSTR and ESTR or LSTR-D and ESTR-D models, respectively. In order to do this consider the parameters of (7.3.2) in terms of the parameters of the corresponding nonlinear model. If (7.3.1) is an LSTR model where F is replaced by its third-order Taylor approximation about $\gamma = 0$, then

$$\boldsymbol{\beta}_1 = (c^2(g_3/2)\gamma^3 + g_1\gamma)\tilde{\boldsymbol{\theta}} - 3\theta_0 c(g_3/6)\gamma^3 \mathbf{e}_0 \qquad (7.3.3)$$

$$\boldsymbol{\beta}_2 = -c(g_3/2)\gamma^3\tilde{\boldsymbol{\theta}} + \theta_0(g_3/6)\gamma^3 \mathbf{e}_0 \qquad (7.3.4)$$

$$\boldsymbol{\beta}_3 = (g_3/6)\gamma^3\tilde{\boldsymbol{\theta}}, \qquad (7.3.5)$$

where again $g_1 = \partial F(0)/\partial z \neq 0$, $g_3 = \partial^3 F(0)/\partial z^3 \neq 0$, $\boldsymbol{\theta} = (\theta_0, \tilde{\boldsymbol{\theta}}')'$ and $\mathbf{e}_0 = (0, \ldots, 0, 1, 0, \ldots, 0)'$ where the unit element corresponds to z_t if z_t is an element of $\mathbf{x}_t$. If (7.3.1) is an ESTR model, we have

$$\boldsymbol{\beta}_1 = 2c\tilde{\boldsymbol{\theta}} - \theta_0\mathbf{e}_0 \qquad (7.3.6)$$

$$\boldsymbol{\beta}_2 = -\tilde{\boldsymbol{\theta}} \qquad (7.3.7)$$

$$\boldsymbol{\beta}_3 = \mathbf{0}. \qquad (7.3.8)$$

as $(1/2)\partial^2 F(0)/\partial z^2 = -1$.

Comparing (7.3.5) and (7.3.8) it is seen that for ESTR models, $\boldsymbol{\beta}_3 = \mathbf{0}$ whereas usually $\boldsymbol{\beta}_3 \neq \mathbf{0}$ if the model is an LSTR model. On the other hand, usually $\boldsymbol{\beta}_2 \neq \mathbf{0}$ if the model is an ESTR model. (We consider ESTR models with $\theta_0 \neq 0$, $\tilde{\boldsymbol{\theta}} = \mathbf{0}$, an exception rather than a rule.) For LSTR models $\boldsymbol{\beta}_2 = \mathbf{0}$ if $\theta_0 = c = 0$, which is fully possible. As to $\boldsymbol{\beta}_1$, in LSTR models generally $\boldsymbol{\beta}_1 \neq \mathbf{0}$ unless $\tilde{\boldsymbol{\theta}} = \mathbf{0}$ (LSTR models with $\theta_0 \neq 0$, $\tilde{\boldsymbol{\theta}} = \mathbf{0}$ are also regarded as an exception), but $\boldsymbol{\beta}_1 = \mathbf{0}$ if (7.3.1) is an ESTR model with $\theta_0 = c = 0$.

This suggests a sequence of nested tests to choose between ESTR and LSTR models. First test

$$H_{03}:\boldsymbol{\beta}_3 = \mathbf{0} \text{ in } (7.3.2) \qquad (7.3.9)$$

against its complement. Then continue by testing

$$H_{02}: \boldsymbol{\beta}_2 = \mathbf{0} | \boldsymbol{\beta}_3 = \mathbf{0} \qquad (7.3.10)$$

and finally

$$H_{01}: \boldsymbol{\beta}_1 = \mathbf{0} | \boldsymbol{\beta}_2 = \boldsymbol{\beta}_3 = \mathbf{0}. \qquad (7.3.11)$$

Comparing this sequence of F tests with (7.3.2–8) makes one conclude that accepting (7.3.9) and rejecting (7.3.10) implies selecting an ESTR model. By the same token, accepting both (7.3.9) and (7.3.10) and rejecting (7.3.11) leads to an LSTR model as well as a rejection of (7.3.9). However, things may not be quite as simple in practice because (7.3.2–8) rely on the third-order Taylor expansion and the higher-order terms are disregarded. Thus, if the true model is ESTR with $c \neq 0$ and/or $\theta_0 \neq 0$, (7.3.9) may sometimes be rejected because of these neglected terms at least if the significance level of the test is high enough and the time-series sufficiently long. However, a rejection of (7.3.9) is more likely and more often stronger for an LSTR model than for an ESTR one. It is therefore a good idea to imitate the procedure for selecting the transition variable and make the choice between ESTR and LSTR models on the basis of the p-values for the F tests of (7.3.9–11). The selection rule is as follows. If the test of (7.3.10) has the smallest p-value, proceed with the ESTR models, otherwise choose the LSTR family.

The procedure simplifies if it is assumed that the transition variable z_t is not an element of x_t. Then the LM-type test statistic based on the logistic transition function does not lose power if $\theta_0 \neq 0$ but $\tilde{\boldsymbol{\theta}} \approx \mathbf{0}$. The third-order Taylor approximation is not needed, and the auxiliary regression (7.3.2) is simply replaced by

$$\hat{u}_t = \boldsymbol{\beta}_0' x_t + \boldsymbol{\beta}_1' \mathbf{x}_t z_{tj} + \boldsymbol{\beta}_2' \mathbf{x}_t z_{tj}^2 + \delta_1 z_{tj} + \delta_2 z_{tj}^2 + \eta_t'. \qquad (7.3.12)$$

The linearity hypothesis is

$$H_0: \boldsymbol{\beta}_1 = \boldsymbol{\beta}_2 = \mathbf{0}, \ \delta_1 = \delta_2 = 0 \qquad (7.3.13)$$

against the alternative that at least one of the equalities is not correct. The choice between ESTR and LSTR models can now be based on a sequence of two nested tests. In (7.3.12),

$$\boldsymbol{\beta}_1 = g_1 \tilde{\boldsymbol{\theta}} \qquad (7.3.14)$$

$$\boldsymbol{\beta}_2 = \mathbf{0} \qquad (7.3.15)$$

$$\delta_1 = g_1 \theta_0 \qquad (7.3.16)$$

$$\delta_2 = 0 \qquad (7.3.17)$$

if the model is LSTR. If it is ESTR, we have

$$\boldsymbol{\beta}_1 = 2c\tilde{\boldsymbol{\theta}} \tag{7.3.18}$$

$$\boldsymbol{\beta}_2 = -\tilde{\boldsymbol{\theta}} \tag{7.3.19}$$

$$\delta_1 = 2c\theta_0 \tag{7.3.20}$$

$$\delta_2 = -\theta_0. \tag{7.3.21}$$

From (7.3.14–21) it is seen that the F tests of

$$H'_{02}:\boldsymbol{\beta}_2 = \mathbf{0}, \; \delta_2 = 0 \tag{7.3.22}$$

and

$$H'_{01}:\boldsymbol{\beta}_1 = \mathbf{0}, \; \delta_1 = 0 | \boldsymbol{\beta}_2 = \mathbf{0}, \; \delta_2 = 0 \tag{7.3.23}$$

in (7.3.12) are useful tests in choosing between the two model families. If the p-value for the F test of (7.3.22) is smaller than that for the corresponding test of (7.3.23) select the ESTR family; in the opposite case choose the LSTR family. A similar rule can be applied to the problem of choosing between ESTR-D and LSTR-D models.

The success of this procedure can be expected to be moderate at best if the number of possible transition variables is large and the number of observations is small. Analysing some well-known univariate time-series like sunspot numbers, different authors have fitted rather different models to the same data, each claiming success. Multivariate modelling problems are hardly simpler than univariate ones, so that uncertainty related to this or any other specification procedure is bound to be substantial.

A small Monte Carlo experiment will illustrate some of the issues here. The attention is restricted to the second stage where the transition variable is selected and the choice between STAR and STAR-D models made. Consider the following LSTR model with transition variable x_{t-1}:

$$y_t = 1 + 2x_t + x_{t-1} + 0.5x_{t-2}$$
$$- (2x_t + x_{t-1} + 0.5x_{t-2})(1 + \exp\{-4(x_{t-1} + 3)\})^{-1} + u_t$$

$$\tag{7.3.24}$$

where $x_t = \alpha x_{t-1} + v_t$, $v_t \sim \text{nid}(0, \sigma_v^2)$ such that $\text{var}(x_t) = 2.78$ ($\sigma_v^2 = 1$ if $\alpha = 0.8$), $\alpha = 0$, 0.8; $u_t \sim \text{nid}(0, \sigma_u^2)$, and $\text{cov}(u_t, v_s) = 0$, $\forall t, s$. The lower regime of (7.3.24) is a linear model with an intercept and two lags of x_t, whereas if $x_{t-1} \gg -3$, y_t is adequately described as white noise with nonzero mean: $y_t = 1 + u_t$. Model (7.3.24) is used to generate time series y_t and x_t of 100 observations, and the process is repeated 1000 times. The first 100 observations of each (u_t, v_t) process are discarded to avoid initialization effects. The linearity is tested against STR using (7.3.2) and x_t, x_{t-1}, x_{t-2} as a transition variable. It is also tested against

STR-D using (7.3.12) and $z_t = \hat{u}_{t-1}$ where $\hat{u}_t$ is the OLS residual of regressing y_t on the intercept, x_t, x_{t-1}, and x_{t-2}. If linearity is rejected, which here is taken to mean $\min p(\theta) < 0.05$ the transition variable for which $p(\theta)$ reaches its minimum is recorded. To give an idea of the 'fit' of the model j, $\hat{R}_j^2 = 1 - \sigma_u^2/\hat{\sigma}_{yj}^2$ where

$$\hat{\sigma}_{yj}^2 = (1/100) \sum_{t=1}^{100} (y_{tj} - \bar{y}_j)^2,$$

is reported as

$$\hat{\bar{R}}^2 = (1/1000) \sum_{j=1}^{1000} \hat{R}_j^2.$$

The results are in Table 7.2. Table 7.2 indicates that for model (7.3.24), the specification strategy works reasonably well already if $T = 100$; roughly two-thirds of the trials in which linearity is rejected yield the right outcome. If $\alpha = 0.8$, an STR-D model would be selected in 15–20% of the cases where linearity is rejected. This result depends on the parameterization in (7.3.24) and can hardly be generalized. An erroneous selection of the transition variable occurs roughly as often as selecting the wrong family of models. If $\alpha = 0$, the performance of the procedure improves considerably, as might be expected, as the possible transition variables are uncorrelated (but x_t, x_{t-1}, x_{t-2} have the same variance as before) and thus easier to distinguish from each other. The

TABLE 7.2. The empirical rejection frequency of linearity and the frequencies of choosing the transition variable x_t, x_{t-1}, x_{t-2}, respectively in (7.3.24) or specifying the model as a STAR-D model given linearity is rejected, based on 1000 replications of 100 observations each and $\sigma_u^2 = 0.0625, 0.25, 1$, x_t generated by $x_t = \alpha x_{t-1} + v_t$, $\mathrm{var}(x_t) = 2.78$, $\alpha = 0.8, 0$.

Error variance σ_u^2	Rejection frequency of linearity	Frequency for choosing				
		x_t	x_{t-1}	x_{t-2}	STR-D	$\hat{\bar{R}}^2$
(a) $\alpha = 0.8$						
0.0625	0.94	0.07	0.68	0.08	0.16	0.822
0.25	0.90	0.09	0.64	0.09	0.19	0.710
1	0.86	0.11	0.60	0.13	0.17	0.532
(b) $\alpha = 0$						
0.0625	0.99	0.05	0.90	0.01	0.04	0.832
0.25	0.96	0.04	0.91	0.02	0.03	0.621
1	0.93	0.05	0.93	0.01	0.02	0.336

probability of erroneously choosing STR-D also decreases compared to the case $\alpha = 0.8$.

Teräsvirta (1994) simulated both the rule for the determination of the delay parameter d and that for choosing between ESTR and LSTR families in the univariate (ESTAR and LSTAR) case. His results showed that the minimum p-value rule worked well in determining d. When it was applied to selecting between the two model families it again worked very well when the models were not close substitutes for each other. If it was possible to approximate an ESTAR model sufficiently well with an LSTAR model, then the rule understandably led to a larger number of incorrect choices. On the other hand, in such a situation making the right choice was not crucial. An ESTR model can be well approximated by an LSTR model if most of the data generated by the model lie above the value of the transition parameter c. Then only the increasing half of the transition function has practical relevance and it can be approximated by a monotonically increasing transition function of LSTR type. Conversely, an LSTR model may be approximated by an ESTR one if its transition function does not grow too rapidly in the neighbourhood of c. No ESTR model offers a reasonable approximation to LSTR models in which the transition from one extreme regime to the other is quick. Teräsvirta (1994) and Teräsvirta and Anderson (1992) contain examples of univariate series for which ESTAR and LSTAR models appear to be close substitutes.

The main attraction of the minimum p-value selection rule for deciding between ESTR and LSTR families lies in the fact that no nonlinear models need be estimated at that stage. This saves time and effort. Nevertheless, it is also possible to postpone the decision further and instead specify and fit both ESTR and LSTR models to the data. The final choice between the best-fitting ESTR and LSTR models may then be based on the results of model evaluation following the parameter estimation.

After specifying the transition variable and the model family, the remaining, and certainly not trivial, task is to specify the lag structure in (7.3.1). Auestad and Tjøstheim (1990, 1991) and Tjøstheim and Auestad (1991b) discussed a nonparametric criterion for determining the order of a general nonlinear model. A closely related approach based on cross-validation appeared in Cheng and Tong (1992). The results can also be generalized to the specification of a multivariate model, see Teräsvirta *et al.* (1994). Such a generalization might prove tedious in practice, however, if the number of candidate variables is large and the number of observations relatively small. The parametric estimation of nonlinear alternatives as such provides quite a lot of useful, if informal, information and for instance helps the model builder to consider restrictions of type $\beta_i = 0$, $\theta_j = 0$, and $\beta_i = -\theta_i$ in STR models. At this stage this is the technique we recommend. The specification could begin by the estimation of the full model and continue by imposing suitable exclusion restrictions of the three kinds just mentioned above. If the model family selected for the application provides a reasonable approximation to the data-generating process, this technique should often produce an adequate model. One could also make use of the auxiliary regression for linearity testing by finding the contributing terms of that equation, but at present there is no systematic experience about the performance of such a procedure.

Generalizations of the above models by allowing linear combinations of variables in f are possible. However, the estimation of such models may often prove very difficult unless the sample size is very large or the variables have predetermined weights. For that reason they are not discussed any further here.

7.4 Estimation of STR Models

The relevant theory needed for the statistical analysis of the estimators of the parameters in STR models is the theory derived for dynamic nonlinear models:

$$y_t = f(y_{t-1}, \ldots, y_{t-p}; x_{t1}, \ldots, x_{tk}; \boldsymbol{\theta}) + u_t, \ t = 0, \pm 1, \pm 2, \ldots.$$

Gallant (1987, ch. 7) contains a complete account of this theory. The variables $x_{t1}, \ldots, x_{tk}$ are assumed to be determined exogenously to the model and independently of the error process u_t, in which serial correlation is allowed. Gallant gives conditions for the consistency and asymptotic normality of least mean distance estimators of which non-linear least squares estimators are a special case. Some of the conditions are difficult to verify in practice, some others may be replaced by even more restrictive ones, e.g. many model builders consider the conditional mean adequately specified only if the errors are i.i.d. or even normal. In practice, the parameters of the STR models can be estimated by nonlinear least squares, and to do that, a suitable iterative optimization algorithm is needed.

The optimization problem in nonlinear least squares is conditional on the starting values $y_0, y_{-1}, \ldots, y_{-p+1}$ and consists of finding the minimum of the criterion function

$$q(\boldsymbol{\theta}) = u(\boldsymbol{\theta})'u(\boldsymbol{\theta}) = (\mathbf{y} - f(\mathbf{x}; \boldsymbol{\theta}))'(\mathbf{y} - f(\mathbf{x}; \boldsymbol{\theta})) \qquad (7.4.1)$$

with respect to the parameter vector $\boldsymbol{\theta}$. Approximating (7.4.1) with a second-order Taylor expansion about $\boldsymbol{\theta}_n$ yields

$$q(\boldsymbol{\theta}) \simeq q(\boldsymbol{\theta}_n) + \mathbf{h}_n'(\boldsymbol{\theta} - \boldsymbol{\theta}_n) + \tfrac{1}{2}(\boldsymbol{\theta} - \boldsymbol{\theta}_n)'\mathbf{H}_n(\boldsymbol{\theta} - \boldsymbol{\theta}_n) \qquad (7.4.2)$$

where the gradient evaluated at $\boldsymbol{\theta}_n$

$$\mathbf{h}_n = \mathbf{h}(\boldsymbol{\theta}_n) = \frac{\partial q(\boldsymbol{\theta}_n)}{\partial \boldsymbol{\theta}}$$

and the Hessian evaluated at $\boldsymbol{\theta}_n$

$$\mathbf{H}_n = \mathbf{H}(\boldsymbol{\theta}_n) = \frac{\partial^2 q(\boldsymbol{\theta}_n)}{\partial \boldsymbol{\theta} \partial \boldsymbol{\theta}'}.$$

The first-order conditions for the minimum obtained by differentiating (7.4.2) with respect to $\boldsymbol{\theta}$ are

$$\mathbf{h}_n + \mathbf{H}_n(\boldsymbol{\theta} - \boldsymbol{\theta}_n) = 0$$

or, assuming $\mathbf{H}_n$ to be nonsingular,

$$\boldsymbol{\theta} = \boldsymbol{\theta}_n - \mathbf{H}_n^{-1}\mathbf{h}_n. \tag{7.4.3}$$

If $q(\boldsymbol{\theta})$ is exactly quadratic (7.4.3) yields the solution directly. More generally, equation (7.4.3) forms the basis of iteration. If we have fixed $\boldsymbol{\theta}_n$ and know how to compute $\mathbf{H}_n^{-1}$ and $\mathbf{h}_n$, (7.4.3) yields a new value of $\boldsymbol{\theta}$: $\boldsymbol{\theta} = \boldsymbol{\theta}_{n+1}$, say. This value forms the starting-point of the next iteration. This is the Newton–Raphson method, see, for example, Bates and Watts (1988, sect. 3.5). The question is how to obtain the updates of $\mathbf{H}_n^{-1}$ (or $\mathbf{H}_n$) and $\mathbf{h}_n$; $\mathbf{H}_{n+1}^{-1}$ and $\mathbf{h}_{n+1}$, respectively, as straightforward computation of all partial derivatives is often very impractical. A host of methods called quasi-Newton methods have been suggested for that with various advantages and disadvantages, see for example Amemiya (1983), Judge *et al.* (1985, Appendix B), Quandt (1983), Seber and Wild (1989, sect. 2.1), or Bates and Watts (1988, sect. 3.5) for details. Another set of algorithms is based on the fact that in nonlinear least squares,

$$\mathbf{h}_n = 2\left(\frac{\partial u(\boldsymbol{\theta}_n)}{\partial \boldsymbol{\theta}}\right)' u(\boldsymbol{\theta}_n) = 2\sum_t \frac{\partial u_t(\boldsymbol{\theta}_n)}{\partial \boldsymbol{\theta}} u_t(\boldsymbol{\theta}_n) = 2\sum_t \mathbf{h}_{tn} u_t(\boldsymbol{\theta}_n)$$

and

$$\mathbf{H}_n = 2\sum_t \left(\mathbf{h}_{tn}\mathbf{h}_{tn}' + \frac{\partial^2 u_t(\boldsymbol{\theta}_n)}{\partial \boldsymbol{\theta} \partial \boldsymbol{\theta}'} u_t(\boldsymbol{\theta}_n)\right). \tag{7.4.4}$$

Ignoring the second terms in (7.4.4) as negligible compared to the first ones we have

$$\boldsymbol{\theta} - \boldsymbol{\theta}_n = \left[\sum_t \mathbf{h}_{tn}\mathbf{h}_{tn}'\right]^{-1} \sum_t \mathbf{h}_{tn} u_t(\boldsymbol{\theta}_n).$$

This suggests that an improvement to $\boldsymbol{\theta}_n$ is obtained by regressing the first derivatives $\mathbf{h}_{tn}$ on the residuals $u_t(\boldsymbol{\theta}_n)$. This is called the Gauss method, and it avoids the computation of the second derivatives altogether. It also has several modifications and generalizations (see for example the references mentioned above).

There are further methods requiring no computation of derivatives. Perhaps the one most frequently used is the conjugate gradient method of Powell (1964). A discussion of this technique can be found for example in Quandt (1983).

Modern statistical software packages contain a variety of algorithms based on the above ideas and often even a possibility to switch from one to the other during the estimation. They also contain built-in stopping rules for ending the iteration when the algorithm has advanced appreciably close to a minimum value. This need not be a global minimum, however, and sometimes several estimations using different sets of starting-values have to be carried out to make sure that a global instead of just a local minimum is found. If convergence is very slow, a grid search in one dimension may sometimes help locate the area where the global minimum can be found.

In the estimation of LSTR models estimating the slope parameter γ in the transition function sometimes causes problems. There is some univariate simulation evidence in Chan and Tong (1986) and Luukkonen (1990) indicating that on the average γ is overestimated in small samples. A more serious worry is that while all the other iterative parameter estimates converge rapidly, $\hat{\gamma}_n$ may do so very slowly. This is often the case if the true parameter is relatively large. The reason is that a large set of γ-values then exist yielding almost the same F. The transition functions corresponding to these γ-values deviate noticeably from each other only in a small neighbourhood of the transition value c. Thus a large number of observations of the transition variable would be needed in that neighbourhood to estimate γ reasonably accurately—see Bates and Watts (1988: 87) and Seber and Wild (1989: 480–1). When γ is large, rescaling it becomes important. Even when the algorithm converges, computing the Hessian is difficult if the elements of the gradient vector are not of the same size. This is the case if γ is considerably larger than any other parameter. Note, however, that the standard deviation estimate of $\hat{\gamma}$ may be sensitive to this rescaling and even to the initial values, which only reflects the uncertainty in estimating γ (and c) if γ is large. A useful idea of what 'large' means here may be obtained by rescaling the argument of F by dividing by $\hat{\sigma}(z_t)$, the standard deviation of the transition variable, and estimating γ in

$$F(z_t) = (1 + \exp\{-\gamma(z_t - c)/\hat{\sigma}(z_t)\})^{-1}.$$

This rescaling is recommended also because it makes the choice of a starting-value for γ easier.

The corresponding standardization in ESTR models consists of using

$$F(z_t) = 1 - \exp\{-\gamma(z_t - c)^2/\hat{\sigma}^2(z_t)\} \qquad (7.4.5)$$

as the scaled transition function. The experience gained so far indicates that $\gamma = 1$ often is a reasonable starting value for iterative nonlinear least squares estimation if F is scaled as in (7.4.5). Straightforward estimation of an ESTR model may be expected to succeed if the model is well specified. If the specification is not adequate, estimating γ may pose problems. Therefore it may be reasonable to keep γ fixed during the specification stage which may involve estimating several ESTR models. Choosing $\gamma = 1$ is often a workable solution. Because the other parameter estimates generally are not very sensible to this choice, fixing γ this way should not be an obstacle to the specification of the dynamic structure of ESTR models. If, however, the final estimation of the model does not lead to an acceptable solution, γ may be estimated using a grid.

At the outset of the specification of the dynamics the ESTR model may often be overparameterized. The estimation of its parameters is likely to reveal this in various ways. Some parameters may be driven to very large or small values during the estimation or pairs of them may move together. This may happen even when γ is fixed. Simplification of the model should then be considered as Bates and Watts (1988: 87) discussed.

7.5 Specification and Estimation of Bilinear Models

In Section 6.2.3 it was pointed out that bilinear and STR-D models are locally equivalent, and in the preceding section the specification of these models was discussed together with other STR models. If, however, there is economic theory or other information suggesting the use of a bilinear model as in Howitt (1988), a specification strategy is needed. A simple one is provided by the auxiliary regression of the LM test (see Section 6.2.3). Let that be the maintained model and remove the redundant bilinear terms by using an appropriate model-selection criterion like AIC. Estimate the selected small model.

Estimation of bilinear models is considered for instance in Subba Rao and Gabr (1984, sect. 5.8). The authors propose a Newton–Raphson algorithm like (7.4.3) to obtain parameter estimates. The difficulty is that the partial derivatives needed for computing (7.4.3) have to be computed recursively because the model contains lagged error terms. To alleviate the computational burden, Subba Rao and Gabr (1984, sect. 5.10) in fact applied the Gauss method, i.e. ignored the second terms in (7.4.4) when computing the Hessian.

A computationally less demanding alternative is to adopt the technique Hannan and Rissanen (1982) proposed for estimating linear ARMA models. First estimate the parameters of a long autoregression by OLS and call the residuals $e_t^{(0)}$. Insert them into the bilinear model

$$y_t = \sum_{j=1}^{p} \pi_j y_{t-j} + e_t^{(r-1)} + \sum_{i=1}^{k} \sum_{j=1}^{m} \phi_{ij} y_{t-j} e_t^{(r-1)} + \varepsilon_t^{(r)} \qquad (7.5.1)$$

($r = 1$) and estimate the parameters. The estimates $e_t^{(1)}$ of $\varepsilon_t^{(1)}$ are inserted into (7.5.1) and the parameters re-estimated ($r = 2$). Iteration is continued to convergence. This simple technique seems to work well if the parameter vector is not near the noninvertibility region. If the model is nearly noninvertible, the algorithm is in trouble.

7.6 Estimation of Neural Network Models

The neural network model was defined in (7.1.3). In this discussion we follow White (1989b) in assuming that the squashing function ϕ is logistic: $\phi(z) = (1 + \exp\{-z\})^{-1}$. Model (7.1.3) is not globally identified as its parameters are exchangeable. Consider $q = 2$ in (7.1.3) which then can be written as

$$y_t = \alpha + \beta_1 \phi(\gamma_1' z_t) + \beta_2 \phi(\gamma_2' z_t) + u_t. \qquad (7.6.1)$$

In (7.6.1), parameter vector $(\beta_1, \gamma_1')'$ can be exchanged with parameters $(\beta_2, \gamma_2')'$ without any effect on y_t, hence these parameters are exchangeable. This is bound to create numerical problems for parameter estimation with techniques described in Section 7.4. Bates and Watts (1988: 78) discussed how to avoid them by transformation. A vector γ_j with large values may cause problems similar to those discussed in connection with the estimation of LSTR models. A simpler and obviously more robust technique is the 'on-line' recursive learning or back-propagation, see White (1989b). It is based on a method called stochastic approximation. If $\tilde{\theta}_T$ is the estimator of $\theta = (\beta_1, \ldots, \beta_q, \gamma_1', \ldots, \gamma_q')'$ after using T observations then the next learning step is defined by

$$\tilde{\theta}_{T+1} = \tilde{\theta}_T + \eta_{T+1} \nabla \tilde{f}_{T+1} (y_{T+1} - \tilde{f}_{T+1}) \qquad (7.6.2)$$

where η_{T+1} is the learning or convergence rate,

$$\tilde{f}_T = f_T(z_T, \tilde{\theta}_{T-1}), \quad \nabla \tilde{f}_T = \left[\frac{\partial}{\partial \theta} f(z_T, \theta) \right]_{\theta = \tilde{\theta}_{T-1}}, \quad \text{and}$$

$$f_T(z_T, \theta) = \sum_{j=1}^{q} \beta_j \phi(\gamma_j' z_T).$$

The learning rate may be constant, $\eta_T \equiv \eta$, $\forall T$, or declining, $\eta_T \propto T^{-1}$ (other declining rates are also possible); for discussion see White (1989b). White showed that under certain conditions, assuming among other things that $\{y_t, \mathbf{z}_t\}$ is a sequence of i.i.d. random vectors and that the learning rate is declining, the sequence $\tilde{\boldsymbol{\theta}}_T$ either converges to a local minimum of $(\mathbf{y} - f(\mathbf{Z}, \boldsymbol{\theta}))'(\mathbf{y} - f(\mathbf{Z}, \boldsymbol{\theta}))$ with probability 1 or $\tilde{\boldsymbol{\theta}}_T \to \infty$ with probability 1. Which local minimum $\tilde{\boldsymbol{\theta}}_T$ converges to depends on the starting-values of the algorithm. A common suggestion has been to carry out the estimation several times from different sets of starting-values. This is advisable as in practice several local minima often exist.

A rather large sample may be required to attain convergence if the data are only used once. Another way to proceed is to do it 'off-line' and resample by bootstrapping (see White 1992). Observation vectors $\{y_t, \mathbf{z}_t\}$ are drawn independently with replacement from the data-set and the updating step (7.6.2) is carried out for each draw. This technique sets no limit to the number of steps. Not much is known about the convergence properties of back-propagation in addition to the theoretical result briefly mentioned above but the algorithm may not be very efficient. White (1989b, 1992) recommended back-propagation for obtaining initial values for subsequent Newton–Raphson nonlinear least squares iteration.

White (1989b) contains an example in which 4000 data points are generated by the Hénon map (e.g. Thompson and Stewart 1986: 177–83)

$$y_t = 1 - 1.4y_{t-1}^2 + 0.3y_{t-2}. \tag{7.6.3}$$

White considered the neural network model (7.1.3) with $\phi(\boldsymbol{\gamma}_j'\mathbf{z}_t)$ being the logistic function, $\mathbf{z}_t = (1, y_{t-1}, y_{t-2})'$ and $q = 5$. Then five realizations using 4000 values of $\mathbf{z}_t$ drawn randomly with replacement from the original data yielded coefficients of determination for the neural network approximation in the range of $[0.9597, 0.9993]$ for back propagation. The fit in the last experiment ($\hat{R}^2 = 0.9925$) improved to $\hat{R}^2 = 0.9984$ as back-propagation with declining learning rate was followed by nonlinear least squares using a Newton–Raphson algorithm.

As a curiosity, note that modelling a time-series of length T generated by (7.6.3), assuming that it can have been generated by a STAR model, leads to a recovery of (7.6.3). Consider a time-series generated by (7.6.3). Selecting a linear AR model to represent the data by AIC most frequently yields an AR(6) model. Linearity testing against STAR based on this model when y_{t-1} is the assumed transition variable leads to an auxiliary regression with perfect fit because 1, y_{t-1}^2 and y_{t-2} appearing in (7.6.3) are also present in the auxiliary regression. Thus the investigator is able to conclude that the data were generated by (7.6.3) and no further steps are necessary.

7.7 Evaluation of Estimated Nonlinear Models

7.7.1 STR models

After an STR model has been estimated, its properties have to be evaluated. A first check is to ensure that the parameter estimates seem reasonable. If the model is not well specified, the estimation procedure may easily converge to a point which in the light of the application is not sensible. For instance, $\hat{c}$ well outside the range of the transition variable indicates misspecification.

If this judgemental check does not indicate problems, the next step is to examine the errors. It is assumed here that the model builder wants to describe the dynamics in such a way that no structure is left in the error term. The residuals have therefore to be checked for autocorrelation. They can also be tested against ARCH as discussed in Chapter 6 and departures from normality using for instance the test suggested by Lomnicki (1961) and Jarque and Bera (1980) or some other test; see for example Spanos (1986, ch. 21). A failure to pass these tests may indicate misspecification. However, the rejection of normality is usually an indication of the presence of outliers among the residuals, and some outliers may have a natural explanation; see for example Teräsvirta and Anderson (1992) for discussion and examples.

The linearity of the error process may be tested against STR to see if the model provides an adequate description of the nonlinearity it was built to capture. Even if there appears to be no error autocorrelation, an AR model has to be used as the basis of the test.

In univariate models, it is of interest to study the dynamic properties of the model, and the same is true in the multivariate case if the model contains lags of the dependent variable. For instance, if the model is the following LSTAR(2) model

$$y_t = \pi_1 y_{t-1} + \pi_2 y_{t-2} + \theta_1 (1 + \exp\{-\gamma(y_{t-1} - c)\})^{-1} y_{t-1} + u_t$$

$$(7.7.1)$$

then we shall compute the roots of the characteristic polynomials corresponding to $F = 0$

$$z^2 - \pi_1 z - \pi_2 = 0$$

and

$$z^2 - (\pi_1 + \theta_1)z - \pi_2 = 0$$

corresponding to $F = 1$. This gives an idea of the local dynamic behaviour of the model in the extreme regimes and helps to understand the functioning of the dynamics. The roots can also be computed for other values of F than zero or one; for instance $F = 1/2$ may be an interesting value if γ is not very large.

Evaluating the long-run dynamic properties of the model is an important diagnostic check. In our example, this amounts to solving the equation

$$z - \pi_1 z - \pi_2 z - \theta_1(1 + \exp\{-\gamma(z - c)\})^{-1} z = 0,$$

see (1.6.5). It cannot be done analytically, so that a numerical solution has to be attempted. We can generate data from (7.7.1) setting the noise $\{u_t\}$ equal to zero and observe the realization. It may converge to a single point which is called the stable equilibrium as in Section 1.6 or the unique stable singular point (see Ozaki 1985). Alternatively, it may display a limit cycle (a set of values repeating themselves for ever) or diverge. In the latter case the model must be rejected as inadequate. Another possibility is that the model generates chaotic realizations, i.e. a small change in the initial values makes the realization diverge from the previous one but the realizations themselves do not diverge. Combinations are possible: a large set of starting values may lead to convergence to a stable singular point, whereas some others create chaotic cycles. Teräsvirta and Anderson (1992) have examples of this. In the multivariate case the same exercise can be repeated after first setting the exogenous variables and their lags to their sample means. (It is assumed that the transition variable is a lagged dependent variable.) By doing this it is implicitly assumed that there is no feedback from the output to these variables. Again, divergence implies rejection of the estimated model. Examples of the use of diagnostic checks are found in Chapter 9.

The estimated model can also be used for forecasting, and comparisons should be made with the forecasts from the corresponding linear model. However, such a comparison may not always be informative. If the nonlinear feature in the data is not present during the prediction period then the nonlinear model cannot be expected to generate more accurate forecasts than the linear one. The check will therefore be negative: if the nonlinear model performs significantly *worse* than the linear one, the specification should be reconsidered. Forecasting with nonlinear models will be discussed in Chapter 8.

7.7.2 Bilinear Models

The residuals of an estimated bilinear model may be subjected to the same tests as those of an STR model. A linearity test may be conducted against bilinearity. A bilinear model has the same long-term solution as an AR model because each bilinear term contains a noise component, so that in the long run these terms lose their significance. One of the consequences of this is that a univariate bilinear model cannot have a limit cycle as its solution.

Because the bilinear model contains lagged errors, checking the invertibility of the model is important. Analytical invertibility conditions are hard to derive if the model is not sufficiently simple; see for example Subba Rao and Gabr (1984, sect. 5.5). The invertibility therefore has to be checked numerically. Only invertible models can be used for forecasting; out-of-sample forecasting of course remains a useful evaluation technique. However, bilinear models are often used for describing processes with occasional strong perturbances. They hardly forecast any better than a linear model if the prediction period does not contain such a perturbance. Maravall (1983) has a good discussion of this point.

8

Forecasting, Aggregation, and Nonsymmetry

Preamble

In this chapter three separate but important topics are discussed. One of the major uses for time-series models is to produce forecasts and nonlinear models have particular difficulties in doing this, especially for several steps ahead. Alternative ways of producing multi-step forecasts are discussed and the possibility of combining forecasts is also considered.

Many observed economic series are actually aggregates over many components—national consumption is the sum of consumption of millions of families, for example. It is shown that nonlinearity in relationships can decrease with aggregation. Series are also often observed at longer periods than those at which they are generated, which is known as temporal aggregation. It is shown that nonlinearity can also be reduced by temporal aggregation.

Nonlinearity is an old topic in business cycle literature where the issue originally was possible asymmetry of business cycles: recessions were thought of as being shorter but more severe than expansions. The interest in the topic has been revised recently, and various approaches have been tried in the empirical investigations of the problem. Some of the recent approaches to nonsymmetry or, more generally, nonlinearity of business cycles are considered. In these, testing linearity of series against nonlinearity has a prominent position but nonlinear modelling of business cycles has also received attention.

8.1 Forecasting from Nonlinear Models

Some of the methods available for forecasting from a nonlinear model can be illustrated by using a simple bivariate model,

$$y_t = g(x_{t-1}) + \varepsilon_t \qquad (8.1.1)$$

for example

$$y_t = x_{t-1}^2 + \varepsilon_t \qquad (8.1.2)$$

where x_t is AR(1), say, where, for the moment ε_t is taken to be zero-mean, independent, and identically distributed. Using a least-squares criterion, the optimal one-step forecast is

$$f_{t,1}^y = E[y_{t+1}|I_t] = g(x_t) \tag{8.1.3}$$

where $I_t{:}x_{t-j},\ y_{t-j},\ j \geqslant 1$ is the information set available at time t. ((8.1.3) follows because $E[\varepsilon_{t+1}|I_t] = 0$). Thus, if one knows $g(\ )$, or has an acceptable approximation for it, one-step forecasts can be achieved with no difficulty.

The two-step case is not as easy. The optimum two-step forecast is

$$f_{t,2}^y = E[y_{t+2}|I_t] = E[g(x_{t+1})|I_t]. \tag{8.1.4}$$

As x_{t+1} is not usually known at time t, it is necessary to specify the generating mechanism for x_t. Suppose that a good approximation to this mechanism is available and, for ease of illustration, let this be the AR(1) model

$$x_t = \alpha x_{t-1} + e_t \tag{8.1.5}$$

where e_t is taken to be i.i.d. with zero mean and distribution D. This gives a one-step OLS forecast

$$f_{t,1}^x = \alpha x_t.$$

Four alternative two-step forecasts using (8.1.4) in the form

$$f_{t,2}^y = E[g(f_{t,1}^x + e_{t+1})|I_t] \tag{8.1.6}$$

are:

    (i) naïve $\qquad\qquad fn_{t,2}^y = g(f_{t,1}^x)$

so that the presence of e_{t+1} in (8.1.6) is ignored by putting its value to zero.

    (ii) exact $\qquad\qquad fe_{t,2}^y = \int_{-\infty}^{\infty} g(f_{t,1}^x + z)d\Phi(z)$

where $\Phi(z)$ is the distribution function of D. Thus, if e_t is $N(0, \sigma^2)$, then $\Phi(z)$ is the normal distribution function with mean zero. The integral will have to be determined at each time-point, by numerical integration, say, or from a comprehensive table of values.

    (iii) Monte Carlo $\quad fm_{t,2}^y = \dfrac{1}{N}\sum_{j=1}^{N} g(f_{t,1}^x + z_j)$

where z_j, $j = 1, \ldots, N$ are random numbers drawn from the distribution D. For N large enough, fm and fe should be virtually identical.

    (iv) bootstrap $\quad fb_{t,2}^y = \dfrac{1}{n-1}\sum_{j=1}^{n-1} g(f_{t,1}^x + e_j)$

where e_j, $j = 1, \ldots, n - 1$ are the $n - 1$ values of the residual e_t observed from (8.1.5) over the sample period.

For the particular model (8.1.2), the four fourcasts will be, effectively

$$fn_{t,2} = \alpha^2 x_t^2$$

$$fe_{t,2} \simeq fm_{t,2} = \alpha^2 x_t^2 + \sigma_e^2$$

$$\text{and } fb_{t,2} = \alpha^2 x_t^2 + \hat{\sigma}_e^2$$

(assuming $\dfrac{1}{n} \displaystyle\sum_{j=1}^{n} e_j$ is near zero).

In practice the function $g(\ )$ is not known and has to be specified and estimated by the techniques discussed in the previous chapters. Thus g has to be replaced by $\hat{g}$ in the four forecasts above. One further forecasting method can be considered:

(v) direct $y_{t+2} = \hat{g}_2(x_t) + e_{t,2}$ or

$y_{t+2} = \hat{g}(x_t, y_t) + e_{t,2}^*$ so that

$fd_{t,2} = \hat{g}(x_t)$,   say

so that the relationships between y_{t+2} and the contents of I_t is modelled directly. A difficulty is that $e_{t,2}$ is not usually a white noise, but has temporal relationships.

For the forecasts from (8.1.2), α^2 is now replaced by $(\hat{\alpha}^2)$, so that

$$fn_{t,2} = (\hat{\alpha})^2 x_t^2, \quad \text{for example}$$

and

$$fd_{t,2} = (\hat{\alpha}^2) x_t^2$$

The five forecasts are quite different and have advantages and disadvantages. The naïve forecast is easy to use but will usually be biased because generally $E[f(\varepsilon)] \neq f[(E\varepsilon)]$. The exact method is computationally complicated and it, and the Monte Carlo forecast, can be biased if an incorrect distribution D is selected, but otherwise should be the best techniques. The bootstrap is both fairly easy to use and should have good properties if $\hat{g}$ is a good approximation to g, but otherwise may be badly biased. The direct method is fairly easy to use but it does involve building a new model for each forecasting horizon.

One other technique is sometimes considered in economics, when x_t is viewed as completely exogenous and potentially x_{t+1} is known at time t. An example is a tax rate set by a governmnet or a price of some good set by a corporation. If applicable, these forecasts should be superior to the others, but are not usually available.

The techniques can clearly be used for multi-step forecasts although some quickly become extremely complex. For example the exact three-step forecast is

$$f_{t,3}^y = E[g(g(f_{t,z}^x + e_{t+2}) + e_{t+3})|I_t].$$

The naïve forecast just ignores e, but the exact forecast now involves a double integral, and the Monte Carlo requires draws from a bivariate distribution, but with independent components. The recommended bootstrap forecast is

$$f_{t,3}^y = \frac{1}{n-2} \sum_{j=1}^{n-2} g(g(f_{t,2}^x + e_j) + e_{j+1})$$

so that the order of the observed residuals is retained, in case the assumption of independence between them is incorrect. As before, if D is well known, the exact and Monte Carlo methods will be the best, but otherwise the bootstrap or possibly the direct forecast is preferred.

Further difficulties arise for all but the naïve method if e_t is heteroskedastic; but this will not be explicitly discussed here. The methods can all be generalized in a fairly straightforward manner to the case where x_t is a vector, possibly including y_t and lags.

The large-sample properties of most of these factors have been discussed by Brown and Mariano (1984, 1989). They consider parametric models for $g(\ )$, where the function is correctly specified but some parameter θ has to be estimated, by maximum likelihood or some asymptotically equivalent method. They show that the naïve forecast is $O(1)$ and thus asymptotically biased, whereas the exact and bootstrap forecasts have bias $O(1/n)$, where n is sample size. Further, the mean squared error for all the methods is $O(1)$. Lin (1991) has found similar results for a nonparametric, kernel estimator with a window h_n that is $o(n^{-1/5})$, although now the bootstrap forecast has bias $O(n^{-2/5})$.

Lin also conducted a simulation study to investigate the comparative performance of these methods for one- and two-step forecast horizons. Data was generated by a first-order LSTAR model:

$$y_t = \pi_0 + \pi_1 y_{t-1} + \theta y_{t-1}(1 + \exp(-\gamma y_{t-1}))^{-1} + \varepsilon_t \qquad (8.1.7)$$

with $\pi_0 = 0$, $\pi_1 = 0.8$, $\theta = -0.8$, and $\gamma = 10$, and where ε_t is a $N(0, 1)$ i.i.d. series. Three methods of estimating the functional relationship were used: (i) 'parametric' in which the correct specification is assumed known, with the five parameters in the STAR model estimated by nonlinear least squares (a search process in the program MIMPACK); (ii) a nonparametric kernel estimator, using the normal cumulative distribution function and windows $h_n = (\frac{4}{3})^{1/5} n^{-1/5} \sigma$; and (iii) a neural network model, with a single hidden unit which is the logistic function so $y_t = 1 + \beta\phi(y_{t-1})$ where $\phi(x) = (1 + \exp(\gamma_0 + \gamma_1 x))^{-1}$.

In each of 200 replications, 700 terms of the series were generated, the first 200 dropped, the next 300 used to estimate the model, and the final 200 used to evaluate one- and two-step forecasts. The basic results are shown in Table 8.1.

For this particular model, and another considered by Granger and Lin (1991) but not reported here, it was found that the kernel-based one-step forecast was nearly as good as the correctly specified, but estimated, model and the kernel bootstrap was the best of the two-step forecasts when the correct specification was not known. Here, the direct two-step forecasts assumed the same STAR model as was used to generate the data, but now relating y_{t+2} to y_t. This is clearly a misspecification.

Some examples of the use of nonlinear models to make forecasts are given in Chapter 9.

In most circumstances there are several possible models that can be used to make forecasts and it follows that in some cases a superior forecast can be achieved by combining forecasts. Let the two models produce one-step forecasts $f_{t,1}^{(1)}$, $f_{t,1}^{(2)}$ made at time t of a variable Y_{t+1}. One method of combining is to run a regression

$$Y_{t+1} = m + \alpha_1 f_{t,1}^{(1)} + \alpha_2 f_{t,1}^{(2)} + \alpha_3 Y_t + \text{error}$$

and the combined forecast consists of the right-hand side, except for the error term, using the estimated coefficients. This and other combinations are discussed in the special issue on combining forecasts of the *Journal of Forecasting*, 8/3 (July 1989).

The procedure can be generalized by considering nonlinear combinations. In Deutsch, Granger, and Teräsvirta (1991) combinations are considered of the form

$$\text{combined forecast} = a_1 f_{t,1}^{(1)} + a_2 f_{t,1}^{(2)} \quad \text{if } I$$
$$= a_3 f_{t,1}^{(1)} + a_4 f_{t,1}^{(2)} \quad \text{if not } I$$

TABLE 8.1.   Forecast bias and mean squared error, model (8.1.1)

Period and forecast	Parametric		Kernel		Neural network	
	Bias	MSE	Bias	MSE	Bias	MSE
1-forecast	.008	1.004	.0159	1.025	−.010	1.076
2-naïve	.172	1.445	.1396	1.442	.003	1.491
2-exact	.014	1.402	.0237	1.424	−.018	1.484
2-bootstrap	.006	1.401	.0255	1.424	−.014	1.456
2-direct	.091	1.433	.0094	1.430	−.018	1.457

where I is some event known at time $t - 1$. The difficult question is how to choose the event I; it may be that some economic variable is positive, or some function of the previous forecast errors is positive, for example. In Deutsch *et al.*, the technique was applied to forecasts from two models of inflation, one a 'monetarist' and the other a 'mark-up pricing' model. The models were estimated, and the combining parameters also selected, using thirty pieces of quarterly data for the period 1969 to 1976, and forecasts evaluated over the following eleven quarters, ending in early 1987. Merely to illustrate the kind of results achieved, the following post-sample sum squared forecast errors were found:

Forecast	Sum squared errors
$f^{(1)}$	155
$f^{(2)}$	93
$f^{(1)}, f^{(2)}$ linearly combined	46
nonlinear comb., $I:e^{(1)}_{t-1,1} > 0$	27
nonlinear comb., $I:w_t > 0$	39

where $e_t^{(1)} = \text{inflation}_t - f^{(1)}_{t-1}$ and $w_t = $ change in the unemployment rate. Overall, the results were not as encouraging as those shown here; some nonlinear combinations did poorly compared to linear ones and it was difficult to decide from the in-sample evidence which particular combination would be superior out-of-sample. Nevertheless, the approach does seem to be promising.

8.2 The Effects of Aggregation and Nonlinearity

Many economic series are seen after aggregation of some form has occurred. If the preaggregated series are nonlinear, the obvious question arises—will this nonlinearity be maintained after aggregation? It should be noted that there are several different types of aggregation:

(*a*) *Cross-sectional*. Here, the original data consist of several series, for each component of an economy, which are summed to form the macro or aggregate variable. For example, aggregate consumption for Texas is the sum of the consumption series for all the individual (or family) consumers living in that state. There may be many individual components—for example aggregate consumption in the USA is the sum of the consumption for about eighty million families; or aggregate profits are for about a million separate firms. This may be thought of as 'cross-section aggregation in the large'. On some occasions aggregation is over components which are already aggregates, for example US consumption is the sum of consumption for the fifty states. This could be called cross-sectional aggregation in the small.

(*b*) *Systematic sampling*. If a series is generated as one time-interval, but only observed over longer time-periods, the original series is said to be systematically sampled to get to the observed series.

(*c*) *Temporal aggregation*. If the original series is generated weekly, say, and is summed to form a monthly series, then it can be said to be temporally aggregated. For example, monthly automobile production is the sum of the daily productions for that month.

Clearly systematic sampling occurs with stock data, such as prices, and inventory levels, whereas temporal aggregation occurs with flow data, such as production, consumption, and imports. There is a substantial literature on the effects of the various types of aggregation on linear systems. A survey is given in Granger (1990); other references include Granger (1987) on cross-sectional aggregation and Weiss (1984) on temporal aggregation and systematic sampling. The results reported here are based on the simulations in Granger and Lee (1993). There is little theory for nonlinear processes, but it is possible to get some useful results for cross-sectional aggregation of bilinear models.

Consider a bilinear model for a series y_{jt} generated by

$$y_{jt} = \alpha y_{j,t-2}\varepsilon_{j,t-1} + \varepsilon_{jt} \qquad (8.2.1)$$

where $j = 1, \ldots, N$. For example y_{jt} may be the savings of the jth family at time t. ε_{jt} is a zero mean, white noise with decomposition

$$\varepsilon_{jt} = e_t + u_{jt}$$

where e_t, u_{jt} are independent and u_{jt}, u_{kt} are independent for all j, k. If ε_{jt} is viewed as the shock to the jth family, this has a shock component e_t common to all families; the common factor, plus an innovation u_{jt} individual to that family. Substituting into (8.2.1) and aggregating over j gives

$$Sy_t = \alpha e_t Sy_{t-2} + Ne_t + \alpha \sum_{j=1}^{N} y_{j,t-2}u_{j,t-1} + \sum_{j=1}^{N} u_{jt} \qquad (8.2.2)$$

where the notation $Sy_t = \sum_{j=1}^{N} y_{jt}$ is used. The last two terms are sums of uncorrelated components and so will have variance $O(N)$ whereas the term Ne_t has variance $O(N^2)$ and so for N large this latter term will dominate. In this case (8.2.2) will be well approximated by

$$Sy_t = \alpha e_t Sy_{t-2} + Ne_t \qquad (8.2.3)$$

and so the aggregate series will still follow a bilinear model to a close approximation. However, if $e_t \equiv 0$, so that there is no common factor the first two terms in (8.2.2) will be absent and there will generally be little or no correlation between terms like $\sum_j y_{j,t-2} u_{j,t-1}$, and powers of Sy_{t-2} or products $Sy_{t-2} Su_{t-1}$, and so little or no nonlinearity will remain in the aggregate.

This theoretical exercise illustrates the importance of the relatedness of the shocks or innovations across the components. Here just a simple form of relatedness has been considered. The analysis can possibly be extended to a few other simple nonlinear models. However, simulations can also be helpful. Those reported here take the following form

   (i) generate a series by some nonlinear model;
   (ii) from these, generate aggregate series;
   (iii) apply some test of linearity to both the original and the aggregate series to the percentage of times the test detects evidence of nonlinearity. It should be noted that these tests do not look for a specific type of nonlinearity, and that aggregation does not necessarily result in the same form of nonlinearity as was in the originally generated series. Granger and Lee (1993) used four different tests, but here the results are reported just for the neural network test of White (1989a), which was described and evaluated in Section 6.3.3. To investigate the effects of cross-sectional aggregation, both univariate and bivariate data-series were generated.

The univariate models were:

(a) Bilinear

$$y_{jt} = \alpha y_{j,t-1} \varepsilon_{j,t-2} + \varepsilon_{jt}$$

with $\alpha = 0.7$.

(b) Threshold Autoregressive (TAR)

$$y_{jt} = \alpha_1 y_{j,t-1} + \varepsilon_{jt} \quad |y_{j,t-1}| \leqslant 1$$
$$= \alpha_2 y_{j,t-1} + \varepsilon_{jt} \quad |y_{j,t-1}| \geqslant 1$$

where $\alpha_1 = 0.9$, $\alpha_2 = -0.3$.

(c) Sign Nonlinear Autoregressive (SGN)

$$y_{jt} = \alpha \operatorname{sgn}(y_{j,t-1}) + \varepsilon_{jt}$$

where

$$\operatorname{sgn}(x) = \begin{cases} 1 & \text{if } x > 0 \\ 0 & \text{if } x = 0 \\ -1 & \text{if } x < 0 \end{cases}$$

and $\alpha = 1$.

(d) Rational Nonlinear Autoregressive (NAR)

$$y_{jt} = \frac{\alpha|y_{j,t-1}|}{|y_{j,t-1}| + 2} + \varepsilon_{jt}$$

with $\alpha = 0.7$.

These series were generated for $t = 1, \ldots, n$ and $j = 1, \ldots, m$, so that n is the sample size and m the extent of the aggregation. The values used are $n = 200$, $m = 1$ (no aggregation), and $m = 20$. The input innovation had three forms, with

$$\text{var}(\varepsilon_{jt}) = 1 \quad \text{all } j$$

and

$$\varepsilon_{jt} = e_t + \eta_{jt}$$

where e_t, η_{jt} are independent, all j, and η_{jt}, η_{kt} are independent for all k, j, and e_t, η_{jt} are always normally distributed with zero mean. The three cases considered are

(i)   var $e_t = 0$ so that var $\eta_{jt} = 1$
(ii) var $e_t = 0.5$ so that var $\eta_{jt} = 0.5$
(iii) var $e_t = 0.9$ so that var $\eta_{jt} = 0.1$.

Thus in case (i) there is no common factor and in cases (ii) and (iii) the common factor exists and is of different level of importance.

The bivariate models take the form

$$y_{jt} = g(x_{jt}) + a_{jt}$$

where $x_{jt} = 0.6x_{j,t-1} + \varepsilon_{jt}$; $a_{jt} \sim N(0, \sigma^2)$; a_{jt}, ε_{jt} are independent and ε_{jt} has the three cases as above. Thus any common factor for the y_{jt} comes through the x_{jt}. Four values of σ are used, $\sigma = 1, 5, 10$, and 20 giving different signal–noise ratios. It is then assumed that both x and y (or their aggregates) are observed, and suitably expanded versions of the tests are used as discussed above. Two forms of $g(x)$ are used, x^2 and $\exp(x)$.

It is assumed that the only quantities observed are

$$S_m y_t = \sum_{j=1}^{m} y_{jt}$$

and equivalently $S_m x_t$, where either $m = 1$ or 20 in the simulation. 100 replications were used in all cases.

Table 8.2 shows a typical set of results, using the neural network test, 5% critical values, and sample size 200. The values shown are the per cent of times that a null hypothesis of linearity is rejected, using the

TABLE 8.2.   Effects of cross-sectional aggregation: neural network test (5%)

Model	case(i) $m = 1$	case(i) $m = 20$	case(ii) $m = 20$	case(iii) $m = 20$
Bilinear	59	19	40	50
	(59)	(16)	(37)	(46)
TAR	59	19	40	50
	(59)	(16)	(37)	(46)
SGN	100	9	20	81
	(99)	(16)	(37)	(46)
NAR	21	7	11	18
	(19)	(6)	(9)	(16)
Square				
$\sigma = 1$	100	68	100	100
	(100)	(67)	(100)	(100)
$\sigma = 5$	100	20	100	100
	(100)	(25)	(100)	(100)
$\sigma = 10$	78	12	100	100
	(78)	(10)	(100)	(100)
$\sigma = 20$	30	8	91	100
	(29)	(8)	(90)	(100)
Exp				
$\sigma = 1$	100	44	100	100
	(100)	(43)	(100)	(100)
$\sigma = 5$	96	24	100	100
	(96)	(22)	(100)	(100)
$\sigma = 10$	80	11	99	100
	(78)	(9)	(99)	(100)
$\sigma = 20$	35	6	88	99
	(33)	(5)	(87)	(98)

Notes: Power(%) using 5% critical value simulated with AR(1) are shown. Power(%) using 5% asymptotic critical value are shown in ( ). Sample size 200, replication 100. The power of the tests seem to be respectable even with a signal–noise ratio of 2% or less.

Source: Granger and Lee (1993).

simulated critical values (results using the theoretical asymptotical critical values are shown in brackets). The first column shows the case of no aggregation, $m = 1$ and here common factors are irrelevant, so the figures just illustrate the power of the neural network test against the various nonlinear models. For the four univariate models the power seems to vary considerably, being low for the nonlinear autoregressive but very high for the sign nonlinear autoregressive models. When applied to the bivariate series, the power is excellent for the higher signal–noise ratios but naturally declines as this ratio gets smaller. For these two bivariate cases, the signal to noise ratio $\text{var}(g(x))/\sigma^2$ is

σ:	1	5	10	20
$\text{var}(x^2)/\sigma^2$	7.0	.28	.07	.019
$\text{var}(\exp(x))/\sigma^2$	2.16	.086	.021	.005

The second column shows similar results when aggregation over 20 micro-units occurs and there is no common factor. In all cases the tests find nonlinearity less often, as suggested by the theory. The final two columns are with aggregation and different levels of common factor presence. As expected, more nonlinearity is found with aggregation and in the bivariate cases even enhances nonlinearity compared to the no aggregation case.

Granger and Lee show that these results do not depend on the test used or the critical value selected, by using other tests and also a 1% critical value.

The simulation to consider the effects of temporal aggregation was organized by first generating series using the univariate models discussed above and then forming temporally aggregated and systematically sampled series of 200 terms after aggregation using $k = 4$ and $k = 10$.

The models used in the simulation may all be classified as short-memory in that their optimum long-run forecasts all tend to the unconditional mean of the series. Thus temporal aggregation leads to a reduction of structure of all types, including nonlinear.

Table 8.3 show the results with sample size 200 and 5% critical values, using the neural network test. It is seen that even when the test is powerful in the no-aggregation case, it finds less evidence of non-

TABLE 8.3.   Effects of temporal aggregation: neural network test (5%)

Model	no agg	Temporal aggregation		Systematic sampling	
		$k = 4$	$k = 10$	$k = 4$	$k = 10$
Bilinear	59	21	9	38	13
	(59)	(21)	(9)	(33)	(13)
TAR	80	3	13	3	3
	(78)	(2)	(11)	(1)	(1)
SGN	100	14	4	11	8
	(99)	(12)	(2)	(9)	(6)
NAR	21	7	3	6	6
	(19)	(5)	(3)	(5)	(6)

Notes: Power(%) using 5% critical value simulated with AR(1) are shown. Power(%) using 5% asymptotic critical value are shown in ( ). Sample size 200, replication 100.

linearity after either temporal aggregation or systematic sampling and generally this effect increases as the extent of the aggregation increases.

Although these simulations consider only a few special models and a few aggregation situations they are certainly suggestive about what can generally be expected to occur. Temporal aggregation will usually reduce nonlinearity and this will also often be true for cross-sectional aggregation. The simulations have used only stationary, short-memory processes. The effects are likely to be less strong with long-memory processes. It is known, for example, that in theory integratedness and cointegration are not affected by temporal aggregation. However, the power of tests of unit roots can be reduced by the use of temporally aggregated data, as indicated by Gokey (1990).

8.3 Business Cycle Asymmetries and Other Nonlinearities

Business cycles are a topic in macroeconomics where nonlinearities have been discussed for a long time. Originally this emerged as an argument that business cycles could be asymmetric. An informal definition of asymmetry is based on the distances from trough to peak and peak to trough in a graph of a business cycle indicator. If these distances on the average are not equal the business cycle is asymmetric. Mitchell (1927: 330–4, 407–12) discussed this possibility and presented evidence both in favour of and against asymmetry by studying graphs of business cycle indicators for different countries and periods. Keynes (1936: 314) argued that contractions in the economy are more violent but also last for shorter periods than the expansions. Burns and Mitchell (1946: 134) regarded this as a common empirical fact. It is not possible to generate asymmetric cyclical time-series by a linear univariate or vector auto-regressive model. A nonlinear model is needed for that. For instance, stochastic STAR or TAR models are capable of generating asymmetric cycles, depending on their parameter values. Some of these and other nonlinear models do it even with the noise suppressed but here the focus will be on stochastic models.

A few years ago, the empirical analysis of cyclical asymmetry was revived. Neftçi (1984) used the theory of Markov chains to consider the problem with US data. He took a stationary business cycle indicator like unemployment, differenced the series, and considered the process consisting of the signs of the differences. This process has to be assumed stationary as well. The symmetry was defined roughly as the probability of moving from a positive to a negative sign in the next period being equal to the probability of the opposite transition from negative to positive. Neftçi modelled the sign process as a second-order Markov chain, which of course made the symmetry definition somewhat more involved than that sketched above. He estimated the two no-transition probabilities and their joint confidence ellipsoid. If the ellipsoid contained points of the 45-degree line in the usual two-dimensional coordinate system spanned by the two probabilities, the symmetry hypothesis was not rejected. Neftçi reported rejections with various US quarterly post-war unemployment series.

A problem in Neftçi's analysis is that information is lost when the original series is transformed into a binary one. Another problem related to his computations is that Sichel (1989) pointed out an error in them. The recomputed confidence ellipsoids did not support the asymmetry assumption. Nevertheless, Rothman (1991) claimed that some US unemployment series, total unemployment among them, were indeed asymmetric. He obtained this result by assuming that the sign process follows a first-order rather than a second-order Markov chain. The choice between the first- and the second-order model was made informally by a likelihood ratio test. Some of these decisions are borderline cases. If AIC had been used to decide between the first-order and the second-order models, the second-order model would have been selected for total unemployment. On the other hand, a more stringent criterion like BIC would have selected the first-order model. If the original unemployment series in Neftçi (1984) are modelled as autoregressive processes, an AR(2) model is a typical choice independent of which of these two model selection criteria is applied. However, in manufacturing where the evidence for asymmetry is strongest, the choice is clear-cut: the data support the first-order model.

When the Markov chain model is applied to other than unemployment series, not much evidence is found to support the asymmetry hypothesis. Falk (1986), noting that the sign process has to be stationary, detrended all trending series before modelling them. He assumed that a second-order Markov chain was an appropriate model to describe the sign process of the detrended series. The US series were real GNP, real gross private investment, and output (real GNP) per worker-hour or productivity, 1948(1) to 1983(4). International industrial production series were considered as well: the data were from Canada, France, Italy, United Kingdom, and West Germany, 1951(1) to 1983(4). All the series were seasonally adjusted. In detrending the industrial production series it was assumed (without testing) that all of them contained a breaking trend with the break-point at 1972(4). These results were therefore conditional on that assumption. No support for asymmetry was found in any of the series.

Westlund and Öhlén (1991) recently extended this analysis by considering detrended seasonally adjusted Swedish industrial production and unemployment series 1960(1) to 1988(4). The industrial production series was assumed (without testing) to have a breaking trend with a break-point at 1974(2). The results indicated no asymmetry. Following DeLong and Summers (1986), the authors also defined asymmetry using the skewness of the detrended series. The symmetry corresponds to zero skewness; if skewness is nonzero the series is asymmetric. Because the observations for testing the null hypothesis of no skewness are correlated, the null distribution is obtained by simulation. The conclusions of Westlund and Öhlén (1991) were the same as those obtained by studying the sign processes and were in agreement with those DeLong and Summers (1986) obtained. In their study, only the US unemployment series showed signs of asymmetry.

Choosing a different approach, Hussey (1992) applied semi-nonparametric techniques to estimate the conditional densities of detrended series of US durable and nondurable production workers and found that the conditional variance of the durable workers' series decreased with increasing employment. This was interpreted to agree with the idea that the unemployment rate changes more slowly in expansions than in recessions. For a similar approach to the differences of the logarithmed post-war quarterly seasonally adjusted US GNP series see Brunner (1992).

In their extensive treatment of the measurement of business cycles, Burns and Mitchell (1946, Appendix A) sought to create a time-scale that would be common to all business cycles by presuming that a typical cycle could be divided into nine successive stages. These stages would be evident in the same order in every cycle. Stock (1987) investigated the existence of this time-scale which he called the economic time. If the economic and calendar time-series were different, then a nonlinear transformation would be necessary to move from one to the other. A linear process in economic time would become a nonlinear process in calendar time. This is called time-deformation. Consider now the idea of testing the hypothesis of no time-deformation or linearity in calendar time. Assume that we have a vector of economic variables, $\mathbf{y}_t$. Let $g(t)$ be the economic time unit and assume that a change in economic time, $\Delta g(t)$, is a function of a vector of economic variables $\mathbf{z}_{t-1}$. The indexation stresses the fact that $\mathbf{z}$ is not allowed to depend on present or future values of $\mathbf{y}$. Economic and calendar time run in the same direction.

Stock developed tests for testing linearity against time-deformation both when $\mathbf{y}_t$ is in levels and when it is expressed in first differences. Consider the latter situation and assume that $\mathbf{z}_t$ is a scalar. The maintained model is

$$\Delta \mathbf{y}_t = \mathbf{C}_0 + \mathbf{C}_1 \Delta \mathbf{y}_{t-1} + \mathbf{C}_2(L)z_{t-1} + \mathbf{C}_3(L)z_{t-1}\Delta \mathbf{y}_{t-1} + \mathbf{u}_t$$

$$(8.3.1)$$

where C_0 and C_1 are coefficient matrices and $C_2(L)$ and $C_3(L)$ lag polynomial matrices, respectively. Note that (8.3.1) resembles the model employed in testing linearity against LSTR in Chapter 6. In the corresponding STR, local dynamics of the model vary with lags of z_t. This allows for the economic time measured in z_t to speed up or slow down in terms of calendar time, the possibility that interested Stock.

The data used were annual US time-series from 1869 to 1975 published in Friedman and Schwartz (1982). The series were income, the money stock, population, the rate of inflation, and an interest rate (nominal short-term commercial paper rate). Income was always assumed to be the z-variable. The results contained a few rejections of linearity, notably in interest rate equations but also in some money equations. The strength of rejection measured in p-values varied considerably across equations. On the other hand, the tests indicated that the equation for the only real variable, income, was linear, which does not support the notion of business cycle nonlinearity. Although linearity was rejected in five out of six two-equation systems considered as well, the idea of a common economic time-scale did not receive support because of the variation in the strength of rejection in the two equations of these systems.

An idea rather different from that of economic time is that the economy may be alternating between a finite number of states and that the discrete switches from one to another are governed not by an observable z_t but by some latent variable(s). Hamilton (1989) assumed that an economy can be in two different regimes, contraction and expansion, and that a shift from one to the other is caused by unobservables modelled as a Markov chain. The estimation results could be used for dating recessions: the National Bureau of Economic Research has been doing this in the USA for a long time by other means. Hamilton applied the idea to US quarterly seasonally adjusted GNP, 1951(2) to 1984(4). The model is

$$y_t = \alpha_0 + \alpha_1 s_t + z_t \qquad (8.3.2)$$

where

$$z_t = \phi_1 z_{t-1} + \phi_2 z_{t-2} + \phi_3 z_{t-3} + \phi_4 y_{t-4} + \varepsilon_t$$

with $\varepsilon_t \sim \text{nid}(0, \sigma^2)$. Furthermore, s_t is the unobservable switching 0–1 variable and z_t is an unobservable linear AR(4) process with fixed coefficients. The estimated model seemed to give a dating of post-war recessions in the US economy well in accordance with that of NBER.

Hamilton did not test linearity of the series he was modelling but that was done later by Hansen (1992) who derived the appropriate test. The testing problem is a very nonstandard one. First, the model is not identified under the null of linearity. This problem was also encountered in connection with some nonlinear models in Chapter 6 where a simple solution was discussed. Second, the information matrix is singular under the null hypothesis. Using Hamilton's data, Hansen was unable to reject linearity. The *p*-value of the test was about 0.7, varying slightly depending on how the test statistic was computed. The result stresses the importance of testing linearity before fitting any nonlinear model. It seems that, although the theoretical model is interesting, Hamilton's application may best serve as an example of the great flexibility of nonlinear models and the possibility of obtaining spuriously good fit with them. If linearity of the post-war US GNP series is tested against STAR it is not rejected either, and as Potter (1991) recently pointed out many other tests applied to this series also accept the linearity hypothesis. However, Tiao and Tsay (1991) were able to reject linearity when testing an AR(2) model against a TAR model using the test described in Section 6.3.4, see (6.3.31), and they then fitted a TAR model to the data as Potter (1991) had done. It is also worth mentioning that Hansen did obtain a rejection when he tested linearity of US GNP against a model resembling the SCAR model of Tyssedal and Tjøstheim (1988) derived in Chapter 2. However, in Hansen's model, the parameter process is not a two-state Markov chain but one in which the state is independent of the previous states. McCulloch and Tsay (1992) fitted a SCAR(4) model to the US GNP series employing informative conjugate priors for the parameters including the two transition probabilities from one regime to the other. They used the Gibbs sampler to obtain marginal posterior distributions of the parameters of which the transition probabilities were of special interest.

Examples of other work testing linearity include those inspired by chaos. Frank *et al.* (1988) used the correlation dimension and the BDS test described in Section 6.3.5 to study four international real seasonally adjusted quarterly GNP series starting in 1960(1). Frank and Stengos (1988) used the same tools to study seasonally adjusted quarterly Canadian macroeconomic series. The only case in the two papers in which linearity was rejected was the Japanese GNP. Frank *et al.* originally seemed to think that rejection of the null implied acceptance of chaos. Nevertheless, their discussion of the Japanese GNP shows that they were also willing to consider stochastic nonlinearity as an alternative to linearity. Brock and Sayers (1988) applied the BDS test to the residuals from AR models of several post-war US macroeconomic series. The i.i.d. hypothesis was rejected neither for the quadratically detrended real GNP nor linearly detrended log GNP. It was rejected for the quarterly unemployment and logarithmic employment series as well as once-differenced monthly logarithmic industrial production. A remarkably strong rejection was obtained for the longest series, the detrended pig-iron production with 715 observations: the values of the asymptotically standard normal statistic under the null hypothesis exceeded 15. Ashley and Patterson (1989) applied the bispectrum test discussed in Section 2.2 to a US aggregate stock-market index as well as an aggregated industrial production index. Both series are relatively long; the stock-market series contains the values of the index for 1000 trading days in the first half of the 1980s and the monthly industrial production series has 456 observations starting from February 1947. The bispectrum test strongly rejected linearity for both series. These and the above results indicate that quite a few US macroeconomic series may be nonlinear but they do not offer much help in modelling these nonlinearities.

Testing linearity against a well-specified nonlinear alternative may give more information about the parametric form of nonlinearity than the BDS test. However, as discussed in Chapter 6, such tests usually have power against alternatives other than the specified one, which complicates the selection of a proper nonlinear alternative. Conducting several tests may nevertheless be useful if one is able and willing to restrict the set of nonlinear alternatives under consideration as in Chapter 7. Luukkonen and Teräsvirta (1991) tested linearity of the US unemployment series in Neftçi (1984) and quarterly international unemployment and industrial production series, 1960(1) to 1986(4), from thirteen OECD countries. The source was OECD Main Economic Indicators. The industrial production series were logarithmic annual growth rates. Linearity was tested against ARCH, bilinearity, and LSTAR using LM and LM-type tests described in Chapter 6. The US unemployment series all seemed nonlinear. Linearity was also rejected for several international unemployment series. Rejections occurred more often against LSTAR and ARCH than bilinearity but as a whole the results were not robust against transformations of the variable. There was a strong surge in the unemployment rate in many OECD countries in the late 1970s. The authors thought that this might bias the results towards nonlinearity and carried out the logistic transformation to dampen the effect. However, although for some of the transformed series linearity could no longer be rejected, some previously linear series appeared nonlinear after the logistic transformation.

The evidence against linearity was less strong in industrial production data. Nevertheless, a few rejections still occurred at the 5% level of significance when linearity was tested against LSTAR or ARCH. In testing against the former most p-values of the tests were below 0.2, the only exceptions being Finland and Sweden. On the other hand, linearity could generally not be rejected against bilinearity and many p-values were high.

Modelling series for which linearity was rejected would have been a natural next step which Luukkonen and Teräsvirta (1991) did not yet consider. That problem was taken up in Teräsvirta and Anderson (1992) instead; see also Teräsvirta (1993). The starting-point of the paper was that possible nonlinearity in the OECD industrial production series Luukkonen and Teräsvirta considered could be adequately described by STAR models. The authors test linearity, specified the delay parameter and the type of model (ESTAR or LSTAR) as discussed in Chapter 7. It turned out to be possible to model several of seven of the series for which linearity was rejected with STAR models. This work is discussed in Chapter 9.

The use of STAR models is based on the assumption that local dynamics of the autoregressive process, characterizing the process, change with the phase of the business cycle. Another possibility, further removed from the original idea of business cycle asymmetry, would be to assume that the dynamic response of the economy to negative shocks is different from its response to positive shocks. At the same time, the response would not depend on at which phase of the cycle the shock occurs. If it is also assumed that the long-term effect of a positive unit shock is the same as that of a negative unit shock, i.e. zero, it is possible to model that kind of nonlinearity by applying the ARAMA model discussed in Chapter 2. Brännäs and De Gooijer (1991) recently tried out this idea with the data-set Teräsvirta and Anderson (1992) analysed. Because the underlying ARAMA model is rather different from STAR models it may not be surprising that the empirical results were also different. Brännäs and De Groijer rejected linearity in favour of ARAMA for France, The Netherlands, Norway, and the USA. On the other hand, the countries for which Teräsvirta and Anderson (1992) did not reject linearity against STAR were France, The Netherlands, and Finland. A possible explanation to the rejection of linearity for the US data against ARAMA is that the largest exogenous shocks entering the US economy between 1960 and 1986 have been negative. The impact of negative shocks to US industrial production may therefore have appeared different from that of the positive ones.

The discussion of this section may be summed up as follows. There seems to be evidence of nonlinearity in many US and other macro-economic time-series. The linearity tests discussed seem to reject linearity both for unemployment and industrial output series, although rejections for the former are more frequent than for the latter. However, the findings are not robust against transformations of the unemployment series. Also, evidence of nonlinearity in quarterly seasonally adjusted post-war US GNP appears rather weak although not totally nonexistent. No economic time scale in the spirit of Burns and Mitchell (1946) with income as the indicator of economic time seems to exist for the US economy.

9

Applications

Preamble

In this chapter, some applications of smooth transition regression models are presented to illustrate uses of the techniques discussed above. The models are potentially useful because they produce economically interpretable results. The first examples, both univariate and bivariate, use international volume of industrial production data and summarize more extensive results found in Teräsvirta and Anderson (1992) and Anderson and Teräsvirta (1992). The second example considers a possible nonlinear relationship between US GNP and an index of leading indicators, and is taken from Granger, Teräsvirta, and Anderson (1993).

9.1 Modelling Industrial Production

Industrial production indices from thirteen countries and a European aggregate were intially modelled with univariate linear and nonlinear forms. This was done to investigate business cycle asymmetries as discussed in Chapter 8. The basic nonlinear model considered is a smooth transition autoregression (STAR) model of order p:

$$y_t = \pi_0 + \pi_1'\mathbf{x}_t + (\theta_0 + \theta_1'\mathbf{x}_t)F(y_{t-d}) + u_t \qquad (9.1.1)$$

where $u_t \sim \text{nid}(0, \sigma^2)$, $\mathbf{x}_t = (y_{t-1}, \ldots, y_{t-p})'$, $\pi_1 = (\pi_{11}, \ldots, \pi_{1p})'$, and $\theta_1 = (\theta_{11}, \ldots, \theta_{1p})'$ and, as in Section 7.3, two different transition functions are considered. The first one is the logistic function

$$F(y_{t-d}) = [1 + \exp[-\gamma(y_{t-d} - c)]]^{-1}, \gamma > 0 \qquad (9.1.2)$$

and the second one is

$$F(y_{t-d}) = 1 - \exp[-\gamma(y_{t-d} - c)^2], \gamma > 0. \qquad (9.1.3)$$

Write

$$y_t = (\pi_0 + \theta_0 F) + (\pi_1 + \theta_1 F)'\mathbf{x}_t + u_t. \qquad (9.1.4)$$

It is clear that (9.1.2) allows the 'parameters' in the state-dependent autoregressive model (9.1.4) to change monotonically with y_{t-d}. Note that when $\gamma \to \infty$ in (9.1.2), $F(y_{t-d})$ becomes a Heaviside function: $F(y_{t-d}) = 0$, $y_{t-d} \leqslant c$, $F(y_{t-d}) = 1$, $y_{t-d} > c$, and (9.1.1) with this transition function becomes a threshold AR(p) model. When $\gamma \to 0$ (9.1.1) becomes a linear AR(p) model. In Section 7.3.1 model (9.1.1) with (9.1.2) is called the logistic STAR (LSTAR) model. Applied to the modelling of business cycle indicators the LSTAR model describes a situation where the contraction and expansion phases of an economy may have rather different dynamics, and a transition (change in dynamics) from one to the other may be smooth.

If (9.1.1) is accompanied by (9.1.3) the result is a model in which the 'parameters' in (9.1.4) change symmetrically about c with y_{t-d}. In Section 7.3, this model was called an exponential STAR (ESTAR) model. It implies that the contraction and expansion have rather similar dynamic structures, whereas the middle ground can have different dynamics. An ESTAR model can therefore represent an economy which returns from high growth towards more 'normal' growth in much the same fashion as it accelerates from low or negative growth towards the middle ground. It may be useful if the growth rate fluctuates rapidly over time. It is obvious that the LSTAR and ESTAR models can describe widely different kinds of dynamic economic behaviour, and this makes the STAR family of models as a whole a promising family for modelling nonlinearities in business cycles.

When using the STAR family of models in this context there is no economic theory to distinguish between LSTAR and ESTAR models, so that the choice between these models has to be based on the data. Likewise, the delay parameter d in (9.1.1), as well as the lag structure of the model, have to be determined from the data. Besides, it is not even known a priori if nonlinearity is required at all to characterize these industrial production series.

As discussed in Section 7.3 the specification of STAR models consists of three steps:

(i) Specification of a linear AR model.
(ii) Testing linearity for different values of the delay parameter d and, if it is rejected, simultaneously determining d.
(iii) Choosing between LSTAR and ESTAR models using a sequence of tests of nested hypotheses.

In the univariate case, the transition variable is a lagged value of y_t. If the delay d is fixed, the linearity test against STAR consists of testing

$$H_0 : \beta_{2j} = \beta_{3j} = \beta_{4j} = 0, \quad j = 1, \ldots, p$$

against H_1 : 'H_0 is not valid' in the artificial regression

$$y_t = \beta_0 + \boldsymbol{\beta}_1' \mathbf{x}_t + \sum_{j=1}^{p} \beta_{2j} y_{t-j} y_{t-d} + \sum_{j=1}^{p} \beta_{3j} y_{t-j} y_{t-d}^2$$

$$+ \sum_{j=1}^{p} \beta_{4j} y_{t-j} y_{t-d}^3 + v_t. \tag{9.1.5}$$

In order to specify d, the test is carried out for the range of values $1 \leq d \leq D$ considered appropriate. If linearity is rejected for more than one value of d, then d is determined as $\hat{d} = \arg\min p(d)$ for $1 \leq d \leq D$ where $p(d)$ is the p-value of the selected test. The rationale behind this rule was discussed in Section 7.3.

After determining d, the purpose of the third stage is to choose between LSTAR and ESTAR by a sequence of tests within (9.1.5). The sequence of hypotheses to be tested is as follows:

$$H_{04}: \beta_{4j} = 0, \quad j = 1, \ldots, p. \tag{9.1.6}$$

$$H_{03}: \beta_{3j} = 0 | \beta_{4j} = 0, \quad j = 1, \ldots, p. \tag{9.1.7}$$

$$H_{02}: \beta_{2j} = 0 | \beta_{3j} = \beta_{4j} = 0, \quad j = 1, \ldots, p. \tag{9.1.8}$$

If the test of H_{03} has the smallest p-value, choose an ESTAR model, otherwise select a LSTAR model. The logic of this sequence was described in Section 7.3. When Teräsvirta and Anderson (1992) used the above test sequence they applied a somewhat different decision rule for choosing between the two model families. Their rule does not always lead to a clear-cut decision but generally yields results similar to the rule presented above.

The Data

The data used for modelling are quarterly observations from the period 1960(1) to 1986(4) and they are seasonally unadjusted values of the logarithmic indices of industrial production for thirteen OECD countries and Europe. The series for Europe is an aggregate of European countries that are OECD members. Observations from 1987(1) to 1988(4) are used for forecasting. The source is the *OECD Main Economic Indicators*.

The original series are made approximately stationary by seasonal (four-quarter) differencing and this annual (four-quarter) growth-rate series is a reasonable business cycle indicator. The French output series is adjusted for strikes in 1963(1) and 1968(2), and the Italian series has also been adjusted to eliminate the effects of widespread industrial action in 1970(4).

Linearity Tests and STAR Models

As is obvious from above, the purpose of linearity testing at the specification stage is twofold. First, one wants to find the countries for which linearity is not rejected so that they can be excluded from model-building efforts. Second, if linearity is rejected, the test provides an estimate for the delay parameter. Note that by carrying out a separate test for each d, the overall significance level of the composite linearity test is not under control. However, the procedure has to be seen as a heuristic model-building device, and then the overall significance level is not a critical issue. If one incorrectly rejects the linearity hypothesis and attempts to estimate a STAR model, a likely outcome is that an appropriate STAR model is not found. Even if one is apparently successfully estimated, despite obvious linearity of the series, its residual variance is not likely to be appreciably smaller than that of the linear AR model. Of course, it is possible to control the overall significance level by assuming that d is unknown. This can be done by modifying the linearity test against STAR as in Luukkonen et al. (1988b) to cover the present situation. However, applying the modified test would require longer series than are presently available, because in the modified test the number of degrees of freedom associated with the test statistic is large if the maximum lag of the AR model is large. Also note that even when d is fixed, the test statistic requires a large number of degrees of freedom if the lag p in the linear AR model is large. It is therefore essential to apply an F-test and not the chi-squared test suggested by the asymptotic theory. The results are in Table 9.1. The use of .05 as a rather arbitrary threshold p-value leads to the classification of the series for Finland, France, and The Netherlands as linear. The series for the remaining countries and that for aggregated Europe are taken to be nonlinear. Note that Canada is not deemed linear at this stage because of a strong rejection of H_{02}.

Table 9.1 also reports the selected values of the delay parameter and the choice between the LSTAR and the ESTAR model without giving details of the choices. For most series the choice is LSTAR, but there are exceptions to be discussed below. We now consider some particular nonlinear models.

(i) USA

The four-quarter differences, y_t, of the logarithms of the US industrial production index contain interesting periods at the recessions of 1970, 1974–5, 1980, and 1982, because these periods are not well explained by the AR(6) model selected using AIC. As seen from Table 9.2, linearity is rejected and $\hat{d} = 3$. As $\hat{d} = 4$ also was a possibility it was considered

TABLE 9.1. Minimum *p*-values of linearity tests, chosen values of the delay parameter and the chosen model family based on fourth differences of industrial production data from 13 OECD countries and Europe (1961(1)–1986(4))

Country	Maximum lag*	Minimum *p*-value over $1 \leqslant d \leqslant 5$	Corresponding delay (quarters)	Type of model
Austria	5	0.010	1	LSTAR
Belgium	5	0.050	1	LSTAR
Canada	5	0.071	2	LSTAR**
FR Germany	9	0.004	4	LSTAR
Finland	1	0.547	—	Linear
France	9	0.156	—	Linear
Italy	5	0.029	3	ESTAR
Japan	5	0.000	1	LSTAR/ESTAR
The Netherlands	1	0.123	—	Linear
Norway	8	0.031	5	LSTAR
Sweden	5	0.015	3	LSTAR
United Kingdom	8	0.047	4	ESTAR
USA	6	0.006	3	LSTAR
Europe	9	0.015	3	ESTAR

Notes: The null hypothesis is linearity. A large value of the *F*-statistic, i.e. a low *p*-value, suggests rejection of the null hypothesis. The tests are *F*-tests as discussed in Chapters 6 and 7.
* The selection was made using AIC. The long lags like 5 or 9 are due to seasonality.
** Although the minimum *p*-value is not low, specification of the non-linear model was attempted, because while H_{04} and H_{03} are clearly accepted with *p*-values of 0.45 and 0.40 respectively, the *p*-value of the test of H_{02} equals 0.013
Source: Teräsvirta and Anderson (1992).

as well but a slightly better-fitting model was obtained when $\hat{d} = 3$. The model choice procedure in Teräsvirta and Anderson (1992) suggested an LSTAR model. Its estimated equation is

$$y_t = - \underset{(0.0072)}{0.021} + \underset{(0.12)}{0.35} \, y_{t-1} + \underset{(0.20)}{0.24} \, y_{t-3} - \underset{(0.19)}{1.03} \, y_{t-4} + \underset{(0.11)}{0.33} \, y_{t-9}$$

$$+ (\underset{(0.0072)}{0.021} + \underset{(0.15)}{1.16} \, y_{t-1} - \underset{(0.10)}{0.57} \, y_{t-2} - \underset{(0.20)}{0.24} \, y_{t-3} + \underset{(0.19)}{1.03} \, y_{t-4}$$

$$- \underset{(0.11)}{0.33} \, y_{t-9})$$

$$\times (1 + \exp[- \underset{(37)}{49} \times 17.5(y_{t-3} - \underset{(0.007)}{0.0061})])^{-1} + \hat{u}_t \qquad (9.1.9)$$

$$s = 0.0176, \quad s^2/s_L^2 = 0.64,$$

TABLE 9.2. The *p*-values of the linearity *F*-test against STAR for delays $d = 1, \ldots, 9$, for the four-quarter differences of the logarithmic US industrial output, 1960(1)–1986(4). The linear baseline model is AR(6).

d	1	2	3	4	5	6	7	8	9
p-value	0.22	0.22	0.0062	0.0086	0.060	0.35	0.65	0.46	0.55

where s is the residual standard deviation (9.1.9), s_L is the corresponding statistic for the AR(6) model, and the figures in parentheses are the estimated standard errors. The restrictions $\pi_{1j} = -\pi_{2j}$, $j = 0, 3, 4, 9$, were suggested by the data and imposed to obtain a more parsimonious model—an important concern in the estimation of STAR models. It is seen that the error variance of (9.1.9) is considerably less than that of the AR(6) model. The interpretable parameter estimates in (9.1.9) are $\hat{\gamma} = 49$ and $\hat{c} = 0.0061$. For the latter, the estimated transition function $\hat{F} = 1/2$ as $y_{t-3} - \hat{c} = 0$, so that $\hat{c}$ marks the half-way point between the recession and the expansion, and it is close to zero at 0.6%. The value of $\hat{\gamma} = 49$ indicates that the transition from one regime to the other is very quick so that the model is very similar to a threshold AR model. (Note that $(y_{t-3} - c)$ has been scaled by dividing it by $\hat{\sigma}(y) = 1/17.5$, see Chapter 7. This makes it possible to judge the size of γ.)

The dynamics of the model are interesting. The most prominent pair of complex roots in the lower or recession regime ($F = 0$) has a modulus of 1.1 and a period of 8.9 quarters, see Table 9.3, so that the process is locally explosive. On the other hand, the upper or expansionary regime ($F = 1$) is completely characterized by a complex pair of roots which have modulus 0.76 and a period of sixty-one quarters. This asymmetry of regimes is the most striking feature of the model. The economy moves from deep recession into higher growth very aggressively, whereas there is nothing in the dynamics of the expansionary regime to suggest a rapid fall into a contraction. Only a sufficiently large negative shock could cause this.

(ii) Japan

Linearity is rejected very strongly for the Japanese industrial production series. A major reason for this is a very deep trough in the growth rate of -0.19 during the first oil crisis and the subsequent rapid recovery which is the dominant feature of the Japanese series. The choice between ESTAR and LSTAR models this time is difficult but both could be fitted successfully. The estimated ESTAR model had a slightly

TABLE 9.3. The most prominent roots of the characteristic polynomials
in both regimes of estimated LSTAR and ESTAR models for logarithmic growth rates of industrial output, 1960(1)–1986(4).

| Country | Most prominent roots | | | |
	Regime	Root(s)	Modulus	Period
USA (LSTAR)	L	$0.85 \pm 0.72i$	1.11	8.9
	U	$0.75 \pm 0.08i$	0.76	61.0
Europe (LSTAR)	L	$0.55 \pm 0.85i$	1.01	6.3
	U	0.95	0.95	
		$0.80 \pm 0.39i$	0.89	13.9
Belgium (LSTAR)	L	$0.77 \pm 0.68i$	1.02	8.6
	U	$0.61 \pm 0.58i$	0.83	8.3
Canada (LSTAR)	L	$0.82 \pm 0.62i$	1.03	9.7
	U	$0.57 \pm 0.51i$	0.76	8.7
FR Germany (LSTAR)	L	$0.81 \pm 0.65i$	1.04	9.2
	U	$0.84 \pm 0.31i$	0.90	18.2
		0.87	0.87	
Italy (ESTAR)	M	1.03	1.03	
	M	-0.55	0.55	
	O	$0.85 \pm 0.53i$	1.00	11.4
Japan (ESTAR)	M	2.48	2.48	
	O	0.94	0.94	
	O	$0.81 \pm 0.48i$	0.94	11.7

Note: L = Lower regime, U = Upper regime, M = Mid-regime, O = Outer regime.
Source: Teräsvirta and Anderson (1992).

better fit and is

$$y_t = \underset{(0.0034)}{0.0075} + \underset{(0.40)}{3.03y_{t-1}} - \underset{(0.19)}{1.31y_{t-2}} - \underset{(0.089)}{0.49\Delta y_{t-4}}$$

$$+ (- \underset{(0.39)}{1.68y_{t-1}} + \underset{(0.24)}{0.87y_{t-2}} - \underset{(0.087)}{0.30 \ \Delta y_{t-8}})$$

$$\times [1 - \exp(- \underset{(0.88)}{1.54} \times 196(y_{t-1} + \underset{(0.012)}{0.082}))^2] + \hat{u}_t$$

$$s = 0.0185, \ s^2/s_L^2 = 0.78. \tag{9.1.10}$$

It should be noted that the transition parameter estimate $\hat{c} = -0.082$ is
low. Most of the observations of the series exceed that value. Thus, the
right-hand tail of the transition function F is mostly in use and that part,
of course, resembles the upper half of a logistic function. This also
suggests that an LSTAR model too might approximate the data-generating process rather well. However, the left-hand tail of F also has a role
to play. As is seen from Table 9.3, the mid-regime $\hat{F} = 0$ contains a

Both (9.1.12) and (9.1.13) in particular are good examples of what may happen when γ is large as discussed in Section 7.4. The lack of sample information in the neighbourhood of c where F grows rapidly is reflected in the very large standard deviation of $\hat{\gamma}$. It indicates that a wide range of γ-values about the (very large) estimated value do produce practically the same F. Furthermore, big changes in $\hat{\gamma}$ have a negligible effect on the other estimates. The value of the transition parameter $\hat{c} = 0.060$ for Canada is considerably higher than those for Belgium or West Germany.

Again, it is found from Table 9.3 that the characteristic polynomials of the lower regimes in each of the three models have an explosive pair of roots, whereas the upper regimes are stationary. All three models suggest possible asymmetry of business cycles in that the dynamics of the recession are different from the dynamics of the expansion. A similar LSTAR model can be estimated for the aggregated European series. Italy (the model is not reproduced here) is the only example of a country with a 'typical' ESTAR model where the transition parameter has its value ($\hat{c} = 0.028$) rather close to the mean of the series, and the observed nonlinearity describes the rapid positive and negative changes in the growth rate in the 1970s. A general conclusion of the study was that during the observation period comprising the years 1960–86, the business cycles in the countries considered have hardly been inherently nonlinear but the response to large negative shocks has been stronger than that predicted by a linear autoregressive model.

Building bivariate nonlinear systems is much more complicated than dealing with linear vector autoregressive ones. Linear VAR models may be easily represented in several observationally equivalent forms, the usual VAR-reduced form and triangular simultaneous form with a diagonal covariance matrix being the most common ones. In nonlinear models it is often very difficult to move from one representation to an observationally equivalent one by a linear transformation as in VAR models. In bilinear systems, mentioned in Section 4.3, this is possible because the system is linear in parameters. If the equations of the system are of STR type, a transition is usually impossible. Thus any choice of the representation is also a choice of the system. Occasionally prior information available about the variables can be used to make a sensible choice. For instance, assume a bivariate two-equation system is being built. Assume furthermore that of the two variables, x is believed to cause y. An obvious representation then is a triangular form, in which the equation for y contains the contemporaneous x, whereas the other equation characterizing x does not contain contemporaneous y. The other possible triangular form would, in that case, be much less informative and harder to interpret. However, if the believed causation is far from certain, it is better to show both possible triangular forms and admit that, using the data alone, it may not be possible to distinguish between them.

(iv) Canada and USA

Keeping this in mind, one can consider bivariate industrial production models to see if the cycles in different countries are related. As an example, take the relationship between Canada and the USA. The individual series were both characterized by LSTAR models (9.1.9) and (9.1.12), respectively. It is natural to assume that if there is dependence between the countries, the US economy is driving the Canadian one rather than the other way round because of differences in size. When linearity of the Canadian model is tested using the procedure for STR models, where the linear baseline model now also contains the US industrial output growth rate and its lags, linearity is not rejected. This suggests a 'common nonlinearity': when the US series is allowed to explain the Canadian series, the univariate nonlinear model becomes a bivariate linear model. On the other hand, the univariate US model is little affected by the possibility of including lagged values of the Canadian industrial production growth rate. Let x_t be the Canadian logarithmic four-quarter difference whereas y_t is the corresponding US one. The equation explaining y_t is

$$
\begin{aligned}
y_t = \ &\underset{(0.0067)}{0.029} + \underset{(0.09)}{0.43y_{t-1}} + \underset{(0.13)}{0.24y_{t-3}} - \underset{(0.14)}{0.84y_{t-4}} + \underset{(0.11)}{0.44y_{t-9}} \\
&- \underset{(0.09)}{0.25x_{t-3}} + (\underset{(0.0067)}{0.029} + \underset{(0.15)}{1.09y_{t-1}} - \underset{(0.17)}{0.74y_{t-2}} + \underset{(0.12)}{0.78y_{t-4}} \\
&- \underset{(0.11)}{0.44y_{t-9}} + \underset{(0.11)}{0.21x_{t-2}}) \\
&\times (1 + \exp[\underset{(28)}{-44} \times 17.5(y_{t-3} - \underset{(0.0008)}{0.0062})]) + \hat{u}_{at}
\end{aligned}
$$

$$(9.1.14)$$

whereas the corresponding equation for x_t (disallowing y_t) is

$$
\begin{aligned}
x_t = \ &\underset{(0.072)}{1.26x_{t-1}} - \underset{(0.12)}{0.44x_{t-3}} - \underset{(0.13)}{0.38y_{t-4}} + \underset{(0.078)}{0.36x_{t-5}} - \underset{(0.074)}{0.17y_{t-2}} \\
&+ (\underset{(0.14)}{-0.46x_{t-1}} + \underset{(0.10)}{0.51x_{t-3}} + \underset{(0.11)}{0.32y_{t-1}}) \\
&\times (1 + \exp[\underset{(5.6)}{-7.3} \times 17.5(y_{t-2} - \underset{(0.0098)}{0.040})]) + \hat{u}_{bt}.
\end{aligned}
$$

$$(9.1.15)$$

The presence of the Canadian variables in the equation for the USA and vice versa shows that each country influences the business cycle of the other, but the transition variable in each case is provided by the USA, suggesting that changes in regime in both countries are generated from within the USA.

The estimates of standardized γ in both equations are high (i.e. 44 and 7.3), and this implies that business cycles in both countries change between recessionary and expansionary regimes quite rapidly. The location parameters for the two equations are 0.0062 and 0.04, and this indicates that the half-way point between expansionary and recessionary regimes in the USA occurs when growth in that country is about 0.6%, while the corresponding half-way point for the Canadian economy occurs when growth in the USA is about 4%. If current y_t is introduced into the model for x_t, nonlinearity is no longer required, leading to the equation

$$x_t = -\underset{(0.0025)}{0.0007} + \underset{(0.07)}{0.82x_{t-1}} - \underset{(0.09)}{0.36x_{t-4}} + \underset{(0.08)}{0.29x_{t-5}}$$

$$+ \underset{(0.07)}{0.50y_t} - \underset{(0.08)}{0.26y_{t-1}} + \hat{u}_t. \tag{9.1.16}$$

(v) Germany and Belgium

These two countries form another interesting pair of neighbouring economies, one small, another large. The two output series were characterized by rather similar LSTAR models. Again, there is reason to assume that economic impulses travel mainly from the large economy to the much smaller one rather than the other way round. Testing linearity of the bivariate model against LSTAR gives the result that linearity is not rejected. The minimum p-value of the test statistic equals 0.12. Letting x_t be the Belgian output variable and y_t the West German one, the linear equation is

$$x_t = \underset{(0.0034)}{0.0066} + \underset{(0.09)}{0.76x_{t-1}} - \underset{(0.09)}{0.59x_{t-4}} + \underset{(0.09)}{0.38x_{t-5}} + \underset{(0.08)}{0.19y_t} + \hat{u}_{bt}.$$
$$\tag{9.1.17}$$

On the other hand, lagged values of the Belgian output growth do not even enter the German LSTAR model (9.1.13). There is the possibility that the cyclical fluctuations in the Belgian output series have at least a part of their origin in the German fluctuations. However, this conclusion is based on the assumption that the economic impulses mainly travel from a big economy to a smaller one. All one can say is that the results obtained do not contradict this assumption. Another possibility is that industries in both countries respond similarly to exogenous shocks for which the West German output acts as a proxy in the Belgian equation.

(vi) USA and Japan

These series proved rather more difficult to model. The reduced form, in which each series is modelled nonlinearly in terms of its own past and the past of the other series, was found to reduce to a univariate model in each case. However, there was a strong contemporaneous correlation between the residuals of these univariate models. Denoting y_t and x_t as the annual growth rates of industrial production in the USA and Japan respectively, these preliminary results suggest building triangular models of the form (a) y_t explained by lagged y and x_t explained by lagged x, plus current and lagged y, and/or (b) x_t explained by lagged x and y_t explained by lagged y plus current and lagged x. It is not possible to distinguish between these alternative 'triangularizations' based on the data and so both are presented.

(a) USA: the equation for y_t is (9.1.9).

Japan: the equation

$$x_t = -0.047 + 1.38x_{t-1} - 2.61x_{t-2} + 3.57x_{t-3} - 1.92x_{t-4}$$
$$ (0.022)\quad (0.08)\qquad (0.80)\qquad (1.32)\qquad (0.65)$$

$$-\ 0.18y_{t-1} + (0.047 + 2.31x_{t-2} - 3.57x_{t-3} + 1.37x_{t-4}$$
$$ (0.07)\qquad (0.022)\quad (0.78)\qquad (1.32)\qquad (0.67)$$

$$+\ 0.41x_{t-5} + 0.25y_t)$$
$$ (0.08)\qquad (0.07)$$

$$\times\ (1 + \exp[-\ 3.5\ \times\ 17.5(y_t +\ 0.0717)])^{-1} + \hat{u}_{bt}. \qquad (9.1.18)$$
$$ (1.6)\qquad\qquad (0.019)$$

The second triangular form is estimated to be

(b) USA: the equation

$$y_t = 0.0061 + 1.34y_{t-1} - 2.14y_{t-2} + 2.22y_{t-3} - 2.88y_{t-4}$$
$$ (0.0033)\quad (0.08)\qquad (0.30)\qquad (0.48)\qquad (0.55)$$

$$+\ 2.34y_{t-5} - 1.51y_{t-6} + 0.28x_t - 0.51x_t + 0.58x_{t-2}$$
$$ (0.46)\qquad (0.30)\qquad (0.08)\qquad (0.13)\qquad (0.13)$$

$$+\ (1.66y_{t-2} - 2.22y_{t-3} + 2.88y_{t-4} - 2.34y_{t-5}$$
$$ (0.28)\qquad (0.48)\qquad (0.55)\qquad (0.46)$$

$$+\ 1.51y_{t-6} - 0.35x_{t-2})$$
$$ (0.30)\qquad (0.13)$$

$$\times\ (1 + \exp[-8.5\ \times\ 13.9x_{t-2}])^{-1} + \hat{u}_{ct}. \qquad (9.1.19)$$
$$ (2.1)$$

Japan: the equation for x_t is (9.1.10).

It is seen from (9.1.17) that the transition variable now is y_t while the estimated location parameter is low $\hat{c} = -0.07$. The US growth rate is this low only during the first oil crisis which suggests that y_t may just be a proxy for the oil price. US output also enters elsewhere in (9.1.18) and of course it is possible to argue that fluctuations in Japanese output are partly caused by US ones. It can be suggested that exogenous factors have contributed to the Japanese output fluctuations in 1974–5, and that hardly contradicts previous knowledge. The low value of c conforms to that of the univariate model (which was ESTAR) indicating that the behaviour of the Japanese series was less exceptional during the second oil crisis in 1979.

Because of the earlier analysis, the second version of the model uses the ESTAR equation (9.1.10) to describe the growth rate of industrial production in Japan, but since most observations are greater than the location parameter (-0.082) and the transition function is therefore virtually monotonic in x_{t-3}, the ESTAR model behaves like an LSTAR model in this case. The US equation (9.1.18) contains some Japanese output variables. In particular, the transition variable is x_{t-2} with a possible interpretation that it acts as a proxy to exogenous perturbations like the oil price. The transition parameter c has been set to zero as its estimate originally was very close to that value.

Table 9.4 compares the standard errors of the residuals of the models shown above with various rival models.

It is seen that generally a superior fit is achieved by the nonlinear models, although these are less parsimonious. The post-sample forecasting results are less clear-cut with linear and nonlinear models, each occasionally providing the better forecasts but with little significant differences.

Table 9.5 contains other summary statistics for the estimated STR, STAR, and linear equations. A conspicuous detail is the negative skewness of the residuals in the US STAR model (9.1.9). As discussed above, according to (9.1.9) the US manufacturing moves from expansion

TABLE 9.4.   Standard errors of models

Dependent country/ Independent country	Model			
	Bivariate STR model	Vector autoregression	Univariate STAR model	Linear autoregression
Japan/USA	.0169	.0186	.0185	.0195
USA/Japan	.0149	.0191	.0176	.0208
USA/Canada	.0165	.0170	.0176	.0208
Canada/USA	.0166	.0169	.0179	.0195
Belgium/Germany	.0206*	.0214	.0231	.0246

* The STR model degenerates to a linear model in this case.

TABLE 9.5.   *p*-values of fourth order ARCH and Jarque–Bera normality tests, and skewness and excess kurtosis measures of residuals from the estimated models

Equation	Country	*p*-values		Other statistics	
		ARCH (4) test	Jarque– Bera test	Skewness	Excess Kurtosis
(9.1.9)	USA	0.41	0.0006	−0.85	1.15
(9.1.17)	Japan	0.47	0.51	−0.16	0.53
(9.1.18)	USA	0.73	0.10	−0.17	1.09
(9.1.10)	Japan	0.18	0.68	−0.17	0.31
(9.1.14)	USA	0.40	0.06	−0.53	0.69
(9.1.16)	Canada	0.83	0.98	−0.02	−0.08
(9.1.13)	Germany	0.19	0.60	−0.23	0.26
(9.1.17)	Belgium	0.17	0.74	−0.19	0.08

to recession mainly as a result of a large negative shock. Since the shocks are exogenous to the system they are not explained by (9.1.9) but show up instead as large negative residuals. In the case of the USA, the observation period contained several rather deep recessions, which is reflected in the size of the residual skewness.

9.2 Nonlinear Relationships between US GNP and Leading Indicators

This section describes an exploratory modelling exercise between y_t = US real GNP and x_t = the US Department of Commerce quarterly index of leading indicators. The objective of the exercise is to consider if a nonlinear model provides better forecasts of GNP. The results are indecisive, with some evidence of nonlinearity being found but no clear-cut improvement in forecastability. The series used are those designated GNP82 and DLEAD in the Citibase data-bank. The series are quarterly, real, and seasonally adjusted, with 166 observations from the period 1948(1) and 1989(2). Models were constructed using the full sample and then twenty terms were held back for use in a forecast comparison, so that the models were re-estimated using just the first 146 observations. The leading indicator series was originally recorded monthly but was summed over the adjacent values to obtain a quarterly series. It was decided to use GNP as the variable of interest, as it is probably the best available approximation to the variable that the leading indicators were designed to lead. The problem is that this variable is available only quarterly. The alternative would be to use the index of industrial production, which is available monthly, but with the growth in the importance of the service industries, the industrial sector now provides a poor approximation of GNP. In what follows, y_t is the GNP series and x_t is the leading indicator. The series were tested for unit roots and cointegration. x_t and y_t and their logs were found to be $I(1)$ but only weak evidence of cointegration was found for the log series. Linear relationships between changes were specified and estimated and tests of linearity applied. In most cases LM-type tests against STR found evidence of nonlinearity. Models involving simple polynomial nonlinear terms produced somewhat superior values for standard errors both in- and post-sample.

As the tests of linearity suggest that nonlinear models are appropriate, a pair of models for the changes in $Ly_t = \log y_t$ are presented and evaluated. A critical decision in the specification of these models is the choice of the transition variable z_t. From the justification of these models presented earlier, this variable should itself be slowly changing and it should not contain a dominant deterministic trend unless the idea is to describe continuous structural change in the parameters of a linear relationship between ΔLy_t and ΔLx_t. The variable selected was the linear detrended log of the index of leading indicators, denoted by:

$$LI_t = \log x_t - 4.73 - 0.008t.$$

A further linear error-correction model was estimated to be:

$$
\begin{aligned}
\Delta Ly_t = \ &0.006 - 0.09\ ECT_{t-1} - 0.08\ \Delta Ly_{t-1} + 0.10\ \Delta Ly_{t-2} \\
&(0.002) \quad (0.02) \qquad\qquad (0.08) \qquad\qquad\quad (0.08) \\[4pt]
&- 0.11\ \Delta Ly_{t-3} - 0.03\ \Delta Ly_{t-4} + 0.02\ \Delta Ly_{t-5} \\
&\ (0.08) \qquad\qquad (0.08) \qquad\qquad (0.07) \\[4pt]
&+ 0.11\ \Delta Ly_{t-6} + 0.06\ \Delta Ly_{t-7} + 0.22\ \Delta Lx_{t-1} \\
&\ (0.07) \qquad\qquad (0.07) \qquad\qquad (0.04) \\[4pt]
&+ \hat{u}_t
\end{aligned}
\tag{9.2.1}
$$

s.e. $= 0.0085$

and where $ECT_t = Ly_t - 2.50 - 0.96Lx_t$. The model is clearly over-parameterized but no standard parameter reduction procedure has been used.

Testing this error-correction model against smooth transition regression alternatives which use lags of the detrended logarithm of the leading indicator index as transition variables found strong evidence of nonlinearity when $z_t = LI_{t-2}$. (The p-value of this test was $p = .001$)

The corresponding STR model was estimated to be:

$$\Delta Ly_t = \underset{(0.002)}{0.011} - \underset{(0.02)}{0.16}\ ECT_{t-1} - \underset{(0.09)}{0.27}\ \Delta Ly_{t-1} - \underset{(0.08)}{0.17}\ \Delta Ly_{t-3}$$

$$- \underset{(0.08)}{0.13}\ \Delta Ly_{t-4} + \underset{(0.07)}{0.13}\ \Delta Ly_{t-6} + \underset{(0.06)}{0.10}\ \Delta Ly_{t-7}$$

$$+ \underset{(0.04)}{0.19}\ \Delta Ly_{x-1}$$

$$+ [\underset{(0.003)}{-0.015} + \underset{(0.06)}{0.14}\ ECT_{t-1} + \underset{(0.19)}{0.54}\ \Delta Ly_{t-1}$$

$$+ \underset{(0.20)}{0.44}\ \Delta Ly_{t-3} + \underset{(0.17)}{0.32}\ \Delta Ly_{t-4}]$$

$$\times\ [1 + \exp\{-221(LI_{t-2} - \underset{(0.005)}{0.036})\}]^{-1} + \hat{u}_t \qquad (9.2.2)$$

$s = 0.0072$.

There are seen to be quite substantial differences in the two regimes corresponding to the values of the transition functions $F = 0$ and $F = 1$, which approximately correspond to the troughs and peaks of the business cycle. An interesting detail is that, according to (9.2.2), the error-correction mechanism only seems to operate when LI_{t-2} remains below 0.036. When it exceeds that value, its coefficient estimate is practically zero. (The estimated transition function changes rather rapidly at 0.036.) The models were constructed using the in-sample data. The forecasting performance of the two models (9.2.1) and (9.2.2) over the following twenty-six quarters (i.e. 1984(3) to 1990(4)) are summarized in Table 9.6.

It is noteworthy that both these models produce forecasts that are too high, giving negative forecast errors on every occasion except for three. Neither model performed satisfactorily in forecasting the most recent downturn. This is partially explained by the lack of movement of the transition variable, z_t, over the post-sample period (i.e. z_t was not helpful in forecasting the downturn).

TABLE 9.6. In-sample and post-sample root mean squared errors of forecasts of the logarithmed US GNP from 1984(3) to 1990(4) using models (9.2.1) and (9.2.2)

	In-sample	Post-sample
Linear (9.21)	.0085	.0072
STR (9.22)	.0072	.0109

9.3 Conclusions

The above applications illustrate both the feasibility of building STR nonlinear models, and their superior in-sample performance. However, there is no guarantee that these models will produce superior forecasts. A necessary condition for that to happen would seem to be that the forecasting period contains 'nonlinear features'. For instance, in predicting US industrial production with a univariate model like (9.1.9), a nonlinear model may be expected to be superior to a linear one only if the forecasting period contains the aftermath of a large negative shock. If that is not the case, a linear autoregressive model is likely to perform as well as a nonlinear one. The success or otherwise of these and other nonlinear models will only become evident as experience with their use accumulates.

10
Strategies for Nonlinear Modelling

The large number of techniques and models available for investigating nonlinear relationships imply that a strategy is required to approach the modelling question. In this final, brief chapter we discuss the various problems that arise and make some suggestions about an appropriate strategy. However, as currently there is little experience with the use of the various methods and models, the proposed strategy is introduced with some hesitation, and it is believed that a better strategy will become available in the future, as more experience is accumulated. It is clear that the strategy to be discussed is not guaranteed to arrive at the best model or even a satisfactory one.

First consider the approach used by a proponent of some particular modelling method, such as projection pursuit or neural networks. They may be thought of as producers of techniques. At present, it is usual to suggest a method to describe its mathematical features and advantages, possibly present a simulation showing that at least in certain circumstances the technique can produce a realistic nonlinear description, and finally it is usual to use the method on one or a few actual economic series and to compare its performance with a linear model. The hope of the producer of an approach is to persuade potential consumers to consider and to use the method for their applied problems. If the technique is easy to understand and to implement, and particularly if a convenient computer program is available, then it is likely to be used. However, what is really required, but is not yet available, is a comparison of the effectiveness of alternative techniques either by simulation or on actual data. Eventually, an accumulation of evidence of the usefulness of methods will occur and then it will presumably be found that some approaches are not useful with economic data and that some pairs or groups of techniques are effectively equivalent. Many of the methods discussed in earlier chapters are 'black boxes', with data inserted into a program, and a 'model' produced, and so are not necessarily easily interpreted in economic terms. A sensible and useful interpretation remains as a further topic to be investigated.

For the consumer of techniques, facing a particular real-world problem and limited data a more sophisticated strategy is required. It will be assumed that a particular relationship is being considered, with a dependent variable y_t and a vector of explanatory variables $\mathbf{x}_t$. The choice of contents of this vector is likely to be critical to the success of the modelling exercise but the decision about the choice has to be left to the discretion of the investigator. Economic theory may be helpful. It is probably a good idea to include at least one lagged dependent variable in $\mathbf{x}_t$, to capture a part of the dynamics of the situation and of course at least one other explanatory variable. What may be included in $\mathbf{x}_t$ is immense, including many lagged dependent variables, many explanatory variables and their lags, and even functions of these variables, such as powers and logs. There are several possible strategies for choosing $\mathbf{x}_t$, including going from simple to general, so that a small $\mathbf{x}_t$ is first used and then larger vectors are explored—as recommended by Box and Jenkins (1970) for linear modellings—or going from general to simple, so that initially $\mathbf{x}_t$ contains many components and these are then reduced by dropping insignificant terms, as advocated by Hendry (see Gilbert 1986). Many of the nonlinear modelling procedures essentially go from simple to general, at least in that they go from linear to nonlinear.

Once y_t and $\mathbf{x}_t$ are selected it is recommended that one or more of the tests of linearity are applied, as described in Chapter 6. Many of the tests are reasonably powerful against wide classes of nonlinearity but will also have limited power against other classes. These properties of the tests need further investigation. If the tests suggest no significant nonlinearity in the relationship, then building a nonlinear model is not recommended, as the techniques are inclined to 'find' nonlinearity even when none is present, as indicated in Section 7.2.

If the tests apparently indicate a significantly nonlinear relation, the difficult question immediately arises, which of the various models and techniques available should be used? There appears to be no simple answer to this question, as so far there is little evidence about which methods work best with economic data. If computer programs are available, it may be worth while building several simple nonlinear models, such as a neural network and projection pursuit with just one or two terms and a simple regime-switching model, such as the STR models illustrated in the previous chapters. These models should be carefully compared and evaluated both in and out of sample. If possible, the post-sample period should be fairly long to allow any nonlinear features of the series to occur and be evident. In particular, the forecasts from the models should be compared. It may also be interesting to consider combinations of forecasts, as the results may suggest the encompassing of some models by others. If there is an important nonlinearity in a relationship, we believe that much of it will be captured by a fairly simple model and that there may be little extra pay-off in moving to more complicated models involving more nonlinear terms. However, this belief is based on quite limited experience with actual data and it may have to be revised later.

If the consumer has to choose a single nonlinear modelling technique, then economic theory has to be used to help make that choice. However many of the techniques such as the nonparametric methods, do not naturally arise from theory. It is thus our inclination to concentrate initially on the regime-switching models, which often do occur in simple theory.

References

AKAIKE, H. (1969), 'Fitting autoregressions for prediction', *Annals of the Institute of Statistical Mathematics*, 21: 243–7.

—— (1970): 'Statistical predictor identification', *Annals of the Institute of Statistical Mathematics*, 22: 203–17.

—— (1974), 'A new look at the statistical model identification', *IEEE Transactions of Automatic Control*, AC-19: 716–23.

AMEMIYA, T. (1983), 'Nonlinear regression models', in Z. Griliches and M. D. Intriligator (eds.) *Handbook of Econometrics*, 1: 339–89 (Amsterdam, North-Holland).

ANDERSON, H. M., and TERÄSVIRTA, T. (1992), 'Nonlinearities in interdependent business cycles', forthcoming.

ANDREWS, D. W. K. (1990), 'Tests for parameter instability and structural change with unknown change point', Cowles Foundation for Research in Economics, unpublished MS.

ASHLEY, R. A., and PATTERSON, D. M. (1989), 'Linear versus nonlinear macroeconomics: a statistical test', *International Economic Review*, 30: 685–704.

—— —— and HINICH, M. J. (1986), 'A diagnostic test for nonlinear serial dependence in time series fitting errors', *Journal of Time Series Analysis*, 7: 165–78.

AUESTAD, B., and TJØSTHEIM, D. (1990), 'Identification of nonlinear time series: first order characterization and order determination'. *Biometrika*, 77: 669–87.

—— —— (1991), 'Functional identification in nonlinear time series', in G. Roussas (ed.), *Nonparametric Functional Estimation and Related Topics* (Amsterdam, Kluwer), 493–507.

BACON, D. W., and WATTS, D. G. (1971), 'Estimating the transition between two intersecting straight lines', *Biometrika*, 58: 525–34.

BANERJEE, A., DOLADO, J. J., GALBRAITH, J. K., and HENDRY, D. F. (1993), *Integration, Cointegration, and Error Correction in Econometrics* (Oxford University Press).

BATES, D. M., and WATTS, D. G. (1988), *Nonlinear Regression Analysis and its Applications* (New York, Wiley).

BERA, A. K., and HIGGINS, M. L. (1993), 'A survey of ARCH models: properties, estimations and testing', *Journal of Economic Surveys*, forthcoming.

—— LEE, S., and HIGGINS, M. L. (1990), 'Interaction between autocorrelation and conditional heteroscedasticity: a random coefficient approach', Discussion Paper 90-25 (Dept. of Economics, University of California, San Diego).

BILLINGSLEY, P. (1968), *Convergence of Probability Measures* (New York, Wiley).

BLATT, J. M. (1983), *Dynamic Economics Systems: A Post-Keynesian Approach* (Armonk, N.Y., M. E. Sharpe).

BOLLERSLEV, T., CHOU, R. Y., and KRONER, K. F. (1992), 'ARCH modelling in finance: a review of the theory and empirical evidence', *Journal of Econometrics*, 52: 5–59.

BOX, G. E. P., and JENKINS, G. M. (1970), *Time Series Analysis, Forecasting and Control* (San Francisco, Holden Day).

BRÄNNÄS, K., and GOOIJER, J. G. de (1991), 'Modelling business cycle data using autoregressive-asymmetric moving average models', Umeå Economic Studies No. 252 (Dept. of Economics, University of Umeå, Sweden).

BREIMAN, L., and FRIEDMAN, J. H. (1985), 'Estimating optimal transitions for multiple regression and correlation', *Journal of American Statistical Association*, 80: 580–97.

BRILLINGER, D. R., and ROSENBLATT, M. (1967*a*, *b*), 'Asymptotic theory of estimates of the kth order spectra', and 'Computation and interpretation of the kth order spectra', in B. Harris (ed.), *Spectral Analysis of Time Series* (New York, Wiley), 153–88, 189–232.

BROCK, W. A., DECHERT, W. D., and SCHEINKMAN, J.-A. (1987), 'A test for independence based on the correlation dimension', SSRI Working Paper No. 8702 (Dept. of Economics, University of Wisconsin).

—— and POTTER, S. M. (1992), 'Diagnostic testing for nonlinearity, chaos, and general dependence in time-series data', in M. Casdagli and S. Eubank (eds.), *Nonlinear Modeling and Forecasting: Proceedings of a Workshop on Nonlinear Modeling and Forecasting held September 1990 in Santa Fe, New Mexico* (Redwood City, Calif., Addison-Wesley), 137–59.

—— and SAYERS, C. L. (1988), 'Is the business cycle characterized by deterministic chaos?' *Journal of Monetary Economics*, 22: 71–90.

BROWN, B. Y., and MARIANO, R. S. (1984), 'Residual-based stochastic predictors and estimation in nonlinear models', *Econometrica*, 52: 321–43.

—— —— (1989), 'Predictors in dynamic nonlinear models: large sample behaviour', *Econometric Theory*, 5: 430–52.

BROWN, R. L., DURBIN, J., and EVANS, J. M. (1975), 'Techniques for testing the constancy of regression coefficients over time', *Journal of the Royal Statistical Society B*, 37: 149–92 (with discussion).

BRUNNER, A. D. (1992), 'Conditional asymmetries in real GNP: a seminonparametric approach', *Journal of Business and Economic Statistics*, 10: 65–72.

BURNS, A. F., and MITCHELL, W. C. (1946), *Measuring Business Cycles* (Columbia University Press).

CHAN, K. S. (1990), 'Testing for threshold autoregression', *Annals of Statistics*, 18: 1886–94.

—— (1991), 'Percentage points of likelihood ratio tests for threshold autoregression'. *Journal of the Royal Statistical Society B*, 53: 691–6.

—— MOEANADDIN, R., and TONG, H. (1988), 'Some difficulties of non-linear time series modelling'. Paper presented to the 17th European Meeting of Statisticians, East Berlin (Aug.).

—— and TONG, H. (1986): 'On estimating thresholds in autoregressive models', *Journal of Time Series Analysis*, 7: 179–94.

—— —— (1990), 'On likelihood ratio tests for threshold autoregression', *Journal of the Royal Statistical Society B*, 52: 469–76.

CHEN, P., and DAY, R. H. (forthcoming) (eds.), *Nonlinear Dynamics and Evolutionary Economics* (Cambridge, Mass., MIT Press).

CHENG, B., and TONG, H. (1992), 'On consistent nonparametric order deter-mination and chaos', *Journal of the Royal Statistical Society B*, 54: 427–49.

CHOW, G. (1984), 'Random and changing coefficient models', in Z. Griliches and M. D. Intriligator (eds.), *Handbook of Econometrics ii* (Amsterdam, North Holland).

DAVIDSON, R., and MACKINNON, J. G. (1985), 'Heteroskedasticity-robust tests in regressions directions', *Annales de l'INSEE*, 59/60, 183–218.

——— (1987), 'Implicit alternatives and the local power of test statistics', *Econometrica*, 55: 1305–29.

——— (1990), 'Specification tests based on artificial regressions'. *Journal of the American Statistical Association*, 85: 220–7.

DAVIES, R. B. (1977), 'Hypothesis testing when a nuisance parameter is present only under the alternative', *Biometrika*, 64: 247–54.

—— (1987), 'Hypothesis testing when a nuisance parameter is present only under the alternative', *Biometrika*, 74: 33–44.

DELGADO, M. A., and ROBINSON, P. M. (1992), 'Nonparametric and semipara-metric methods for economic research', *Journal of Economic Surveys*, 6: 201–49.

DELONG, J. B., and SUMMERS, L. H. (1986), 'Are business cycles asymmetric?' in R. J. Gordon (ed.), *The American Business Cycle: Continuity and Change* (Chicago University Press).

DESAI, M. (1984), 'Econometric models of the share of wages in national income, UK, 1855–1965', in R. M. Goodwin, M. Kruger, and A. Vercelli (eds.), *Nonlinear Models of Fluctuating Growth*, Lecture notes in Economics and Mathematical Systems, No. 228 (New York, Springer-Verlag).

DEUTSCH, M., GRANGER, C. W. J., and TERÄSVIRTA, T. (1991), 'The combina-tion of forecasts using switching regressions', UCSD Working Paper (Dept. of Economics, University of California, San Diego).

DOUKHAN, P., and GHINDÉS, M. (1980), 'Étude du processus $x_{n+1} = f(x_n) + \varepsilon_n$', *Comptes Rendus de l'Académie des Sciences de Paris A*, 290: 921–3.

ENGLE, R. F. (1982), 'Autoregressive conditional heteroskedasticity with esti-mates of the variance of UK inflation', *Econometrica*, 50: 987–1008.

—— (1987), 'Multivariate ARCH with factor structure: cointegration in vari-ances', Discussion Paper No. 87-68 (Dept. of Economics, University of California, San Diego).

—— and BOLLERSLEV, T. (1986), 'Modelling the persistence of conditional variances', *Econometric Reviews*, 5: 1–50.

—— and GRANGER, C. W. J. (1987), 'Cointegration and error-correction repre-sentation, estimation and testing', *Econometrica*, 55: 251–76.

——— (1991) (eds.) *Long-run Economic Relationships: Readings in Cointe-gration* (Oxford University Press).

——— RICE, J., and WEISS, A. (1986), 'Semiparametric estimates of the relation between weather and electricity sales', *Journal of American Statistical Association*, 81: 310–20.

—— LILLIAN, D., and ROBINS, R. (1987), 'Estimation of time-varying risk premia in the term structure: the ARCH-M models', *Econometrica*, 55: 391–407.

ERMINI, L., and GRANGER, C. W. J. (1991), 'Some generalisations on the algebra of I(1) processes', Discussion Paper (Dept. of Economics, University of California, San Diego).

ERTEL, J. E., and FOWLKES, E. B. (1976), 'Some algorithms for linear spline and piecewise multiple linear regression', *Journal of the American Statistical Association*, 71: 640–8.

ESCRIBANO, A. (1986), 'Identification and modelling of economic relationships in a growing economy', Ph.D. diss., University of California, San Diego.

—— (1987), 'Cointegration, time co-trends and error-correction systems: an alternative approach', CORE Discussion Paper No. 8715.

FALK, B. (1986), 'Further evidence on the asymmetric behavior of economic time series over the business cycle', *Journal of Political Economy*, 94: 1097–109.

FERRI, P., and GREENBERG, E. (1989), *The Labor Market and Business Cycle Theories*, Lecture Notes in Economics and Mathematical Systems, No. 325 (New York, Springer-Verlag).

FRANK, M., GENCAY, R., and STENGOS, T. (1988), 'International chaos?' *European Economic Review*, 32: 1569–84.

—— and STENGOS, T. (1988), 'Some evidence concerning macroeconomic chaos', *Journal of Monetary Economics*, 22: 423–38.

FRIEDMAN, J. H., and STUETZLE, W. (1981), 'Projection pursuit regression', *Journal of the American Statistical Association*, 76: 817–23.

FRIEDMAN, M., and SCHWARTZ, A. (1982), *Monetary Trends in the United States and the United Kingdom: Their Relation to Income, Prices, and Interest Rates, 1867–1975* (University of Chicago Press).

GALLANT, A. R. (1987), *Nonlinear Statistical Models* (New York, Wiley).

—— and WHITE, H. (1988), *A Unified Theory of Estimation and Inference for Nonlinear Dynamic Models* (Oxford University Press).

GILBERT, C. L. (1986), 'Professor Hendry's Econometric Methodology', *Oxford Bulletin of Economics and Statistics*, 48: 283–307.

GLEICK, J. (1987), *Chaos: Making a New Science* (New York, Viking Books).

GLOMBOWSKI, J., and KRUGER, M. (1986), 'Some extensions of a classical growth cycle model', in W. Semmler (ed.), *Competition, Instability and Nonlinear Cycles*, Lecture Notes in Economics and Mathematical Systems, No. 275 (New York, Springer-Verlag) 212–51.

GODFREY, L. G. (1988), *Misspecification Tests in Econometrics* (Cambridge University Press).

GODFREY, M. D. (1965), 'An exploratory study of the bispectrum of economic time series', *Applied Statistics*, 14: 48–69.

GOKEY, T. C. (1990), 'Stationarity of nominal interest rates, inflation and real interest rates', Working Paper No. 105 (Institute of Economics and Statistics, University of Oxford).

GOLDFELD, S. M., and QUANDT, R. (1973), 'The estimation of structural shifts by switching regressions', *Annals of Economic and Social Measurement*, 2: 475–85.

———— (1976), *Studies in Non-Linear Estimation* (Cambridge, Mass., Ballinger).

GOODWIN, R. M., KRUGER, M., and VERCELLI, A. (1986) (eds.), *Nonlinear Models of Fluctuating Growth*, Lecture Notes in Economics and Mathematical

Systems, No. 228 (New York, Springer-Verlag).

GOOIJER, J. G. de, ABRAHAM, B., GOULD, A., and ROBINSON, L. (1985), 'Methods for determining the order of an autoregressive-moving average process: a survey', *International Statistical Review*, 53: 301–29.

GOURIÉROUX, C., and MONFORT, A. (1990): *Séries temporelles et modèles dynamiques* (Paris, Economica).

GRANGER, C. W. J. (1986), 'Developments in the study of cointegrated economic variables', *Oxford Bulletin of Economics and Statistics*, 48: 213–28.

—— (1987), 'Implications of aggregation with common factors', *Econometric Theory*, 3: 208–22.

—— (1990), 'Aggregation of time series variables: a survey', in T. Barker and M. H. Pesaran (eds.), *Disaggregation in Econometric Modelling* (London, Routledge).

—— (1991), 'Developments in the nonlinear analysis of economic series', *Scandinavian Journal of Economics*, 93: 263–76.

—— (1992), 'Forecasting stock market prices: lessons for forecasters', *International Journal of Forecasting*, 8: 3–13.

—— and ANDERSEN, A. P. (1978), *An Introduction to Bilinear Time Series Models* (Göttingen, Vandenhoeck & Ruprecht).

—— and HALLMAN, J. J. (1989), 'The algebra of $I(1)$', Finance and Economics Discussion Paper Series, Division of Research and Statistics (Washington DC, Federal Reserve Board).

—— —— (1991a), 'Nonlinear transformations of integrated time series', *Journal of Time Series Analysis*, 12: 207–24.

—— —— (1991b), 'Long memory processes with attractors', *Oxford Bulletin of Economics and Statistics*, 53: 11–26.

—— and HATANAKA, M. (1964), *Spectral Analysis of Economic Time Series* (Princeton University Press).

—— and LEE, T.-H. (1989), 'Investigation of production, sales and inventory relationships using multicointegration and nonsymmetric error correction models', *Journal of Applied Econometrics*, 4: S145–S159.

—— —— (1993), 'The effects of aggregation on nonlinearity', in R. Mariano (ed.), *Advances in Statistical Analysis and Statistics Computing*, iii (Greenwich, Conn., JAI Press).

—— and LIN, J.-L. (1991), 'Using the mutual coefficient to identify lags in non-linear models', Working Paper (Dept. of Economics, University of California, San Diego).

—— and NEWBOLD, P. (1986), *Forecasting Economic Time Series*, 2nd edn. (San Diego, Academic Press).

—— and TERÄSVIRTA, T. (1992), 'Experiments in modeling nonlinear relationships between time series', in M. Casdagli and S. Eubank (eds.), *Nonlinear Modeling and Forecasting, Proceedings of a workshop on nonlinear modeling and forecasting held September, 1990, in Santa Fe, New Mexico* (Redwood City, Calif., Addison-Wesley), 189–97.

—— —— and ANDERSON, H. (1993), 'Modelling non-linearity over the business cycle', in J. H. Stock and M. W. Watson (eds.), *New Research on Business Cycles, Indicators and Forecasting* (Chicago University Press), 311–25.

GUÉGAN, D. (1987), 'Different representations for bilinear models', *Journal of Time Series Analysis*, 8: 389–408.

—— and PHAM, D. T. (1989), 'A note on the estimation of the parameters of the diagonal bilinear model by the method of least squares', *Scandinavian Journal of Statistics*, 16: 129–36.

HAGGAN, V., HERAVI, S. M., and PRIESTLEY, M. B. (1984), 'A study of the application of state-dependent models in non-linear time series analysis', *Journal of Time Series Analysis* 5: 69–102.

—— and OZAKI, T. (1981), 'Modelling non-linear random vibrations using an amplitude-dependent autoregressive time series model', *Biometrika*, 68: 189–96.

HALLMAN, J. J. (1990), 'Nonlinear Integrated Series, Cointegration and Application', Ph.D. thesis, University of California, San Diego.

HAMILTON, J. D. (1989), 'A new approach to the economic analysis of nonstationary time series and the business cycle', *Econometrica*, 57: 357–84.

HANNAN, E. J. (1970), *Multiple Time Series* (New York, Wiley).

—— and RISSANEN, J. (1982), 'Recursive estimation of mixed autoregressive-moving average order', *Biometrika*, 69: 81–96.

HANSEN, B. (1992), 'The likelihood ratio test under non-standard conditions: testing the Markov trend model of GNP', *Journal of Applied Econometrics*, 7: S61–S82.

HÄRDLE, W. (1990), *Applied Nonparametric Regression* (Cambridge University Press).

HARVEY, A. C. (1981), *The Econometric Analysis of Time Series* (Deddington, nr. Oxford, Philip Allan).

—— (1990), *The Econometric Analysis of Time Series*, 2nd edn. (Cambridge, Mass., MIT Press).

HASTIE, T. J., and TIBSHIRANI, R. J. (1990), *Generalized Additive Models* (London, Chapman & Hall).

HATANAKA, M., and SUZUKI, M. (1967), 'The theory of the pseudospectrum and its application to non-stationary dynamic economic models', in E. Shabik (ed.), *Essays in Mathematical Economics: In Honor of Oskar Morgenstern* (Princeton University Press), 443–66.

HIGGINS, M. L., and BERA, A. K. (1989), 'A joint test for ARCH and bilinearity', *Econometric Reviews*, 7: 171–81.

HOWITT, P. (1988), 'Business cycles with costly search and recruiting', *Quarterly Journal of Economics*, 103: 146–65.

HUBER, P. J. (1985), 'Projection pursuit (with discussion)', *Annals of Statistics*, 13: 435–525.

HUSSEY, R. (1992), 'Nonparametric evidence on asymmetry in business cycles using aggregate employment time series', *Journal of Econometrics*, 50: 217–31.

JARQUE, C. M., and BERA, A. K. (1980), 'Efficient tests for normality, homoscedasticity and serial independence of regression residuals', *Economics Letters*, 6: 255–9.

JOHANSEN, S. (1991), 'Estimation and hypothesis testing of cointegration vectors in Gaussian vector autoregressive models', *Econometrica*, 59: 1551–80.

JUDGE, G. G., GRIFFITHS, W. E., HILL, R. C., LÜTKEPOHL, H., and LEE, T.-C. (1985), '*The Theory and Practice of Econometrics*', 2nd edn. (New York, Wiley).

KARLSEN, H. A., and TJØSTHEIM, D. (1990), 'Autoregressive segmentation of signal traces with application to geological dipmeter measurements', *IEEE Transactions on Geoscience and Remote Sensing*, 28: 171–81.

KEENAN, D. M. (1985), 'A Tukey non-additivity-type test for time series nonlinearity', *Biometrika*, 72: 39–44.

KEYNES, J. M. (1936), *The General Theory of Employment, Interest and Money* (London, Macmillan).

KIMELDORF, G., and SAMPSON, A. R. (1978), 'Monotone dependence', *Annals of Statistics*, 6: 895–903.

KLIMKO, L. A., and NELSON, P. I. (1978), 'On conditional least squares estimation for stochastic processes', *Annals of Statistics*, 6: 629–42.

KOOPMANS, L. H. (1974), *The Spectral Analysis of Time Series* (New York, Academic Press).

KRÄMER, W., PLOBERGER, W., and ALT, R. (1988), 'Testing for structural change in dynamic models', *Econometrica*, 56: 1335–70.

—— and SONNBERGER, H. (1986), *The Linear Model under Test* (Heidelberg, Physica-Verlag).

LASOTA, A., and MACKEY, M. C. (1989), 'Stochastic perturbation of dynamical systems: the weak convergence of measures', *Journal of Mathematical Analysis and Applications*, 138: 232–48.

LAU, L. J. (1986), 'Functional forms in econometric model building', in Z. Griliches and M. D. Intriligator (eds.), *Handbook of Econometrics*, vol. 3 (Amsterdam, Elsevier), ch. 3, 1515–1566.

LeBARON, B. (1990), 'Some relationships between volatility and serial correlations in stock returns' (Soc. Systems Research Inst., University of Wisconsin).

LEE, T.-H., WHITE, H., and GRANGER C. W. J. (1993), 'Testing for neglected nonlinearity in time series models: a comparison of neural network methods and alternative tests', *Journal of Econometrics*, 56: 269–90.

LIN, J.-L. (1991), 'Three essays on nonlinear time series', Ph.D. thesis, University of California, San Diego.

LIU, S.-I. (1985), 'Theory of bilinear time series models', *Communications in Statistics: Theory and Methods*, 14: 1549–61.

LIU, T. (1990), 'Time series analysis of synchronization and chaos', Ph.D. thesis, University of California, San Diego.

—— GRANGER, C. W. J., and HELLER, W. (1992), 'Using the correlation exponent to decide if an economic series is chaotic', *Journal of Applied Econometrics*, 7: S25–S39.

LJUNG, G. M., and BOX, G. E. P. (1978), 'On a measure of lack of fit in time-series models', *Biometrika*, 65: 297–303.

LOMNICKI, Z. A. (1961), 'Tests for departure from normality in the case of linear stochastic processes', *Metrika*, 4: 37–62.

LORD, M. E. (1979), 'The method of non-linear variation of constants for difference equations', *Journal of the Institute of Maths and Applications*, 23: 285–90.

LORENZ, H.-W. (1989), *Nonlinear Dynamic Economics and Chaotic Motion*, Lecture Notes in Economic and Mathematical Systems, No. 334 (New York, Springer-Verlag).

LUUKKONEN, R. (1990), 'Estimating smooth transition autoregressive models by conditional least squares', in R. Luukkonen: *On Linearity Testing and Model*

Estimation in Non-Linear Time Series Analysis (Helsinki, Finnish Statistical Society).

—— and TERÄSVIRTA, T. (1991), 'Testing linearity of economic time series against cyclical asymmetry', *Annales d'économie et de statistique*, 20/21: 125–42.

—— SAIKKONEN, P., and TERÄSVIRTA, T. (1988a), 'Testing linearity in univariate time series models', *Scandinavian Journal of Statistics*, 15: 161–75.

—— —— —— (1988b), 'Testing linearity against smooth transition autoregressive models', *Biometrika*, 75: 491–9.

McCULLOCH, R. E., and TSAY, R. S. (1992), 'Statistical inference of Markov switching models with application to US GNP', Technical report no. 125 (Statistics Research Center, Graduate School of Business, University of Chicago).

McELIECE, R. J. (1977), *The Theory of Information and Coding* (New York, Addison-Wesley).

McLEOD, A. I., and LI, W. K. (1983), 'Diagnostic checking ARMA time series models using squared residual autocorrelations', *Journal of Time Series Analysis*, 4: 269–73.

MADDALA, G. S. (1977), *Econometrics* (New York, McGraw-Hill).

MARAVALL, A. (1983), 'An application of nonlinear time series forecasting', *Journal of Business and Economic Statistics*, 1: 66–74.

MELLIN, I., and TERÄSVIRTA, T. (1992), 'Estimating the smoothing parameter in piecewise linear regression', in W. E. Griffiths, H. Lütkepohl, and M. E. Bock (eds.), *Readings in Econometric Theory and Practice: A Volume in Honor of George Judge* (Amsterdam, North-Holland), 215–41.

MILLER, M. H., and ORR, D. (1966), 'A model of the demand for money of firms', *Quarterly Journal of Economics*, 80: 413–34.

MITCHELL, W. C. (1927), *Business Cycles: The Problem and its Setting* (New York, National Bureau of Economic Research).

MOFFIT, R. (1990), 'The econometrics of kinked budget constraints', *Journal of Economic Perspectives*, 4: 119–34.

NEFTÇI, S. N. (1984), 'Are economic time series asymmetric over the business cycles?' *Journal of Political Economy*, 92: 307–28.

NELSON, C. R., and PLOSSER, C. I. (1982), 'Trends and random walks in macroeconomic time series: some evidence and implications', *Journal of Monetary Economics*, 10: 139–62.

NELSON, D. B. (1990), 'Conditional heteroskedasticity in asset returns: a new approach', *Econometrica*, 59: 347–70.

NICHOLLS, D. F., and QUINN, B. G. (1982), *Random Coefficient Autoregressive Models: An Introduction*, Lecture Notes in Statistics, No. 11 (New York, Springer-Verlag).

OZAKI, T. (1978), 'Non-linear models for non-linear random vibrations', Technical Report No. 92 (Dept. of Mathematics, University of Manchester Institute of Science and Technology).

OZAKI, T. (1985), 'Non-linear time series models and dynamical systems', in E. J. Hannan, P. R. Krishnaiah, and M. M. Rao (eds.), *Handbook of Statistics*, v (Amsterdam, Elsevier) 25–83.

PAGAN, A. R. (1978), 'Some simple tests for non-linear time series models',

CORE Discussion Paper No. 7812.

—— and HALL, A. D. (1983), 'Diagnostic tests as residual analysis', *Econometric Reviews*, 2: 159–218.

PEARSON, E. S., and HARTLEY, H. O. (1972) (eds.): *Biometrika Tables for Statisticians*, ii (Cambridge University Press).

PETRUCCELLI, J. (1990), 'On tests for SETAR-type nonlinearity in time series', *Journal of Forecasting*, 9: 25–36.

—— and DAVIES, N. (1986), 'A portmanteau test for self-exciting threshold autoregressive-type nonlinearity', *Biometrika*, 73: 687–94.

PHAM, D. T. (1985), 'Bilinear Markovian representation and bilinear models', *Stochastic Processes and their Applications*, 20: 295–306.

PINSKER, M. S. (1964), *Information and Information Stability of Random Variables and Processes* (San Francisco, Holden Day).

PLOBERGER, W., and KRÄMER, W. (1992): 'The CUSUM-test with OLS residuals', *Econometrica*, 60: 271–85.

POTTER, S. (1991), 'A nonlinear approach to US GNP' (Dept. of Economics, University of California, Los Angeles), unpublished paper.

POWELL, M. J. D. (1964), 'An efficient method of finding the minimum of a function of several variables without calculating derivatives', *Computer Journal*, 7: 155–62.

PRIESTLEY, M. B. (1980), 'State-dependent models: a general approach to non-linear time series analysis', *Journal of Time Series Analysis*, 1: 47–71.

—— (1981), *Spectral Analysis and Time Series* (New York, Academic Press).

—— (1988), *Non-Linear and Non-Stationary Time Series Analysis* (London and San Diego, Academic Press).

PUU, T. (1989), *Nonlinear Economic Dynamics*, Lecture Notes in Economics and Mathematical Systems No. 336 (New York, Springer-Verlag).

QUADE, D. (1967), 'Rank analysis of covariance', *Journal of the American Statistical Association*, 62: 1187–200.

QUANDT, R. E. (1960), 'Tests of the hypothesis that a linear regression system obeys two separate regimes', *Journal of the American Statistical Association*, 55: 324–30.

—— (1982), 'Econometric disequilibrium models', *Econometric Reviews*, 1: 1–63.

—— (1983), 'Computational problems and methods', in Z. Griliches and M. Intriligator (eds.), *Handbook of Econometrics*, 1: 699–746 (Amsterdam, North-Holland).

QUINN, B. G. (1982), 'Stationarity and invertibility of simple bilinear models', *Stochastic Processes and their Applications*, 12: 225–30.

RAMSEY, J. B. (1969), 'Tests for specification errors in classical linear least-squares regression analysis', *Journal of the Royal Statistical Society* B, 31: 350–71.

RISSANEN, J. (1978), 'Modeling by shortest data description', *Automatica*, 14: 465–71.

—— (1987), 'Stochastic complexity and the MDL principle', *Econometric Reviews*, 6: 85–102.

—— (1989), *Stochastic Complexity in Statistical Inquiry* (Singapore, World Scientific Publishers).

ROBINSON, P. M. (1977), 'The estimation of a nonlinear moving average model', *Stochastic Processes and their Applications*, 5: 81–90.

—— (1988), 'Semiparametric econometrics: a survey', *Journal of Applied Econometrics*, 3: 35–51.

ROCKE, D. M. (1982), 'Inference for response-limited time series models', *Communications in Statistics, Theory and Methods*, 11: 2587–96.

ROSTOW, W. W. (1992), 'Nonlinear dynamics: implications for economics in historical perspective', in Chen and Day (1992).

ROTHMAN, P. (1991), 'Further evidence on the asymmetric behavior of unemployment rates over the business cycle', *Journal of Macroeconomics*, 13: 291–8.

RUGH, W. J. (1981), *Non-linear System Theory: The Volterra–Wiener Approach* (Baltimore, Johns Hopkins University Press).

SAIKKONEN, P. (1989), 'Asymptotic relative efficiency of the classical test statistics under misspecification', *Journal of Econometrics*, 42: 351–69.

—— and LUUKKONEN, R. (1988), 'Lagrange multiplier tests for testing nonlinearities in time series models', *Scandinavian Journal of Statistics*, 15: 55–68.

SCHWARZ, G. (1978), 'Estimating the dimension of a model', *Annals of Statistics*, 4: 461–4.

SEBER, G. A. F., and WILD, C. J. (1989), *Nonlinear Regression* (New York, Wiley).

SHILLER, R. (1984), 'Smoothness priors and nonlinear regression', *Journal of the American Statistical Association*, 79: 609–15.

SICHEL, D. E. (1989), 'Are business cycles asymmetric? A correction', *Journal of Political Economy*, 97: 1055–60.

SONTAG, E. D. (1979), 'Realization theory of discrete time nonlinear systems I: the bounded case', *IEEE Transactions Circuits and Systems*, 26: 342–56.

SPANOS, A. (1986), *Statistical Foundations of Econometric Modelling* (Cambridge University Press).

STENSHOLT, B. K., and SUBBA RAO, T. (1987), 'On the theory of multivariate bilinear time series models', Technical Report No. 183 (Dept. of Mathematics, Institute of Science and Technology, University of Manchester).

—— and TJØSTHEIM, D. (1987), 'Multiple bilinear time series models', *Journal of Time Series Analysis*, 8: 221–33.

STOCK, J. H. (1987), 'Measuring business cycle time', *Journal of Political Economy*, 95: 1240–61.

SUBBA RAO, T. (1985), 'On the theory of bilinear time series models', *Journal of the Royal Statistical Society B*, 43: 244–55.

—— and GABR, M. M. (1984), *Introduction to Bispectral Analysis and Bilinear Time Series Models*, Lecture Notes in Statistics No. 24 (New York, Springer-Verlag).

—— and NUNES, A. M. D. (1985), 'Identification of non-linear (quadratic) systems using higher order spectra', *7th IFAC Symposium on Identification and System Parameter Estimation* (University of York).

TERÄSVIRTA, T. (1990a), 'Power properties of linearity tests for time series', Discussion Paper No. 90-15 (Dept. of Economics, University of California, San Diego).

—— (1990b), 'Generalizing threshold autoregressive models', Discussion Paper

No. 90-44 (Dept. of Economics, University of California, San Diego).

TERASVIRTA, T. (1994), 'Specification, estimation, and evaluation of smooth transition autoregressive models', *Journal of the American Statistical Association*, forthcoming.

—— and ANDERSON, H. M. (1992), 'Characterizing nonlinearities in business cycles using smooth transition autoregressive models', *Journal of Applied Econometrics*, 7: S119–S139.

—— LIN, C.-F., and GRANGER, C. W. J. (1993), 'Power of the neural network linearity test', *Journal of Time Series Analysis*, 14: 209–20.

—— and MELLIN, I. (1986), 'Model selection criteria and model selection tests in regression models', *Scandinavian Journal of Statistics*, 13: 159–71.

—— TJØSTHEIM, D., and GRANGER, C. W. J. (1994), 'Aspects of modelling nonlinear time series', in R. F. Engle and D. McFadden (eds.), *Handbook of Econometrics* Vol. 4 (Amsterdam, Elsevier), forthcoming.

TERDIK, G. (1985), 'Transfer functions and conditions for stationarity of bilinear models with Gaussian residuals', *Proceedings of the Royal Society, London*, PC400: 315–36.

THIO, K. B. T. (1986), 'Cyclical and structural aspects of unemployment and growth in a non-linear model of cyclical growth', in R. M. Goodwin, M. Kruger, and A. Vercelli (eds.), *Nonlinear Models of Fluctuating Growth*, Notes in Economics and Mathematical Systems No. 228 (New York, Springer-Verlag), 127–45.

THOMPSON, J. M. T. and STEWART, H. B. (1986), *Nonlinear Dynamics and Chaos* (New York, Wiley).

THURSBY, J. G., and SCHMIDT, P. (1977), 'Some properties of tests for specification error in a linear regression model', *Journal of the American Statistical Association*, 72: 635–41.

TIAO, G. C., and TSAY, R. S. (1991), 'Some advances in nonlinear and adaptive modeling in time series analysis', Technical Report No. 118 (Statistics Research Center, Graduate School of Business, University of Chicago).

TIBSHIRANI, R. (1988), 'Estimating transformations for regression via additivity and variance stabilization', *Journal of the American Statistical Association*, 83: 394–405.

TJØSTHEIM, D. (1986), 'Estimation in nonlinear time series models', *Stochastic Processes and their Applications*, 21: 251–73.

—— (1986), 'Some doubly stochastic time series models', *Journal of Time Series Analysis*, 7: 51–72.

—— (1993), 'Nonlinear time series: a selective review', *Scandinavian Journal of Statistics*, forthcoming.

—— and AUESTAD, B. (1991a), 'Nonparametric identification of nonlinear time series: projections' (Dept. of Mathematics, University of Bergen), preprint.

—— —— (1991b), 'Nonparametric identification of nonlinear time series: selecting significant lags' (Dept. of Mathematics, University of Bergen), preprint.

TONG, H. (1983), *Threshold Models in Non-Linear Time Series Analysis* (New York, Springer-Verlag).

—— (1990), *Non-Linear Time Series: A Dynamical System Approach* (Oxford University Press).

TSAY, R. S. (1986), 'Non-linearity tests for time series', *Biometrika*, 73: 461–6.
—— (1987), 'Conditional Heteroskedastic time series models', *Journal of the American Statistical Association*, 82: 590–604.
—— (1989), 'Testing and modeling threshold autoregressive processes', *Journal of the American Statistical Association*, 84: 231–40.
TUKEY, J. W. (1959), 'An introduction to the measurement of spectra', in U. Grenander (ed.), *Probability and Statistics* (New York, Wiley), 300–30.
TWEEDIE, R. L. (1975), 'Sufficient conditions for egodicity and recurrence of Markov chain on a general state space', *Stochastic Processes and their Applications*, 3: 385–403.
TYSSEDAL, J. S., and TJØSTHEIM, D. (1988), 'An autoregressive model with suddenly changing parameters and an application to stock market prices', *Applied Statistics*, 37: 353–69.
ULLAH, A. (1989a), 'Nonparametric estimation and hypothesis testing in econometric models', in Ullah (1989b).
—— (1989b), *Semiparametric and Nonparametric Econometrics* (Heidelberg, Physica-Verlag).
WECKER, W. E. (1981), 'Asymmetric time series', *Journal of the American Statistical Association*, 76: 16–21.
WEISS, A. A. (1984), 'Systematic sampling and temporal aggregation in time series models', *Journal of Econometrics*, 26: 271–81.
—— (1986), 'ARCH and bilinear time series models: combination and comparison', *Journal of Business and Economic Statistics*, 4: 59–70.
WESTLUND, A., and ÖHLÉN, S. (1991), 'On testing for symmetry in business cycles', *Empirical Economics*, 16: 479–502.
WHITE, H. (1984), *Asymptotic Theory for Econometricians* (Orlando, Fla., Academic Press).
—— (1989a), 'An additional hidden unit test for neglected nonlinearity in multilayer feedforward networks', Proceedings of the International Joint Conference on Neural Networks, Washington, DC (San Diego, SOS Printing), vol. 2: 451–5.
—— (1989b), 'Some asymptotic results for learning in single hidden-layer feedforward network models', *Journal of the American Statistical Association*, 84: 1003–13.
—— (1992), 'Parametric statistical estimation with artificial neural networks', Discussion Paper No. 92–13 (Dept. of Economics, University of California, San Diego).
WIENER, N. (1958), *Nonlinear Problems in Random Theory* (Cambridge, Mass., MIT Press).
WOOLDRIDGE, J. M. (1990), 'A unified approach to robust, regression-based specification tests', *Econometric Theory*, 6: 17–43.

Index